Paul Waldner

A Constant
Immigrant

1st edition

LEUZE VERLAG
seit 1902

Fachverlag für ▨ Oberflächentechnik –
Galvanotechnik

▨ Produktion von Leiter-
platten und Systemen

Author:
Paul Waldner

1st edition 2024

All rights, including those of translation and the organisation of a foreign-language edition, are reserved by the owners of the publishing rights.

Reprinting, even in part, is prohibited. No part of this work may be reproduced in any form (photocopy, microfilm or any other process) or processed, duplicated or distributed using electronic systems without the written consent of the publisher.

© 2024 EUGEN G. LEUZE VERLAG GMBH & CO. KG
www.leuze-verlag.de
Overall production: Eugen G. Leuze Verlag GmbH & Co. KG,
88348 Bad Saulgau
Print: Druck & Kalendermarketing Sosset GmbH

ISBN 978-3-87480-396-0

Table of contents

Preface

Most of us go through life without much thought as to why. Some of us go through phases where life just goes by automatically. Then there are those phases where life seems purposeful and full of meaning. We often don't give much thought to the "why or wherefore". We get up. We shower. We read the paper with a cup of morning coffee. We get ready for our day and go to work. We work, lunch, work, and, perhaps, have a couple of beers with friends before going home. At home we have dinner and time with our mates or our family. If we have family, we may have convinced ourselves that family is the reason for our lives. If not, we have other reasons to live but we don't, generally, give a lot of thought to it all except perhaps at a worship service, at funerals, at the birth of another grand-child, after a serious accident or sickness or discovering a life-threatening health issue. Some of us live much more considered lives or perhaps it's just much more nervous-about-missing-something-about-life lives. Being in my late-sixties and having always wondered what it was all about, this is my story and my take on what it's all about.

As a 14-year-old, I began working in a small drive-thru grocery store. Nicky was my boss and I have no idea what the rest of his life was like because I only knew him from that store – appropriately "Nicky's". He lived quite far away from the store, in a town called Shirley and drove about 45 minutes every day from his home to the shop to open the store at 8:00 a.m. and then drove home every evening either at 5:00 p.m. or at 8:00 p.m. Before knowing Nicky, I had always pictured the shop owner living above, next to or behind his shop. Never-the-less, Nicky's shop was Nicky's life. There, he was not only the boss but the center of a small local community. Around the neighborhood of the shop was a mixture of the old, original Polish and Ukrainian farmer-settlers of the area and the more newly moved-in-gentrification wave of people escaping the city to live the suburban life in East Meadow, Long Island, New York.

I'm at an impasse in my life right now. I've run my own business, more-or-less by myself, for more than 35 years. I didn't know it at the time, but the basis of my business life began in the summer of 1974, when I was 20 years old. Through a summer job, I learned about printed circuit boards (PCBs). I've had bosses and partners throughout the years but I've always felt like Multiline International Europe, my company, was a product of my energy, my creativity and my will, but now it all seems to be running out of steam. The days are full of stress. Thoughts of failure and a deep concern for my employees nag me. I am doing what I admonish all others not to do – worrying.

Perhaps Nicky comes to my mind as the opening scene in my story because he was my first role model as a boss. A business owner doesn't just provide a place to work. He creates an eco-system. Nicky's was a tiny eco-system within a small space on a small building lot along Newbridge Avenue. Before my time there, Nicky's was a traditional delicatessen. In those days delicatessens in our area had a high glass-front counter behind which stood a man in a white apron. His main product, mostly comprised of cold meats, were arrayed before him in a refrigerated vitrine displayed so that the customer could be impressed by the size and quality of the meats, sausages, cold cuts and cheeses on offer. On the other side of the vitrine the store was stocked with canned vegetables and other foods, a selection of soft-drinks, household cleaning supplies, bread, milk products, beer and boxes of cereal, cookies and packaged cakes.

At some point the deli model didn't work for Nicky anymore. There was a grocery store right next door called the "IGA" (short for Independent Grocer's Association) with just about every product that Nicky had, but selling at a price at least 20 % cheaper. Another deli opened less than two blocks away from him, on Newbridge Avenue, and it attracted a more up-class clientele who were willing to pay more for a better brand of cold cuts. Nicky decided, in the late 1960s, to change his business model and turned his deli into a drive-through convenience store. In a deli, the proprietor must handle unpackaged foods according to strict standards. A certain level of employee is required to meet hygiene standards and the expectations of a deli's customers. With the addition of a drive-way that wrapped around the store in a "U" form and a sliding door punched into the wall of the shop that adjoined the exit side of the "U", Nicky's Deli became Nicky's Milk Drive-In. The large cuts of roasted meats, sausage, bologna, cheeses and other cold cuts along with the vitrine itself gave way to pre-packaged cold cuts and cheese in a low refrigerated display case and the store became one in which the customer's orders were taken off the store's shelves, stacks of boxes or coolers and placed into paper sacks by the store employees in response to the barked commands of the driver of each car that came around the "U" in turn. The fact that the store's employees needed no special training in handling unpackaged food and the fact that the greatest attribute of a store attendant at Nicky's was speed and a projection of energetic helpfulness, led to my being hired by Nicky as a store helper at 14. Asked later why he hired me, he answered, "Because you asked and I needed somebody!"

Paul Waldner

Spring 2024

Immigration to America

August 10th 1959 is the date of my first memory in color. There are black and white images from before that date but this first memory I'll always remember (hopefully) in full, living color. I was on my first flight. The plane stopped in Hawaii on its way from Seoul to Portland, Oregon. Hawaii was celebrating coming USA statehood. All of us were led from the plane to a room in the airport where each of us kids were given some crackers, an American flag with 50 stars and something to drink. There wasn't anything special about the drink and the flag was kinda cool – colorful, paper, but those crackers were a taste of heaven – buttery and salty – I'll never forget the first taste of Ritz Crackers!

The next day I was in America for the first time. The former Kim Flo and I, became the younger Waldner siblings, Sharon (Sherry) and Paul. I met my mother and my father and my new older sisters Barbara and Nancy. I can't remember the 11th of August so well except how impressed I was with my father's house. The huge maple trees all around the house, the black wrought iron fence that looked as if it were freed from a cemetery, the stucco coated house that some of my friends later said looked "kinda haunted" made an impression, if not a really sharp memory like those Ritz Crackers!

My American period ended on the 4th of January 1987, but that's another journey – another adventure with a whole other cast of characters.

For my sister, Sherry, and me the 11th of August has always been a day to remember. My parents would never say anything about the day that I can recall. It was always our Nana and Opa, my mother's parents, who reminded us by coming by with ice cream or a pie or both. They reminded us and told us we should always celebrate the day.

Now, after 36 years in Germany (more than half of my life!) I am still thankful for my years in America. Those 27 and a half years gave me my second and third families, my education, western civilization, uncountable friends, baseball and basketball.

An East Meadow Childhood

My early known life is shrouded in mystery because the only truth that can be known about it is based on what my parents thought they knew from the narrative given by the orphanage and assumptions that came through what my parents' imagination came up with based on my actions as a little boy and total stranger in their house. There must have been letters between the orphanage and them, but I've never seen any, nor has my little [adopted] sister (that I know of). What is certainly known is that about five years after my birth it was estimated that I was probably born in Seoul, South Korea in 1954. I was lost or abandoned by my parents. I was found in dire straits-delivered to a hospital and from there landed in an orphanage. I was given a name; Choi Bibum. My birthday became the day that my identity papers were generated upon my release from the hospital into the care of the Holt Children's Service in Seoul. There I spent several months before I was delivered to America at an estimated five years old. The orphanage wrote a report to my adoptive parents just before I made the trip to them of my being sick with whooping cough, ring worm and chicken pox when admitted into the hospital prior to my stay at the orphanage. Up until the moment of an intervention of a good-Samaritan-stranger, there was little hope for a bright future for me. Someone had found me with a large, bleeding cut that traversed the full length of my right leg, beginning at my right buttock and descending to my heel. Conjecture has it that I was a street urchin of the type that populates Dickens' story of Oliver Twist. What is the support for this narrative? I was small, quick, charming and a good thief! My parents were constantly taking me back to the candy store or the grocery store or some other place of business where I had to return that which I had taken when I knew that nobody was looking. Even if I knew that someone was looking, I had the presence of mind, peripheral vision, and just plain confidence that my hands and pockets were hidden from view and that I could take what I wanted. I never really stole anything of real value in money terms. It was normally some candy, baseball cards, some kind of snack food or cheese but I always came away from the stores clean and was constantly being caught by my parents (mostly my mother) when I got home (bulging pockets) or at the point of consumption (crumbs on the floor) or after consumption (wrappers in the dust bin). My mother was, I must admit, a very good reader of my larcenous soul. She nearly always caught me until she forced me into ever more creative ways to avoid being caught the next time! Of course, for every action she took, there was a reaction on my part.

I often went to the IGA (Independent Grocers' Association) store on the corner with a note from my mother and a 5- or 10-dollar bill in hand, both of which I handed over to someone in the store who went around the store with a paper bag in hand, filling it and then putting the change and the note back into the bag before handing it over to me to carry back home to my mother. I often left the store with more merchandise than was in that bag.

In time, I was subjected to a mandatory incoming "pocket control." This was roughly analogous with today's pat down, light frisk that the airport security people do. My reaction to being subjected to this pat-down was to sneak up to our house unseen and to hide any stolen goods outside where I could recover the booty at some later, un-surveilled, time. For example, one time shortly after the implementation of the pocket control policy, my mother was in the back yard, and I was near the front of the house. I silently snuck out the front door, unseen and unheard, I recovered an eight-ounce brick of Kraft Sharp Cheddar Cheese from under the bush I'd hidden it and took it to my room to enjoy. I did enjoy the first four ounces but, I must admit, the second half of that brick of cheese was torture to get down. But I ate the whole thing. This only left me with the conundrum of the "wrapper problem." Well before the "pocket control" policy, there was a "wrapper check policy" for the illicit leftover evidence of candy wrappers, baseball card cellophane or Ding-dong packaging sometimes found in the dustbin in my bedroom. To empty my dustbin, I had to go into a hallway past all the bedrooms, down the stairs into the living room then onward to the kitchen and through what became the "family room" (although we never really called that room anything except the back room) to go out the backdoor, onto the patio, at the end of which were the garbage pails. It was nearly impossible to get away clean, getting rid of evidence, unless I was home alone, which was a very infrequent occurrence.

Sitting on the edge of my bed, feeling a little sick from forcing so much cheese down my gullet so quickly, I found a great solution. I simply balled up the wrapper as densely as possible and threw it out my bedroom window on the second floor. The wrapper bounced on the roof of the downstairs bathroom which sloped down and away from the outside of my window toward where the garbage pails stood. It was my job to empty the bathroom and kitchen garbage each morning and evening, so the goal was to have the wrapper lying there until the completion of my evening chores. How could I know that my mother was standing directly at the back wall of the bathroom next to the garbage pails when the evidence landed on the patio next to the garbage pails and right at her feet!? My father and I had another trip to the grocery store where I had to apologize to the store manager and pay for the cheese out of my saved up Birthday and Christmas gift money.

The fact of the consumed cheese and the cheese wrapper got my mother to thinking about how I got that cheese into the house. At the same time, I began to make a plan about how I'd get rid of the wrapper without putting myself into jeopardy of being caught again. Sometime later, I stole some baseball cards on my way home from school and hid them again in the same bush on my way into the house. The plan was to launder the stolen cards at school by playing "colors" with them mixed into my own, given-to-me-as-gifts, baseball cards. "Colors" was a kind of gambling game that kids played with baseball cards to win cards away from another, opposing, card collector. Two opposing players laid the cards alternately on top of each either until the colors bordering the picture on the card matched. When a match was achieved, the one that laid down the matching card took the whole pile of cards just played and on it went until one player didn't have any cards to play anymore. So, all I needed to do was to collect my cards from the hiding place and go to school, throw the wrapper away where nobody checked me for stolen goods and then get myself a game to launder the goods. I waited until my mother was on her way upstairs, said goodbye, let the screen door bang shut, bolted to my cache, collected the goods and then, to my surprise, I heard my mother's voice at the door inquiring about what I had just stuffed into my pockets. Another trip to another store, this time without my gift money (I had to return the stolen goods), was what I had to look forward to when I got home from school.

All of this happened from the time I was about 6 or 7 years old until I was about 10 or so. It never occurred to my parents to give me a weekly allowance until one time when I was perhaps 10 when they decided to give me an allowance of 10 cents per week. To put this into perspective; a penny (one cent) bought a piece of bubble gum, a pack of chewing gum or a Mar's bar was a nickel (5 cents) and an ice cream bar or a pack of baseball cards (5 cards I think to recall) with a flat piece of dried out bubble gum was a dime (10 cents) – all at Eats-n-Sweets, the candy store with the luncheonette counter on the corner. The allowance policy lasted about two weeks. The allowance was rescinded when my parents were disappointed that I always spent my money so quickly and frivolously for baseball cards or candy.

Life wasn't simple for me or for my parents. My mother came to the conclusion that boys have to be kept busy in order to keep them out of trouble – perhaps she was, in my case, right. I often wonder how my mother arrived at any of the conclusions that she arrived at or how she came to believe what she believed. Discussions about stuff just didn't occur in our house. The back and forth about one's day or about the news or about the people in one's lives were simply not the subject of our dinnertime discussions. I don't recall any real conversations between my parents. I can't recall discussions about my mother's dogs or my father's project around the house. Discussions that mined the realm of ideas, the flooding and ebbing of time or what was in their minds, hearts or souls are simply not in my recollection. I doubt they happened at all. Whether that is because of my disinterest or because my parents' lived truly unconsidered lives is a discussion I'll have to have with one of my sisters.

For much of the time that I lived in my parent's home, my mother bred and raised dogs. At the beginning, there were Chihuahuas, at some points of time in there, there were a couple of Boston Terriers, Pekingese, and Maltese. From the time I was 11 or 12 or so there were Japanese Spaniels. For all the time from 7 or 8 years old, I was my mother's dog-keeping "helper." This involved cleaning the dogs' cages, which involved removing the soiled newspaper making sure to roll up the dog-shit with the piss-laden paper and discarding it in the trash. Washing down the floor of the cages with a soapy ammonia, pine sol solution, rinsing the soap away and drying the floor, leaving the floor slightly damp. The job was completed by the laying down of two to three layers of old newspaper so that the Masonite floors of the cages were fully covered. As I recall from the Chihuahua days, there were about 12 or so separate individual cages and a couple of larger whelping pens where a new mother and her pups were held until the pups were old and large enough to be sold.

Puppies were born at regular intervals. Being present at the birth of these helpless tiny creatures was a wonder. They were blind at birth and about the size of my thumb. I learned about the beginnings of life from those puppies, and I learned about the end of life from them as well. Some were still born, some died later on the day of their birth and some died several weeks later. There was a place behind the garage where I buried them in paper bags for caskets and a prayer hoping they would get into dog heaven.

My routine was to get up in the morning about six, clean the dogs' pens, take the garbage out and have canned fruit and cereal with milk for breakfast, then walk to school. I had a similar routine during my summer vacations except that the yard needed mowing or weeding, or some other chores needed to be done instead of my traipsing off to school. My mother thought that keeping me busy was the only way to keep me out of trouble. At some point my mother thought I was taking too long with the dogs. I came down from my room and saw that my breakfast was already there. I went to sit down but my mother told me that I could have my breakfast after the pens were clean then she poured my milk onto my cereal. I, like most people, liked my cereal a little crispy with some milk and sugar in it. By the time I got done with the dogs, my Wheaties were the consistency of pudding. I rebelled. "I ain't eatin' that!" She said either eat it or wear it. I raced for the door, but she caught up with me as I struggled with the latch on the door and dumped that cereal mush on my head. Life was complicated for her. I don't know where her mind was sometimes.

We had so many dogs – through my young years there must have been a couple of hundred dogs that entered and exited my life but for me there was only one that I loved without condition and that was our Doberman Pincher, Misty. She was, before I came, my father's dog. I took her for my own. She growled and barked at paperboys and mailman when I first came. She was so dangerous seeming that she was relegated to stay in the pantry which had a back door to an outdoor dog pen ringed with five-foot-high wooden fences. She was such a majestic dog in such a tiny space. I learned how empty death leaves you feeling when she, at the age of 10, died of a heart attack at my feet in that small pantry. She rolled around the floor in pain until she stopped and laid there on her side. My father scooped her up and took her to the vet. When he came back to the house an hour or two later, he came back without her and told me she was dead. We both wept tears of grief and consoled each other. I was 10 as well.

The Japanese Spaniels came around then. The Japanese Spaniels had the run of the back half of the house. My mother had a closer attachment to the Japanese Spaniels so they weren't confined to the cages as were the Chihuahuas. This was fine with me because I was freed from cleaning the dogs' cages each morning and evening. The Japanese Spaniels were let out into an enclosed dog-pen out behind our house, so pen cleaning was replaced by more infrequently done "pooper-scooper" duty to rid the outdoor dog pen of their excrement.

My Father

My father was full of energy to get things done. I had the feeling that he felt that a minute sitting in peace was wasted time. While my mother read or watched television in the living room, my father was in the basement working on this or that or outside in the driveway working on the car. My father had no fear of failing at whatever he tried. Sometimes the results of his labors indicated that he should have had more fear of failing, but he always assumed at the beginning that all would turn out well. I learned the idea of hiring professionals to do things from my experiences of helping my father do it himself! There was the time that we paneled the basement together and we went through 3 sheets of 4 x 8 foot paneling on this one part where the slope of the stairway and a light switch had to be cut away. The first piece would have fit perfectly if the back of the panel had the finishing on as well as the front. The second piece would have been perfect had the light switch been up the stairway a bit. The third piece fit perfectly in every way. Along the way, I learned some new vocabulary words.

Then there was the time of the car tune-up and taking and putting back together of the carburetor. My father couldn't see the timing light no matter how many blankets he put up around the hood of the car. He set the timing as best he could and then decided that the problem had to be in the float of the carburetor, and he tore into that marvel of a mechanical assembly. Putting it back together was harder than taking it apart. We had three pieces left over. A screw, a little bracket and a spring. After reassembly, the car ran just about as well as it did before the tune up and along the way I learned some more and even some "blue" vocabulary.

Haircuts were 75 cents at the Twenty Barbers Shop (never a wait) in Levittown. We went for haircuts just about every other week. My father decided that he might save the 75 cents for my haircut when I was nine or ten. He took these electrical sheep shears to my head and got into this situation where he was cutting one side a little too much and over-compensating on the other side and then over-compensating again on the original side. The result was fear of shaving me clean in little steps. While one side was clearly higher than the other, a baseball cap was plopped on my head and we went to the Twenty Barbers Shop for a repair job.

The man was impatient, but then again I have been told I am impatient as well. Perhaps I got it from him – either that or we were just born impatient and came to cross each other's paths for 11 years.

There was a time in the mid to late 1960s that I absolutely feared my father. There were sessions in the basement or in the family room or in my bedroom or the kitchen where he would absolutely try to beat me into submission. This was well past the time of my petty thievery. The sessions always began with me being a disappointment or displaying some sort of 'disrespect.' The shoes weren't polished well enough, I didn't arrive home at a suitable time after delivering my papers – the rosy blush on my cheeks from playing ball along my paper route looked like I was taking drugs. Sometimes it began with a remark I made that didn't suit his views or his mood. Sometimes it was a burst of angry violence that came from frustration and anger at my mother or something else in his life that he expressed with flailing arms and flung projectiles, the results of which could be blood from my nose and mouth mingled with spaghetti sauce finger-painted on the kitchen table, walls and refrigerator – Me escaping through the living room and up the stairs to the refuge of the bathroom. The house becoming a place of four silent beings each trapped in a kind of numb, psychological prison with nowhere to go. Then there was the more ritual corporeal punishment that we went through with me having to bare my buttocks and he giving me a certain number of whacks with the coal shovel – the last time I submitted to that version of parenting, I was 14, and he struck me 14 times with that coal shovel – hard – like swinging a baseball bat. After the third or fourth blow, the pain was intense and he must have seen the angry redness that would turn to dark purple with green fringes in the following hours, but it went on – through seven, and ten, and finally 12…13 and 14! He never used his fists – always an open hand or a belt or that coal shovel, but there were days afterward that I could not sit without pain. There were days afterward that my ear would run with a combination of some kind of fluid and blood. No broken bones but angry technicolor bruises the size of melons covered by clothes and my nose constantly bleeding, then stopping with a clotted scab hanging-on inside one nostril or the other. The hardened blood clot remained there, waiting to be dislodged by another blow on another day or evening to start the bleeding again. Sometimes I shed tears, but as I grew older, I learned to just take it. I escaped into my inner self and let my body take the blows knowing that, at some point, each session would end and there would be a kind of peace when it was over. I fled such scenes when I fled my home. My life has been peaceful ever since.

Those horrible years of violence at home at the hands (and feet) of my father was preceded by a period of time between the ages of about 8 until about 12 years old in which I had a relatively good relationship with my father. I sometimes wonder if it was only because I was too small to hit hard or if there was indeed genuine affection that passed between us in those days. I know that there were certain things that my father was proud of me for. I was smarter than the average kid and did relatively well in school, although I was more of an attentive pupil than a hard-working one. I listened in class and read the texts but almost never did my homework as requested. This single-mindedness did not do my relationship with my parents any good. They were constantly trying to get me to do what the teachers wanted me to do, but, like the cat and mouse that we had with my klepto-manic ways, there was a constant struggle of wills with home-work and my attitude about school's busy-work, in general. I know that my parents knew, as my teachers knew, that I was severely underperforming in school. Instead of being one of the high-flying two or three "smartest and best", I was one of five or six kids that always got As and Bs on school quizzes and tests but let my grades slip to Bs, mostly and the occasional A or C on my report cards when my visible efforts were calculated in. In other words, I was learning everything I needed to learn but not showing it in terms of class participation, homework, and classwork. Still, by the time I was 12, I had become much better educated than my parents. I was an extremely curious child. Despite the horrors of living in their home, I learned well.

I read incessantly. This led to a broadening of my interests beyond anything that my parents could match. I liked and read about horses, the wild west, American History, America's engagement in wars, baseball books, John Kennedy's "Profiles in Courage", Thomas Hughes' "Tom Brown's Schooldays" and other novels about young spunky, altruistic but quietly understated heroes. My parents were working class people happy to maintain a working-class life without the curiosity that drives incessant readers. Not that they never read. I do remember my father once reading a book about Douglas MacArthur (a hero of his) and my mother reading books by or about the Evangelical leader, Billy Graham. In general, if they read, they read books about or by people they liked. I think to recall my mother reading books about or written by Shirley MacLaine, Peggy Lee and Judy Garland.

My father and I were bonded together in our love of baseball. I came to love the New York Yankees because my father loved the New York Yankees. I came to love Mickey Mantle as my boyhood hero because my father loved Mickey Mantle. My parents weren't the kind to ferry us kids around for school activities or boy scouts or even church activities. At the age of about 9 or so, I became quite proficient at getting around on my bicycle. The one exception was baseball and my participation in the Little League. When it came time for me to join the Little League, my Dad was all in. He always drove me to practices and games. I loved baseball more than anything as a little boy up until I was about 14 years old. We didn't go to Yankees games, because they were in the Bronx (my father thought the Bronx a little too far, a little too inconvenient and a little too dangerous for us.) We have a father/son tradition in some American families of "playing catch". One stands about 10 to 30 meters apart from each other, depending on the age of the son; each wearing baseball mitts, and throw a baseball back and forth and "shoot the breeze" – just chat. It's an activity that usually lasts about 10 minutes to a half an hour. I tried to get my son interested in playing catch with me when I became a father, but he just didn't take to it like I did. Playing catch with my father in the side and back yards in the early years and then in the street in front of the house as I got older was heaven to me. "Come on, Dad, give me a grounder!" "Throw it high!" "Oww! – I can throw it harder!" If I could just condense all my memories of my father into those sessions of playing catch, I would be weeping now. The love of the Yankees remains with me still. Baseball is part of my soul and my father planted it there.

It was through baseball that I learned of my father's innate sense of fairness and the sense that the weak should be protected and helped. He was one of the baseball coaches all the time I played Little League from the age of nine or so until about fourteen. There were always three or four good players that, had they always played all of every game, we would not have lost so much! But my father insisted that the good guys played only half the game and that the others had an equal, or better than equal, chance to play and get better. I often came home after games in tears for losing, but my father was unmoved from his principle that every kid played and I being his son, was always the first to come out if I started or the last to be shuffled in if I didn't. He was proud of my toughness and my refusal to leave a game if I had hurt myself. Once, having slid my hand up my bat to bunt and not knowing the right way to keep my fingers behind the bat, the ball crushed my right index finger. It was a great bunt and I raced to first base and was declared safe. Although I knew that I had been stung by the ball, I didn't realize that I had left a trail of blood down the first base line. My father was coaching and it looked like he was going to faint and he was amazed that I didn't feel like fainting. He grabbed his handkerchief out of his pocket to try to stanch the bleeding and couldn't believe I didn't feel anything. I felt great, but he made me leave the game and drove me to the hospital.

The source of my fear became a little shriveled up old man of 80-something when I went to visit him in Florida. He had a touch of age-related dementia that drove Ada, his third wife, a bit nuts but didn't seem so bad to me. He had a little Chihuahua that was always in his arms or on his lap. We went to dinner at a local Cracker Barrel restaurant and, although I could afford to pay full price, he insisted on going at 5:00 pm when it was still possible to eat for half price with the so-called "Early Bird Special", a common fixture for restaurants in retirement communities all over Florida. He ordered the cheapest thing on the menu, ate very little of it and had the rest packed up to take home. The Cracker Barrel has a kind of souvenir shop that one must wend through on the way to the cash register. He picked out some little tacky decorative thing that he fancied that I bought for him. He asked me to drive him to the local Walmart so that he could get some exercise and have me pick up some groceries for him. He didn't really walk as much as he shuffled. If he picked his feet up at all it was negligible. His rate of forward progress, and therefore mine as well, was perhaps ¼ of a normal adult gait. He insisted on pushing the cart. It took me a while to figure out that he used the cart as a kind of walker. He told me his stories about being the fastest kid in New York in his youth and about his friend who called to talk to him almost every day. When we got around to our relationship, he said that he was proud of me and what I'd made of myself. I mentioned how I hated being at home because of all the violence, he protested and told me that he had never laid a hand on any of us kids. I learned a lesson in how utterly complete self-delusion can be that day and I learned that one's memory of life is, for some, an act of renovation where something ugly and unkempt can be turned into something respectable and pristine.

He died a short while later. None of us kids went to his wake in Florida, although we did gather for a burial ceremony in Oneonta the next summer. He wanted the urn that bore his ashes to be placed in the same square hole in the ground (about 2 feet wide x 2 feet long x 2 feet deep) that his little Chihuahua's ashes would be buried. The workers at the cemetery had already placed the dog's remains in the hole when it came time for us to place his remains in his "final resting place." The actual job of lowering him into that ridiculously small hole in the ground fell to me. The package was a cube-shaped sturdy box of a kind of ceramic that was about 8" per side. The dog's box already occupied a space on the right side of the hole as I got to my knees and tried to elegantly place my father to his eternal resting place. The hole was too small to allow my elbows to fit easily into the hole and I had to jockey around a little and kind of let him slip gently from my fingers into the designated place. My sister, Nancy, standing to my right, bent down and whispered in my ear, "This is your chance for revenge, Paul. Just drop him!" My heart smiled that my sister knew enough of my time in that home of his when she wasn't there anymore, to be able to bring some humor to such an absolutely bizarre moment of life. I didn't drop him and I don't regret not having dropped him.

Nicky's

Minimum wage in the summer of 1968 in New York State was $ 1.60 per hour. I think that Nicky offered to pay me $ 1.65 per hour at the time and that he raised my pay in increments to about $ 2.50 per hour by the time I stopped working there in the spring of 1972 when minimum wage was $ 1.85. At the beginning my job was to sweep floors, clean the display cases and the refrigerated cases, dust and restock (marking every item with a price) the shelves, sweeping the outside sidewalk and driveway areas. By beginning with this work, Nicky reinforced to me that this work always needed to be done, no matter what else intervenes in the business of the store. This was the work of shop-keeping. According to Nicky, taking care of the customers was important to do as the 1st priority but that wasn't work – that was the bonus for just being there with a shop prepared with all the stuff, ready to buy. The real work of shop-keeping was taking care of the store and making sure it was as easy and quick as possible for the customer to make his purchase. One can debate the wisdom of this theory of shop-keeping. You'll get no argument from me; it was Nicky's theory! When customers weren't there, there was always shop-keeping work to do and Nick paid me to be busy. Not that he was a hard boss or a slave-driver, he just wanted me to make a good impression on the customers and he wanted his shop to have a clean, prepared and well-stocked look about it. To this day, I always rate the quality of a store that sells drinks in cans by the amount of dust found on the tops of the cans. Cleaning the tops of cans and bottles was a big part of my job as beverages seemed to be what people went to drive-ins most to buy – at least then.

The store was laid out so that there was a free area in the back of the store among the stock of crates of canned goods and soft drinks of about six feet by four feet where people could sit on the one chair and a card-table that were there or on overturned plastic milk crates or beer crates. Nicky had a small stove top to warm up canned food or hot dogs or some such prepared foods to eat during his time at the shop. Up to three people could carry on a conversation there but they had to be prepared to be interrupted or shuffle from side to side as whoever was actually working squeezed by. We had to enter the walk-in refrigerator from this back area regularly to recharge the display at the front of the refrigerator's glass doors. Less regularly, we needed to recharge the cash register with small bills and coins because Nicky used to hide his cash in a small paper sack tucked between the beer and the sodas in the refrigerator. There were a "cast of characters" that belonged to Nicky's back space. Nicky had a brother, Artie, who came in a few times per week and would sit and chat with Nicky in the back of the store while I (or the other helper,

Ray) tended the front of the store. Periodically, neighbors would stop by, particularly an old man called George, who lived in the house that abutted the rear of Nicky's parking lot. Most of these neighbors were of Polish or Ukrainian descent. Much of Long Island had been peopled by duck farming or potato farming east and central Europeans who had migrated to the US at the turn of the 20th century. Oftentimes the neighbors would bring sausages or pierogis they had made as a treat for Nicky and sometimes he shared these gifts with us who were either working or just hanging out at the back of the store. One constant visitor was a man called Spotsy. Spotsy was a bachelor of nearly 80 years old. He made the impression on me to be like a character out of a Melville novel. He often wore the kind of flat peaked cap made famous by the Andy Capp cartoon character and was always chewing on or smoking a cigar. He had been a long shore-man (stevedore) in his working life and even at nearly 80, he was a very wiry, muscular man. I loved Spotsy's company and I think he liked me as an audience for the stories he had to tell. Two particular stories still stick out in my memory. Spotsy had been born sometime around 1890. He was the only person I ever knew that participated in the 1st World War. He said they called him a mule skinner, although his work was exclusively with horses. I didn't have any idea why they needed mule skinners in the army. "Well", he said, "At the beginning of the Great War, they needed horses to pull the cannons up to the front lines. They didn't use jeeps and trucks like they do today! They needed horses who weren't afraid to pull heavy loads in the direction of incoming barrages and fools like me to lead the horses! Most of my time was spent with the horses, taking care of them and making sure that the carriages and wagons were in good order. The trip over on the ship was awful. I was sea-sick for the week it took us to make the crossing over to England – I thought that I wanted to die – and then they sent us to the front! I missed being sea-sick, I was so scared!" He often had a hacking cough that I always attributed to a lifetime of puffing on or chewing on cigars, but he insisted that he had been gassed with mustard gas during the 1st World War and that was the cause of his constant cough.

I'm sitting in a cafe in Bad Homburg writing these reminisces down as the cleaning lady finishes the apartment. I got to my place and realized that it was Tuesday. She still had the kitchen and the bathrooms to do. I left the office early because I couldn't stand sitting there waiting for somebody to call or for money to enter the accounts so that I could pay some bills and animate the people in the office some. Sometimes I find myself painted into a corner in my life. I find myself paying a psychological price for seemingly to have done everything wrong. I've long ago learned that beating myself up doesn't help. More recently I've learned that taking my frustrated feelings out on somebody else makes me feel even worse than I originally felt when I knew it was only my own damned fault. I find myself returning to my youth and asking a question to myself. I ask, "Are you running with me Jesus?"

Running Away,
Freedom and Restaurant Work

April 3, 1971 is a day that I will never forget. It was the day that I grew up – or at least the day that began an adventure that would lead to my having the confidence of an adult. It was the end of Easter vacation of that year – a Friday – I'd scrubbed the floors in the kitchen, family room, bathroom, pantry and dining room and had a "run-in" with my mother after she let the dogs in from the back-yard before the floors had dried. Dog paw-prints everywhere – the entire floor looked leopard-spotted. (It was a lot of little dogs!) Upset and exasperated, I yelled, "Did you have to let them in now!" The answer was a slap to the face from behind as I walked away in disgust and, "You don't talk to me like that!" She was aiming for my fresh mouth, but she caught my nose and it proceeded to run red. I caught the blood in my hands, made it upstairs to my room, laid back on the bed. I waited for the bleed-ing to stop and the blood to harden into a clot that didn't run anymore. She didn't mean to hit me hard – it was meant more as a remark than a blow. My nose had remained bloodied for more-or-less the entire time since Good Friday, a week earlier, when I'd had a "run-in" with my father. Touch it and it would bleed; lay back and it would stop until the next touch. Eventually I raised myself to a sitting position and my thoughts ran to getting away from there.

I came downstairs with some library books that needed return-ing and told my mother that I was going to the library. On my way to the library, I stopped at Nicky's. Nicky owed me $65 in back pay. He gave me the money in cash and I was on my way. "When are you working again?" he asked. "I don't know, I'll call," I replied.

From the Library, I crossed the street and waited at the bus stop until a bus came to take me to Hempstead. From Hempstead, I took the Long Island Railroad train to Penn Station in New York City. It was the first train ride of my life. Most of us, who are not commuters, go everywhere that is beyond walking distance by car on Long Island. I only began to feel the pressure to find an-other destination than New York once I was actually in the city. I discovered I had no idea where I wanted to go. There were two thoughts driving me: I didn't want to be found and I didn't want to stay in New York. I had heard and read too much about how dangerous New York was for youth. The whole time I was away, one thing was always in my head to hear and that was, "Are you running with me Jesus?" It was a book that had been mentioned several times in Church and although I'd never read it, the ques-tion haunted me constantly on this trip.

I thought that a bus ticket to St. Louis could work. I walked to the Port Authority bus station and asked, "How much does a one way ticket to St. Louis cost?" He said, "$32,50!" I said "OK" and walked back to Penn Station. I saw a schedule card for the Silver Meteor – a train that went from NYC to Miami. The train stopped in Philadelphia, Baltimore, Washington DC among other places and after DC, Richmond, VA. I asked the ticket salesman, "How much does a one way ticket to Richmond cost?" He said, "$ 21.50." I said, "Please give me one of those."

A great train-ride. Finally free. I had a meal on the train. The first time in my life that I ate with a knife and fork on a moving vehicle. So, on the train, I reviewed my finances. I started with $ 65. Hempstead to NYC $ 3.00; $ 21.50 train-ride; $ 2.50 meal on the train. I still have $ 38.00. Good.

The Silver Meteor arrived in Richmond at around 11:00 pm. The freshness of the warm spring air, the green lawn stretching down the hill from the Broad Street Station and the smell of Magnolias forms the indelible impression I still carry as I exited the station! It was a change from the weather in NY – warm and fragrant had replaced damp and cool! I was elated by the change in climate but tired and needed sleep. I crossed the street to the William Byrd Hotel – a large building that simply could not be missed as I exited the Station – and paid $ 16 for a room in advance. The next morning, I awoke refreshed and had this delicious feeling that I knew not where I was. I was free, somewhere strange and had no idea what I should do. I felt freedom wake and energize me as I slowly came to the realization that I was in a place far removed from yesterday's waking. "$ 16 per night is too expensive," I thought. The realization that I needed to find a cheaper place to live and a job propelled me out of bed!

I bought a local newspaper and went to have some breakfast at a diner downtown and scanned for possible jobs and a place to live that cost less than $ 16 per night. I don't know what motivated me to think that I could possibly qualify as a grill-helper at a place out on Parham Road, but I made that my first destination. I asked at the diner how I could get to Parham Road and they directed me to Main Street and told me that if I headed northwest out from downtown and then did a dog-leg onto Cary Street that I would eventually come to Parham Road. "Thanks," I said, paid for my food and was on my way. When I got to Main Street, I didn't know if northwest was right or left so I asked a lady who was washing her jalousie storm door if she knew which way I had to go to get to Parham Road. Her answer will remain with me for the rest of my life. "Weyull, it's a riiught good ways down the road a bit..." indicating a direction, "if ya stick your thumb out mebbe ya'll getta riiud." It was an accent foreign to my Long Island ears! It was southern – some people speak southern here! Besides that, it was an adult middle-aged woman telling a youngster like me to hitch-hike which no adult I knew would advise in the New York area! Oh, brave new world!

I did what she told me to do and crossed the street and hitched a ride. In almost no time a man in a big car picked me up and asked me where I was headed. I gave him the address on Parham Road. He said it was fine and he could drive me there. He drove and as he drove, he asked me where I came from. I asked, "Originally or just now?" He said, "Tell me both." "Originally Korea, just came from Long Island." "Ahh – I was in Korea, in the army – whaddya doing here in Richmond?" "Looking for a job and a place to stay." "Well, I can't help you with a place to stay, but I can definitely help you with a job" he said as he handed me a business card. The card said his name was Mr. Boyer and he worked as a job counselor for the Commonwealth of Virginia unemployment office. I said, "Really – you can definitely find me a job?" "Yep! Come see me first thing Monday morning – you promise?" "OK – I guess you can let me out right here then and I'll head back downtown." "See ya on Monday morning, nine-o-clock sharp – OK?" "Yep, thanks."

The second stop was a house on 223 North Blvd which advertised that it was a boarding house and had a single room to let for $15 a week. I walked up North Blvd from Main Street. The house and neighborhood were impressive. Across the street from my destination, 223, was the Fine Arts Museum of the Commonwealth of Virginia. An impressive building across a wide Avenue with a sloping green lawn. 223 itself was a large house with a covered front porch. Rocking on a swinging love-seat type swing on the porch was an old man who watched me as I came up the walk. I greeted him, told him my name, shook his hand as he paused his swing, and told him I was inquiring about the room I saw advertised in the paper. He said, "My name is Redford, my wife takes care of that – one moment." He called into the house for his wife and out she came. She was beautiful – I can remember that – beautiful and not old – perhaps in her 30s or early 40s – but beautiful. She looked me up and down and said, "You look mighty young." "I am, that's why I need a place to stay." "You do realize that it's $15.00 a week and you need to pay each week in advance. If you wanna eat, that's extra." "OK. Here's my $15.00 for my first week. I won't be eating (I couldn't afford it right now, even if I wanted to)." "I'll show you the room."

There is a painting (or several) by Van Gogh where he shows a room that he had let (in France, I think). Had I known of the painting at that time, I might have been reminded of it at the moment I laid eyes on my room. As it is, I'm reminded of the room every time I see the painting, except Van Gogh's room was more colorful. My room was all dark wood. A straight back chair, a twin bed, a wardrobe and a table. It was simple stuff and less than I had on Long Island, but I was happy. The bathroom was down the hall and shared with three or four other single men who had their own rooms just like me. I hardly ever saw anyone because of the hours I wound up keeping and the fact that my room, although it was a great place to sleep, depressed me whenever it was lighter outside than in.

I needed to buy some clothes, a tooth brush, hairbrush – I didn't shave yet so I was spared that expense – so I went out shopping. I found I only had enough money for a towel, three sets of underwear, three pairs of socks, the tooth brush, tooth paste, hair brush and a package of cookies. Mrs. Redford lent me bedding and a blanket until I could buy my own. I had twelve cents left – a dime and two pennies!

For the rest of Saturday, I explored Richmond on foot. It was warm – girls – young women, I should say – were in the park sunning themselves in bikinis! VCU, Virginia Commonwealth University, was in the area and the students were enjoying the weather and I was enjoying the sight of them! I walked and walked and walked until it was dark. I remember seeing a movie theater that was showing the movie "A New Leaf" and I thought that I would have to see that when I could afford to. We weren't a movie-going family and the idea of planning to see a movie made me feel both mature and free. Monument Avenue in Richmond is just what it claims to be – more boulevard than avenue but with monuments to the Confederacy – Jefferson Davis, Stonewall Jackson – I suppose that Robert E Lee should be there somewhere, but I never did see him there. I'd never seen an Avenue like that! The cookies were long gone and I was getting a little hungry, but I still was filled with feelings of freedom and fresh possibilities. I don't recall talking to anybody that day after the exchange with the Redfords, but all-in-all I was contented and full of peace of mind as I fell asleep in my room that night.

Most Sunday mornings my mother or father would drop my little sister and me off for Sunday School in my sister's case and the church service in my case. I enjoyed the hour-and-a-half away from home – the music, the hymn singing, the standing-up-and-sitting-down rhythm of the traditional Lutheran liturgy as well as the simple peace brought by worship. Sometimes my father would stay for the service, although mostly not. My first Richmond Sunday had none of that. I wandered around the town. I can't recall if it was indeed overcast on that day or if my mood was just gray, but my memory of the morning was just that – gray and overcast. I missed my Sunday morning traditions: Picking up two bags of rolls at the bakery and two sets of newspapers (Times and Daily News in those days) at the candy store on the corner, delivering one set to my Uncle's doorstep around the corner, going home, having rolls with butter and jam with my usual cereal and canned fruit for breakfast and reading the baseball news before going to church. My mother wasn't a great cook but she did go out of her way to make a roast for Sunday afternoon dinner – the only day of the week we had anything other than sandwiches at lunch-time. I was simply alone and lonely this Sunday in Richmond. I remember asking myself the question, "Are you running with me, Jesus?" As a tall and lanky southerner passed me by on the street and said, "Ya'all look lahk ya got da weight of the wooorld on those little shoulduhs. You OK?" "I'm fine, sir. Good morning!"

That afternoon, I summoned the courage to walk into the Fine Arts museum across the street. I didn't know how museums worked but I had nothing else to do and all the time in the world. I found out, as I found out many years later about the Metropolitan Museum of Art in New York, that one made a donation upon entering which was voluntary and that there was, therefore, no fixed price of entry. I gave my dime, leaving me two pennies and I was entertained for the afternoon as I'd never imagined entertainment could ever be. Paintings with depictions of southern scenes and southern history. Sculptures from the classical age. Scenes of battles, murder, death, families, embraces, landscapes and fruits – Paintings of astonishing color, astonishing size, fascinating subjects, naked people! Room after room with a hushed atmosphere and quiet foot-steps while the walls cried out with the passion of life, spoke with the cool detachment of posed portraits or narrated the natural beauty of representations of life in all its forms. I learned to appreciate the artists' power to move the soul on that Richmond Sunday afternoon.

Monday I awoke with only one thing on my mind and in my body and that was hunger. I hadn't eaten since I'd finished those cookies on Saturday afternoon. I knew that I had that appointment with Mr. Boyer at nine-o-clock, but I was too hungry – I couldn't imagine doing anything until I'd eaten. Saturday's newspaper had advertised a temporary job agency where you would be given a job for the day and be paid at the end of the day. I made my way there at 7:00 a.m. I sat in a room full of ragged and time-worn men – black and white, young and old but all looking like they were used up, lost and totally different from the people of my experience. There were two exceptions to my perception of these men and they were a young man – I can't remember his name – I'll call him Patrick because he had that hard-scrabble Irish way about him – the kind of optimistic view he had no right to have given the hard luck he was experiencing – and me. I went to a counter at a hole in the wall of the waiting room when it came my turn and gave my name, my address, my age as 18 – I knew I had to lie – for someone to write on a form – (many of these people didn't write, I supposed). I then sat down and waited. A group of men went out to work on a construction site, others were picked up in pick-up trucks to work on farms and others were picked up to work at factories. Patrick, who told me he was 18, and I, were the last in the place to be picked up at around 8:30 and we were driven to a dirty old factory not very far from downtown.

We were walked through the factory to an area outside the back of the factory that looked kind of like a junk yard. There was a huge pile of car batteries near a contraption that I could only describe at the time as an electric industrial guillotine (now I know it was a shear). On the other side of the contraption was a large barrel and still farther away was a pile of old empty battery casings. Patrick and I were given rubber aprons that covered our torsos and upper legs (but did nothing for our arms and bottoms of our pants below the knees), shoe coverings and instructions to line up six batteries at a time on the contraption, pull the lever to chop the tops of the batteries off, pound the contents of the batteries into the large barrel and throw the empty casings onto the empty casings-pile. This we did. Patrick was a hard working guy and proud of his strength (as he should have been). He was not much bigger than I and wiry, built like a wrestler, didn't speak a southern accent, more a mountain-folk accent. He had come to Richmond to build a life for his girl-friend, himself and his new-born baby boy. We took turns placing the batteries on the contraption, I always pulled the lever, we both slammed the sludge into the barrel and threw the casings on the casings-pile. At the time I was about 5'-4" tall and around 100 pounds dripping wet. I hadn't eaten in nearly two days and this was not a job I was made for doing (not like Patrick). The minimum one could work in order to be paid was four hours. I am ashamed to say that I lasted the four hours and then left Patrick to do the job by himself for the afternoon. I picked up my time sheet. I walked back to the temp agency, I collected my pay and went to eat. I should have found a way back to Patrick somehow – just to keep in touch, but I didn't.

Six dollars is a lot of money when you only have two cents in your pocket! I ate a meal of hot dogs, potato salad, beans and a dessert of jello with whipped cream for $ 1,09. I was full and still had nearly five dollars. I threw away my ruined shirt (the sleeves were full of holes and splattered from the battery acid). My pants weren't too bad so I was now down to a white tee-shirt and dark pants when I went looking for Mr. Boyer. I found him sitting at a desk in an office which was the destination of a queue of about 40 or 50 mostly black people. As I had walked past this line of bright white eyes staring at me passing them by, I had no idea that it was the queue that I was supposed to be standing on! (Nine-o-clock sharp rang in my mind!) Fortunately, Mr. Boyer raised his head and saw me the instant I recognized him – "Stop, don't move. I'll be done here in a minute and then you are to come in!" "OK"

"So what happened this morning?" he asked. Looking down, I answered, " – couldn't come, had to do something else." He left it at that and asked about my work experience. "I've delivered newspapers – I was an honor carrier for Newsday! I've worked in a small grocery store. I've helped out on a farm sometimes during summers.." He asked if I'd ever worked in a kitchen. "I worked in my Mom's kitchen all the time!" I enthusiastically replied. He then said sternly, "I'm going to send you to work in the kitchen for a good friend of mine called Mr. Potter. I've never sent him a bad worker. I've never disappointed Mr. Potter, so do not disappoint him or me." He then made a phone call and told me that I could take the bus out there that afternoon and introduce myself.

Mr. Potter was a very impressive man. Dressed in a gray business suit with a silk tie, he cut the perfect figure of a serious manager. When he opened his mouth and a plush English accent cascaded out in a comforting baritone, he became even more impressive. Mr. Potter was the boss of the Restaurant and Catering at the Willow Oaks Country Club of Richmond, VA. He met me in the kitchen of the club where I had been led, offered me his hand and almost immediately told me that Mondays were to be my day off. He showed me around, told me I would be a washer of pots and pans (the guys that had had that job had simply not shown up on Sunday), pointed out a soup-maker – a kind of silver pedestal in the floor with a stainless steel dome covering a huge stock pot full of a hardened glop that must have been soup at some point in the (hopefully) not too distant past, and said, "Ohh ... you can clean that up tomorrow when you get in – do you like pie?" He introduced me to a hunched-backed black man – his name has faded from memory, but I think his name was Bill, so I'll call him Bill here, who, having been injured in World War II, couldn't straighten up anymore. They built him a big butcher block work-table which must have been about five feet by five feet with a working height only about two feet off the floor. Bill could work perfectly on a table of that height. The ovens were all low in any case. Mr. Potter expansively called out, "You have any pie for this young man, Bill?" Bill, to me, "How's about apple pie, boy?" Me, "Sure!" Mr. Pot-

ter, "Have a cup of coffee – here's how you use the machine…."
Me, "Sure, thanks." I'd never had coffee before in my life, but it
smelled and tasted delicious and I had the first of many pieces
of Richmond "breakfast pie" and coffee. After the pie and coffee, as I checked in with Mr. Potter, wanting to check out, it being my day off, Mr. Potter handed me $ 20 and told me that he
figured I could use it until I got paid on Friday. All I could do
was thank him and promise him he'd have the money back on
Friday. He told me who to check in with the next morning and
that I shouldn't forget about the soup-maker.

I took the bus back downtown feeling flush with cash. I went
shopping for clothes. I found a sidewalk sale at a Woolworth's
downtown and bought a pair of pants, some more underwear
and socks, a couple of shirts and still had some money left over
for the rest of the week. I really didn't need money until Saturday
when it was my time to pay the next week's rent on my room. I'd
be doing all my eating at work according to Mr. Potter (we could
order anything from the a' la carte menu before or between our
shifts except for the fish, shad-roe or the steak). I felt very lucky,
and, in my vernacular of that time, I knew that Jesus was running with me. Peace of mind was mine.

Tuesday morning brought with it my first taste of my regular
schedule as a Willow Oaks employee. Mr. Potter had arranged
for me to be picked up before work and dropped off after work by
the number two guy (not being able to remember his name either, let's call him Tony) at the club. His nominal position at the
club was maître-d'; seating people, arranging the wait and bus
staff for the various restaurant rooms in the club and all around
'look-arounder' to make sure all ran smoothly. Tony was a long
way from having the aura of confidence of Mr. Potter, but he was
friendly, competent and dependable. He was, along with Mr. Potter, the only white, male member of the permanent staff. There
was a white woman (busty, blonde piled up hair, about 45 years
old – I remember her only as Dolly, but I'm sure that wasn't her

name – perhaps it was Doris) who worked lunchtimes in the a' la carte room. Other than her, there was me who looked east-Asian (even if I felt lily-white), there was Willie Joga, the bartender, who looked and sounded kind of India-Indian, although I never had that absolutely confirmed, and black people. White, young people would come in as pot washers and dishwashers sometimes (several times, in fact, while I was there – it seems pot washers and dishwashers are hard to keep), but generally, the stable working staff was black. In any case, Tony would pick me up every morning and drop me back home the next morning sometime after one in the morning when we were finished. I wasn't working the whole time I was at the club each day. When I wasn't working, I'd just hang around listening to or talking mostly with Bill, Willie or Dolly – especially Willie because, oftentimes there really wasn't much for Willie to do at the bar but he had to stand there, look busy and wait for drinking club members. I get ahead of myself though.

Tony was right on time picking me up for my first morning of work. I arrived to find Bill was already at his baking station rolling out dough. He called to me and offered to give me a piece of "breakfast pie" as soon as it was done provided, I went into the provisions room and reached up on the shelves there to haul down a couple of large cans of fruit preserves and bring them to him. This became a daily chore – the way every work day began during my time in Richmond. When setting the cans down on Bill's butcher block table, I set about cleaning that soup-maker. It was the only work I could imagine that was worse than busting and gutting car batteries! Soup, after a couple of days standing at room temperature takes on a thick, slick, pasty consistency and a funky smell from up close. I devised a strategy of scooping and scraping with a ladle and then using soapy, hot water to cut the grease. Even though the water was plenty hot, I had to go through several iterations of scooping, emptying, pouring and scrubbing before the machine was truly squeaky clean. The folks in the kitchen were impressed though and were effusive in their praise. It seems they wanted this pot washer to stay. I felt good as I ate my pie and drank my coffee. As I finished my coffee, Tommy, the grill chef, came up to me and in a gruff, blustering way, introduced himself. He was dark black, must have been about 40, built like a sprinter or a halfback, had a wonderful smile and gripped my hand hard as he said, "So's yous da new kid Mistuh Potter tole me about – good ta meedjuh! Sho did a good job on dat Soup-makuh! Man shee shiiines!" I was and remained in awe of Tommy, the grill chef. He was full of energy. He worked as if possessed and every time he would throw a steak or a burger on that grill and it sizzled and spat, he'd jump back and yell, "Hot Damn!"

Tuesday and Wednesday were filled with washing pots and pans and helping the dish washer(s) if it got busy there and I was caught up with pots and pans. I spent all my time in the kitchen watching the controlled chaos of waiters rushing in and out, of cooks and cooks' helpers scrambling to get food out, of the dishes coming in, stacked, piled high, topped with left-over food and used napkins, being converted into stacks of steaming clean dishes waiting to be filled with food again. Pots and pans are in constant use in a kitchen like that and I remained busy from start of day until around four in the afternoon and from five until around eleven during the evening shift. At first, during my time in the kitchen, if I wasn't busy, I just hung around Bill and his bake station or sat on a stool near my work station waiting for incoming pots and pans. If I emptied the soup-maker in the evenings and cleaned it before the end of my evening shift, I had rather leisurely mornings where I could have my breakfast pie and coffee and read a paper without any pressure as long as Bill had his preserves and Tommy didn't need me to do anything. The Country Club always seemed to have two or three events going on in the various rooms set aside for meetings and banquets. The a' la carte room was open for members and their guests from noon to three and in the evenings from six until one in the morning. Members all had their own accounts so money was normally never asked for, seen or exchanged that I could see during my entire time there. Even the waiters were not tipped. They received 15 % of all the orders they put into the kitchen. Tony had to be there until closing, and as he was my ride home every evening except Thursdays (his off day), I spent my entire time in Richmond at the Willow Oaks Country Club from around 10:00 a.m. until 1:00 a.m. (except for Mondays).

My career as a pot washer ended on Thursday evening. There was a big party in the banquet room that evening. The dishwashers who had left after the afternoon shift didn't come back for the evening shift and the need for someone to man the dish washing station out-weighed the need for someone to clean pots and pans after about nine-o-clock when the glasses started piling up and the first dirty dishes started coming. I had already learned how the cleaning line worked from helping on the previous two evenings. Scrape the dishes out into a large container, throw the napkins into a cleaning bin, use the overhead spray head to get most of the food and grease off of the plates before placing them onto their edges between the tines of a square transport bin. The more compact the better but try to keep a separation between every surface so that the spray of the machine can rinse every surface without any hindrance. Push the bin onto the conveyor belt that guides the dishes under the hot caustic spray of the machine. Prepare the next bin. As the previous bin exits the machine (the plates so hot that they're already practically dry), stack the plates onto bins that can be transported to the food stations or to the dish storage. From 9:00 p.m. until 2:00 a.m., I repeated this process over and over again until the dishes from a five course meal for 275 people were all clean. I was the hero of the day at the Willow Oaks Country Club – (at least among the waiting and kitchen staff).

The next morning when Tony picked me up, he told me that he'd heard that I had worked extra hard the previous night. He said that I would now wash dishes for the next couple of days but that before the weekend was over he and Mr. Potter had discussed that I would begin training to be a waiter by busing tables. They just needed to get people into the jobs of washing pots and washing dishes. True to their word, I worked washing dishes and pots and pans for Friday and Saturday, but on Sunday, they found a uniform that fit me and put me out front in the a' la carte room to bus tables there. I learned to set tables, fold napkins, keep my attention spread out across all the tables in my area, refill water glasses and coffee cups, get the waiter to come to take orders if asked to do so. It was easy work compared to washing pots, pans, dishes, and soup-makers. Smiling at people was part of the job and I found I enjoyed it.

The work got a little harder on Sunday evening when I had to work a big banquet. There were almost 200 people dining that evening with a fixed menu. The waiting and bus staff was about 10 or 12 black men, Tony, and me. One of the waiters was a distinguished looking man (picture Uncle Ben of rice fame in a waiter's black tux) who, having suffered a nervous break-down as a teacher in the Richmond schools, decided that he would try to make some money as a waiter. There are a lot of positive things one can say about being a waiter, but it is a job not without its own various forms of stress. Add to this normal stress the varied personalities of people who work as waiters at banquets. Waiters who work such jobs are often people who like the money from working two or three shifts a weekend but are not dedicated to waiting as a profession. They are often what you might call "characters." One tall example of this type of waiter liked to tease people by reaching in as one raced by carrying a tray-load of glasses and deftly removing one glass out of the middle of the tray. The ensuing struggle to maintain balance and keep from dropping anything was snicker-inducing to those who witnessed the event but absolutely terrifying to the poor sod carrying the tray. A short victim such as I had it a bit easier than a taller guy like "Uncle Ben" because the wise guy was so tall he could indeed get a glass out of the middle of my tray and over-all balance was maintained as long as I maintained my cool. Uncle Ben being taller, the glass removed from his tray absolutely unbalanced the tray and poor Uncle Ben became positively unhinged. His water glasses – about 25 to 30 of them, filled with ice, slid to the floor after a quite sad and desperate dance, with "Uncle Ben" still gripping the large oval tray by its rim. He surveyed the scene, dropped the tray, walked out and was never seen again. I got to separate the ice from the glass, sweep up the glass and mop up the melted water. The wise guy got to cover Uncle Ben's station. Uncle Ben's share of the 15 % service fee was split by the rest of us.

I returned the $ 20 to Mr. Potter that weekend when I saw him and thanked him for the opportunity of working at the Club and for the opportunity to become a waiter. He said that I should stick with the job and stick with him because it was a good career path I was on if I wanted it. I said thanks and didn't tell him that I was still hopeful of completing high school somehow and go to college. I settled into life in Richmond. I paid my rent every Saturday. I rode to the country club every day with Tony where I took down preserves for the pies and set them on Bill's butcher block worktable each morning. I had breakfast pie and coffee every day except Mondays. I worked lunch shifts with Dolly and evening shifts with Tony. I talked with Willie at the end of every day and I did my job waiting on the club members of the Willow Oaks Country Club.

One night, after a particularly busy shift, I got back to the neighborhood where I lived and not wanting to go right to bed, I took a walk. I discovered a pick-up basketball game populated by young-to-middle aged black men, who all, like me had just finished their shifts at work and were blowing off steam. I watched a bit and was eventually asked if I wanted to play. I did and was accepted as one of them – the New Yawkuh – they called me. Car headlights illuminated the court, and no one complained about the noise and it was a great way to shake away the remnants of a work day before heading to bed. It became a nightly ritual, and I became one of the regulars.

A few days later, I was taking orders as a waiter in the a' la carte room. After a week or so, Dolly and I worked the lunch shifts and the evening shifts were handled by one or two of the black waiters, Tony, and me. If it was a quiet evening, it was just Tony and me. I only worked the banquets when they were short-handed. In general, the a' la carte room was my workplace. Willie worked the bar. Willie Joga (or Yoga – I only ever heard the name – never saw it written) was an immigrant. I only assumed he came from India because of his slightly lilting accent and his dark complexion but he might have been from anywhere in south Asia or the eastern middle east. I spent more time with him than anyone else because my duties in the restaurant were generally over about 10:30 most evenings and I had to hang around until 1:00 for my ride back downtown. He would stand behind the bar and I would sit under the bar, facing toward him and talk to him while he served his customers on the other side of the bar. Several times the confused customer thought the discussion strange as they thought Willie was addressing them when in fact, he was responding to something I had quietly said. Willie was proud to be older and wiser than I and was generous in his advice. He gave me a book – a small, black-bound book that fits into the inside breast pocket of a blazer or suit jacket with the title, "The Secrets to Success, Power and Love." He told me that he had read it and he thought that it might be useful to me. It was full of one line or short paragraph anecdotes about what it means to be a gentleman of the sort that our parents tried to make of us young folks in the 50s and 60s. When my time was over in Richmond, Willie gave me a silver Kennedy half-dollar which he told me would bring me luck and which I should always carry with me and never spend. I carried that coin around in my pocket for five or six years. One day, my sister told me I should put the coin on a chain and wear it so as not to lose it by carrying it around in my pocket like that! It sounded like a good idea, and I did so. One evening a few weeks later, I discovered that the chain had somehow slipped off my neck and was gone. It was the saddest I've ever been at losing any amount of money. The memory of Willie – and the coin – remains with me though.

After I had gotten into my routine in Richmond and life became ordinary and routine, I took a fistful of coins and some time out to call my sister, Nancy. She asked, naturally, about where I was, was I fine, what was I doing, etc., etc. I didn't answer any of the direct questions except to say that I was fine, I was working and taking good care of myself and was healthy and happy but missing her and our other sisters. She told me to call again the following week at the same time. This I did. On the second call, she told me that our sister Barbara had found a way that I could come back to Long Island, live with Barbara, and return to school. I should arrange things so that I could return. Because Nancy lived very close to a train station in Hicksville, Long Island, I told her that I'd come to her house when I could arrange it. I then talked to Mr. Potter about leaving my job after the following weekend but didn't tell him why. He told me that I didn't have to stay for him. He said I could leave whenever it was convenient for me, he'd give me whatever I was owed for the time I'd worked in cash on my departure, and I shouldn't worry about anything else. We decided that Friday would be good then. I was thinking that I wouldn't have to pay Mrs. Redford for another week then. I wanted to tell him everything, but I didn't. I had a suspicion though that he somehow knew most of it anyway.

We go through life as immigrants. We go from one place to another either physically, emotionally or psychologically. Some beginnings are more memorable than others. Many of us never move to another country but we've all gone from one place or state-of-mind to another – from a place where all was familiar to a place where all was different. My first immigration was from Asia to America. My second from Long Island to Richmond. I didn't stay in Richmond long, but Richmond remains in me to this day. The easy manner of Mr. Boyer asking me where I'd come from; Mr. Potter's generosity and apparent ability to look into me and see who I was; Bill's joy at making me happy with a piece of breakfast pie; Tommy's exuberance in his work and an energy that I never saw wane; Tony's quiet way and competence although he knew he'd never be Mr. Potter; Uncle Ben's making another go at handling stress; the wise guy; Willie, the advice, the book and the coin; the pictures and naked sculptures in the museum; the basketball players; Patrick, his girl, his kid and Mrs. Redford, her beauty and her quiet old husband rocking back-and-forth on that porch – they're all a part of me until the day I breathe my last.

At my "home-coming," Nancy saw me walking up her street and she, crying and blubbering gave me the hardest hug I had ever gotten. She was so excited, her head accidently bumped my nose and set it bleeding again, but I just sniffed it back until we could get into her house. My return to Long Island from Richmond precipitated a chain of events that caused my family to splinter apart. My parents separated and divorced and sold the house I'd lived in. My mother would eventually move to Florida taking Sherry, my little sister, with her, and my father would move upstate New York and re-marry rather quickly. I was able to return to school and my former job at Nicky's because my oldest sister took the step to petition the court in Nassau County to declare me an emancipated minor. By the court ruling I became freed of my parents and could make decisions for myself. Best of all and most importantly, I didn't have to go back to my parents' home. I was in the 11th grade at the time of my Richmond experience. I had one more year of high school to complete and the last remaining month of the 11th grade. Returning after being away for a month was a mixed bag of experience and feelings. My friends, of course, were happy to see me back and curious about what I'd done while I was away, but the stories, I think, seemed far-fetched to them. I had stepped out of my life, entered another, and returned, as far as they were concerned. What happened in between simply didn't impress them. The fact that I was breathing more freely and that my inner life had completely changed didn't register on them because no one had an idea how my life had been in the home of my parents. I went from being spiritually crushed and physically abused at home to living free, going to a home without fear of what would happen there, and learning that my life's light cast a good and satisfying glow.

Pots and Pans and Learning to Sell

When I finished high school in June of 1972, I knew I would be college bound in September. I had been accepted into the State University of New York's College of Environmental Science and Forestry at Syracuse. I received a scholarship from New York State which would pay for my entire tuition, but I needed to worry about paying for my living expenses. I answered an advertisement in the jobs section of the local newspaper. The advertisement promised minimum earnings of $ 800 for eight weeks' work and claimed only to want to hire college kids on their summer vacations. I wasn't technically a college kid yet, but I answered the ad and was directed to come to a presentation and an "interview". The presentation was a very slick and well put together recruiting piece designed to impress us gullible young people into believing that we could earn relatively large sums of money by participating in a revolutionary new marketing promotion for a company called American Foresight. Besides the already mentioned stipulation that one was supposed to be a college student, successful recruits needed to have their own cars. We were told that a bright future awaited those who participated in the summer program. The company was owned by Drum Corporation, a division of Fidelity Investments Corporation. The President of American Foresight had convinced Fidelity managers to buy his company and finance it as training ground for future investment salespeople. The thinking behind Fidelity's purchase of American Foresight was to train hundreds of young college students through summers of direct sales to have a ready-made recruiting pool for future sales professionals who could sell investments after their time in college. Some of the older students who had been in the program for more than one summer and who had already completed their junior year of college were looking forward to being able to fall back on a job offer from Fidelity investments upon graduation from college. Those that wished to take on this challenge for this summer job were invited to a four-day training camp that took place at a college campus near Philadelphia. I had been working at Nicky's all the years since I was 14 on a part-time basis but I felt the need to work a full-time job and 40 hours of working at a department store or a fast-food restaurant didn't appeal to me. At Nicky's 20 to 25 hours per week was the most I could work and that paid me about $ 60 per week. Working 40-hour weeks at a fast-food place or a department store would only bring me about $ 80 per week. I had loftier hopes for a summer of work and the possibility of earning over $ 2000 for the summer and the guarantee that I would receive at least $ 800 which would translate to $ 100 per week convinced me to take American Foresight up on their offer to train me into a successful businessman.

I hadn't yet been to college so the experience of visiting a college for the training program and being in a place with people who were all slightly older than I was completely new. I felt like an imposter at first because all these people that I was now involved with were truly students and all had already been to college. The person who recruited me was a young lady whose name I can't remember. She was a student that had just completed her junior year at Bryn Mawr College. She would be my manager for the summer. The training program was a grueling affair. We started every one of the four mornings at 8:00 a.m. and worked late into the evening for the first three days and were released to return to our homes on the afternoon of the fourth day. We learned that American Foresight's product was cookware – pots and pans – and fine China (or porcelain) dinnerware. Our sales strategy was to target single working girls who were still living at home. The ideal sales presentation was to the single working girl herself along with her mother. This ideal presentation was called a "qualified presentation." To collect the minimum of $ 800 at the end of the summer, one had to do 10 qualified presentations every week for the 8 weeks of the summer. A small set of pots and pans (called "Wonder Ware") went for $ 220. A large set of Wonder Ware cost $ 300 and 8 place settings of China, a choice of one of two patterns cost $ 280. As an inducement for the young lady to decide to purchase the cookware, a free gift of either 4 place settings (for the purchase of the small set of Wonder Ware) or 8 place settings (for the purchase of the large set of Wonder Ware) of one of two patterns of stainless-steel flatware was given for no additional cost. One received a 20 % commission on every sale. The first sale was commission free but was compensated to the recruit with the ownership of his "sample kit."

On the first day of the training, we were introduced to the "Gold-spot" card. It was a postcard with a gold colored "rub-off" field – a rectangular area in the middle of the card which covered the name or description of a promised prize. The printing on the face of the card asked the recipient not to rub the field off until the "Gold-spot" representative came to call on them to introduce them to a new marketing campaign. The promised prize was for participating in the campaign. We were each given 10 of these cards and told to hand-write to 10 girls we knew from our home-towns who we knew worked full-time jobs and who lived with their mothers. Our message was that we would come and visit to reveal the prize and ask for their participation in our market-ing campaign. We were then trained on how to introduce our-selves as the "Gold-spot" representative (or man) and introduce ourselves as people trying to raise the awareness of the brand-name "Wonder Ware". We learned the following dialogue with the theoretical potential customer:

GSM*:   Hi is Mary home? (Holding up a Gold-spot card) I'm Paul, the Gold-spot Man.

Mary: Yes, I'm Mary.

GSM: Oh great, Mary. We are here in East Meadow doing a marketing campaign to raise awareness of our brand. When I say Aspirin, Mary, what comes to mind?

                                                 * GSM = (Gold-spot Man)

Mary: Bayer.

GSM: (writing on a pre-printed form) OK, very good! When I say car, whaddya think?

Mary: Chevrolet

GSM: (writing) – OK – Not Ford or Chrysler?

Mary: Well, yes, but Chevrolet just came to mind first because that's what I drive.

GSM: Now if I ask you what brand comes to mind when I say cookware, what do you think of?

Mary: I don't know any brands of cookware.

GSM: Well, our marketing campaign is for a brand of cookware called Wonder Ware. Our goal is that whenever you hear cookware, you'll automatically think of Wonder Ware just as you just identified with Bayer and Chevrolet. Mary, I'd like to make a presentation of my product to you. To thank you for your time and attention, I am here to rub off the "Gold-spot" on the card you received in the mail and present you with your free gift.

Mary: OK.

GSM: Mary, who does the cooking in the family.

Mary: My mother, of course.

GSM: We'd like to present our brand to you and your mom. We'll need a half an hour to an hour of your time. Would that be possible now or should I come back another time?

Mary: OK, I think it'll be OK now. Please wait a minute and I'll ask my mother.

The "Gold-spot" opening was for beginners, and it forced the new recruit to overcome his uncomfortableness with talking himself into the house. The program was set up to force the recruit into action directly after the training session as he had already sent 10 cards out. As time passed and the recruit became more confident the card was simply a prop and often was not sent in advance.

After a successful "opening" I had to go back to the car and haul out the suitcase sized sample kit which contained a complete set of Wonder Ware as well as samples of the flatware and china. Also in the suitcase was a small tripod and a "pitchbook." The pitchbook was a large hard covered flip chart with pictures, charts and content for Mary and her mother to look at on their side of the tripod set-up. The other side of flip chart (the salesman's side) had every word that the recruit was to say along with advice printed along the bottom of each page such as "Be Positive!;" "Smile!"; "What is your body language saying?;"etc.

The training session covered every step of the process: from the door-opening, to presenting the free gift, to every page of the pitchbook presentation including the close. Equally important, we were trained to stay with the customer after the sale in a process called "solidifying the sale." We then were to ask Mary and her mother who else we might be able to talk to among Mary's friends and work colleagues. The training was extremely in-depth and complete. I have never encountered a more effective sales training since. Every element of the sales process was discussed in detail. Through the training and the experience that followed I learned the lessons of the professional salesman, which I still consider, to this day, are the same lessons that every politician, pastor, successful businessman and conman must learn. I learned that the sales process is indeed a process which needs to be controlled. The narrative needed to be formed, practiced, and stated to the potential customer effectively, sincerely and as if it was coming from the heart. The key was to have practiced every word that was printed on the salesman's side of the pitch book and committed it all to memory through constant practice so that the sales demonstration flowed like a performance in which Mary and her mother had parts as well.

When I returned to the house from my car, having just retrieved my sample set from my car, I needed to ask for a kitchen or dining room chair to be placed in front of the sofa and the mother's easy chair where Mary and her mother invariably sat. My sample case was placed about one foot to the right of chair with the case open toward me. The lid of the case acted as a sight barrier to Mary and her mother's side of the room restricting their view into the sample case. The sample kit was set up with the contents placed in FILO order (first in last out). The stainless steel table ware was in the bottom of the case, then came the china samples and then the set of Wonder Ware that included a frying pan, a 6 quart stock pot, with a pot lid that fit both, "Dutch Oven" domed lid that fit both pan and stock pot, a four quart sauce pan, a three quart sauce pan and a one quart sauce pan all with their own lids, a set of six poach-egg cups and a rack to hold them which could also be used to hold ears of corn or asparagus on end for steaming when placed in the stock pot and used with the domed lid. A black velvet covering hid the contents from view until it was time for each element of the demo to be revealed. I then placed a tripod between the chair and sample case with one leg directly between the chair and the sample kit and the two legs forward pointed, usually, one toward Mary and the other toward her mother. The tripod had a rail supported on these forward two legs which held the pitchbook. The pitchbook's pages were all flipped to my side of the tripod at the beginning of the presentation with the opening remarks printed on the first page I could see. As the contents of each page were spoken by me, I would flip the page to show Mary and her mother an image on the reverse side of the page I'd just recited. That image matched the words I saw on the next page on my side of the tripod.

So, one page after the next I would flip the images to make each point in its proper order. As I spoke, the images Mary and her mother saw were designed to reinforce every point. There were images of the hodge-podge of cheap pots and pans most mothers used to cook the evening meals in these lower-middle to middle class homes. There were images and graphs to show the health of "waterless" cooking. There were images of healthful food lovingly prepared by perfect wives and there were images of the well-ordered lives lived by people who save and plan well. At some point in the presentation the pots would be introduced, one by one. Mary and her mother would be made to be impressed by their heft. They would remark about the beauty of the surfaces of polished or brushed stainless steel. They would feel how heavy they were, and I would show them how strong they were by standing on one while it rested on its edge and showing after standing on the edge that the pot lid still fit perfectly (which would have been impossible if my weight had deformed the roundness of the pot).

Wonder Ware was designed to cook with little water and lower temperatures. It was also designed to be used as stackable cookware. That domed lid, that came with the six-quart stock-pot, allowed one to stack a saucepan on top of the stock pot or the frying pan to preserve burner space on the stove top. I would later learn that Wonder Ware was one brand name for a premium set of cookware made by Regal Ware Inc. and sold under various brand names with modest changes in design. The ideas brought forth during the presentation spoke of the future responsibilities that Mary dreamed about having when she would be the lady of her own house and be providing for the health and welfare of her own family. The presentation spoke to the different arc that Mary's life might take as compared to the arc her mother's life took as expressed in the nearly universal stack of cheap, non-matching-bought-as-required, usually aluminum and with a worn-out Teflon coating, often dented and deformed pots and pans in the kitchen of Mary's house. What I want to convey here is the degree to which this program was thought out. The mastermind behind this company and the sales program was a man called Ed Satell, a Philadelphia area businessman who was always present during the training programs and at sales meetings. He was a man of unbridled enthusiasm and had an extremely active imagination and an unsurpassed ability to think through a sales campaign to its success. I have to say, I learned much from his concept.

During the winter of that year, American Foresight became American Future. I didn't know it at the time, but the relationship between the American Foresight management and the Fidelity management soured during my first summer of work at the company. It became clear through a recent review of documents that described a court case involving Regal Ware seeking to collect funds from both American Foresight and Fidelity that Ed Satell's companies were both less than and more than what met my eyes and touched my experience in my two summers of selling Wonder Ware. Despite the shadiness that the entire enterprise now exudes in my memory, that I learned the nuts and bolts of sales in a way few people have had the opportunity to learn, in such a compact and intensive manner, is absolutely undeniable.

There are certain things all salespeople must learn and here is a short list of the lessons I learned in that original four-day training session, and which were solidified into my consciousness over the following weeks of the summer of 1972:

1. Being positive and remaining positive is the most basic work of selling.
2. Being totally into the presentation or demo with all your senses open to the communications [both verbal and nonverbal] coming from the potential customer is mandatory. Selling is the practice of purposeful empathy.
3. Selling is a numbers game. Putting oneself into selling situations as often as possible is the first step to selling (therefore the promise of a minimum income if a recruit did 10 demos per week for each of the 8 weeks of the American Foresight selling season). A beginning salesperson with a mediocre presentation will have a success rate or "closing average" of about 20 %. A great salesperson might increase his closing average to as high as 60 %. The difference is making $ 100 per week or making more than $ 300 per week. Doing more demos put a salesman on a road to more success as well as more failure.

4. Each time a customer says no to your product, the successful salesman knows that he is getting closer to his next sale. Direct selling is a practice in constant self-motivation.
5. The salesman can control the narrative to shape and manage expectations. In the Wonder Ware demo, the salesman was forming a narrative of how a $ 400 or $ 500 investment in a good set of cookware was worth it because of the health benefits of waterless cooking, the lifetime character of the investment, the satisfaction that the customer was doing something good for her future and was being given an opportunity to avoid at least one of the mistakes that her mother made. At the end of the demo, when she learned that a small set of Wonder Ware only cost $ 220 and the large set was only $ 300 and that she could pay the purchase off in a relatively painless $ 20 per month, purchasing didn't seem like such a bad idea.

I learned my lessons well. After taking a few days to shake the jitters of having to speak to people that I didn't know, I felt confident in my line of patter. I went from the Gold-Spot-Postcard openings to cold calling in a matter of a week or two. Whenever a demo was completed, I sat with the "Mary" and her mother for a few minutes and, whether she had bought the Wonder Ware or not, would inquire about other young women she might know that might be interested in hearing about our brand of cookware. The process of developing leads and qualifying them had been taught in the training session and ingrained in our psyche as an important part of every visit or exchange with anybody we met along our way. Throughout that first summer, I made at least 10 demos per week and sometimes as many as 14 or 15 over six-day weeks. I travelled all around the area around my hometown of East Meadow and the neighboring towns of Levittown, Westbury and Uniondale visiting single working girls and their mothers. That summer I earned about $ 3000 in commissions (which was about 55 sets of Wonder Ware and 5 sets of

China or about 6 or 7 sales per week). The highlight of the summer was winning a four-day trip to Bermuda where a group of about 15 of us stayed at the then famous Bermudiana Hotel in Hamilton. I was also asked to come back the following summer to be a sales manager.

The trip to Bermuda was, for a working-class kid like me that had never stayed at a hotel except for my first night of my runaway experience in Richmond, an experience of stepping out of normal life and into a dream. The people who planned the trip thought of everything to make us feel like we belonged in "high society." We were handed rum swizzles immediately upon landing. I wasn't a drinker in those days, but these tasted very good and I drank them for the next four days. American Foresight had booked a penthouse suite which was always open to us and always stocked with snacks, fruit, and drinks as a kind of "party room". We all were provided with mopeds to get around the island on. I suppose that the experience was both a reward for good service and our success for the company, but it also served to make us hungry for more. I can't remember a more carefree experience in my life. We were in paradise with a group of other high achievers with nothing to do but visit the beaches, enjoy the weather and each other, eat great food, drink rum swizzles, and race our mopeds around the island (if racing is what you can call it when the speed limit is 20 mph and when one always was in the wrong lane when turning a corner! I, being one of the smallest, almost always won). We had all gone through a remarkably similar experience of a summer spent alone in our cars or in front of "Marys and their mothers," trying to internalize a new system of making money and living someone else's idea for our summers and now we had these four days before returning to our normal lives.

The difference for me from all those other kids in the American Foresight summer program was that I didn't have a normal life anymore. I wasn't returning to college as all the others were. I was going away to school for the first time. The four days in Bermuda were like an emphatic end to my years of saving and planning and the beginning of my time spending what I had saved and moving forward with my plan for my life.

After that summer of learning to be what was known in those days as a "door-to-door salesman" and coming to a realization that earning money was something within my own power to influence, I packed up all of my stuff into my car at my sister's house and drove to Syracuse to begin my life as a college student.

Getting an Education

The SUNY College of Forestry occupied a tract of land adjacent to Syracuse University (SU). SUNY (State University of New York) was and is one of the biggest public Universities in the US. Today SUNY has 64 campuses, over 440,000 full-time enrollment and over 2,000,000 people who are enrolled in continuing education programs at its community colleges, major university centers and specialty colleges. What is a wonder to me is that CUNY (City University of New York) is a parallel public university that serves New York City and a further 275,000 degree seeking enrollees. There was a special relationship between the College of Forestry (since renamed the College of Environmental Science and Forestry or simply ES & F) and Syracuse University. Anyone enrolled at the College of Forestry was also entitled to take classes, participate in social activities and sports, use the facilities and more-or-less have most of the privileges of Syracuse University students. All of this even though Syracuse was a private university with significantly higher tuition costs than the public SUNY College of Forestry. There was a social and cultural distinction between students that were SUNY ES&F students and SU students. From an ES&F perspective, the average Stumpy (as the ES&F students were called) was less well-to-do, less sophisticated and perhaps a little less cool than the SU students. We saw ourselves as a little smarter than the SU students, a bit more serious as students and definitely more down to earth than 'they' were. From the perspective of the SU student, we Stumpies were just plain dull and socially backward. SU students tended to come from urban and suburban communities from all over the northeast whereas ES&F students tended to come from upstate New York. In any case, I fit in really well with the Stumpies. I was admittedly a bit socially backward (not at all cool) and I did indeed identify easily with the Stumpies although I came from downstate New York's Long Island. We Long Islanders were also a bit out of place as Stumpies and were easily identified as nearly imposters because of the way we 'tawked'. The typical upstate Stumpy 'tokked'.

During the years I attended, tuition at the College of Forestry was, I believe, $ 600 per year for the first two years and then $ 900 for subsequent years. The tuition at Syracuse University was much more expensive. I was fortunate enough to have received a scholarship from the State of New York which would have paid up to $ 2000 per year of tuition for the full time that I was matriculated in a University. I would, however, need to pay for my living expenses (the dormitory and my meal plan) and all the costs of living on my own. During my years of high school in East Meadow, there were at least two kinds of High School diplomas. One was meant for kids who wanted to go on to university and the other for kids for whom finishing High School was enough. About half the kids in High School went for the diploma, issued by the New York State Board of Regents, which would allow them to apply to college and have a chance of being accepted. In those days, as now, the rankings in a High School graduating class, the results of the SAT standardized test, the recommendations of teachers and other community leaders as well as participation in after school activities were all criterion by which a potential college student's applications were evaluated for possible acceptance. The same Board of Regents gave a standardized test to all college bound students in New York which was also a means of colleges and universities of evaluating potential students who had applied. A third standardized test that all of us headed toward colleges were subjected to was the National Merit Scholarship Test. In all those standardized tests I did very well scoring in the 98th percentile or better every time. What they did was to underscore my teachers and my parents evaluation of me as an underachiever – someone who was performing at a level far below his capability. There was one redeeming value to the tests and that was that the New York State Regents Exam result came with a 99th percentile ranking and a scholarship. One either won a scholarship or didn't and if one did, the amount of the scholarship was based on financial need. Since I was an emancipated minor under the law and had no parents that supported me, I received the highest amount which meant that I never needed to pay for my tuition at Syracuse. In addition, the financial aid office at the college always found me some money in the form of a private scholarship which helped out with the books and other supplies or the defrayment of the costs of living, traveling or simply being.

I remember receiving a package of information Syracuse University sent me which was meant to inform me about the possibilities for activities open to students. All the various clubs and groups involving music, arts and crafts, religious organizations, civic organizations, political affiliations and sports activities were introduced to the incoming freshmen. The one flyer that appealed to me was one from the Hendricks Chapel Choir which invited all interested singers to an audition. Up to that time, I hadn't really been involved in any organized music but the thought of being involved in a choir appealed to me. During a visit to my mother, I told her that I was making my plans to go to Syracuse and mentioned to her all the various activities on offer and indicated that I was interested in auditioning for a choir that, according to its own advertising, was quite demanding and had a very good reputation. Her response was that I shouldn't be disappointed if I didn't get accepted into such a good choir at such a big school. My music performance career up to that time involved taking part in a variety show in our high school which involved clowning around, telling jokes and some singing but she hadn't ever really seen me perform. There was the one time that my parents did come to see me play at an accordion recital when I was nine years old. I had been one of the best in the group of kids who took after-school lessons at the local public shool. We had learned on small student accordions with only 12 so-called "bass" buttons for the left hand. My older sister had a real, adult, 120 "bass" button accordion and my parents, not wanting to continue to rent the student accordion, gave me my sister's accordion to use for my lessons. At the recital, I walked out onto the stage strapped to this monster of an instrument. To the vantage point of the people looking up at the stage, it looked like a headless accordion walked out onto the stage by itself and the audience simply broke into tittering, restrained, but undeniably, genuine, laughter. The program seemed to aid the comedic effect. The piece which appeared to have played itself was called "Monkey Business". My mother seldom went to church with me, so, unlike my father, she never really heard me sing out the way I loved to during a church service. Her general impression was simply that I was probably not going to be good enough (no matter what the task was). When she made these subtle putdowns, it wasn't meant to be a rebuke. Just as a point of fact. I learned to keep my mouth shut.

My roommate, Tim, and I shared a room on the fourth floor of Lawrinson Hall. This particular dormitory was mostly populated with fairly well-to-do kids from all over the northeast of the US and athletes who were on scholarship from all over the country. Syracuse gave out scholarships in sports like Basketball, Football (American), Crew (rowing), Track and Field, Wrestling, LaCrosse, Women's Soccer, Women's Field Hockey and probably a couple of other sports, but I can't remember which.

Lawrinson was an all men's dorm. Next door was an all women's dorm called Sadler Hall where both men and women (boys and girls?) from the neighboring dormitories would have their meals. I do recall how bitter cold it was sometimes. It would get so cold that, no matter how hungry we were, we waited until the last minute to walk across a walkway of about 70 yards to Sadler and food. We waited until the wind and driving snow (that often came sideways, driven by a freezing wind with temperatures approaching -20° F, that made each snowflake feel like the cutting edge of a razor) would somehow relent to make the walk over to Sadler a bit less uncomfortable and stingingly, bitingly cold. We never remembered later (after enjoying the warmth of Sadler's dining hall, with its abundance of food and the proximity to co-eds) if it had relented or not. We still had to walk back. Funny how we were always surprised by the cold when we returned to Lawrinson after dinner although the idea of the cold going to Sadler was a major hurdle to us getting over there in the first place.

The Syracuse University campus and the SUNY College of Forestry campus were located next to each other. At that time, the College of Forestry occupied six buildings located around its own quadrangle. Lawrinson Hall was the closest dormitory to the College of Forestry. There was only a field about the size of a football field which separated my dorm from the ES&F campus. The field served as our playground for occasional pick up games of touch football, frisbee or impromptu snowball fights.

Lawrinson Hall had 20 floors. Each floor had 16 rooms, two of which were single rooms and the rest double rooms. I would spend two years living in Lawrinson Hall. The SU rules stated that freshmen and sophomores needed to live on-campus in dormitories and older students could live in off-campus apartments. My first year was spent with Tim as my roommate. My sophomore year was spent with a slightly older Syracuse University student named Gary Stephenson. Gary was from the Philadelphia suburbs of Southern New Jersey and studying business administration. He was a much more serious student than Tim and came from a completely different family background than Tim or me. Gary came from an upper middle-class family and grew up playing tennis and not really worrying about money the way that I needed to do. He was also an extremely organized person whereas Tim and I were normal young men with a tendency toward sloppiness and disorder. If Gary were sitting at his desk reading a text for homework and he was called to the telephone which occupied a space in the central hallway near the elevator banks, he'd put a bookmark in his book, put his book on a shelf, fix his hair and then go to take his phone call. Although we were roommates, we didn't have a very close relationship. It was cordial and respectful but not particularly warm.

The memory of my Lawrinson life is the memory of being the innocent (as in inexperienced) character standing by as an observer to something like a John Irving novel. A multitude of characters passed through my time there. Our fourth floor didn't contain any real "high flyers" that captured the attention of the campus newspaper or anything like that but we did have a blind guy, a Casanova (make love, not war) type, an earnest Roman Catholic theological, intellectual type, a political, equally earnest, conservative William Buckley Republican type (complete with bow ties – at least in my memory), the local-boy-just-trying to do good type, several others who didn't make much of an impression at all and a small group of just plain, everyday types without girl-friends who just kind of hung out together. We didn't have any of the big, bulky football players or the really tall basketball players on our floor. What we had were a collection of young men who were mostly coming home from classes everyday without much to do except hangout with each other and play cards. At the beginning, card playing was limited to poker. The people who played poker there, played for more money than most of us could afford to lose at one sitting and it was uncool for us to play for pennies when others were playing for 10s of dollars per hand. Our solution was to learn how to play bridge. Sometime in October or November of my first year a group of 16 of us all learned to play bridge together. From that point on, there was hardly a day that went by when between 12 and 16 young men didn't sit and play bridge every late afternoon and evening, often until the early hours of the morning. It became a habit that we couldn't break. It got so bad that I often dreamt of bridge hands in the fitful sleep I managed during those nights that followed five or six hours of playing cards. The card playing influenced our grade-point averages as well. I did OK in my classes but many of us that played regularly (like Tim, my roommate) were failing many of their courses. I was never a high-flying student with high grades – I was satisfied to be a B or C student in a grading system that awarded A as the best grade possible and an F to the those who failed. For me, what was important was that I maintained my grade-point average in the two to three (Bs and Cs) area which would mean that I would always be able to go on to the next level courses that were necessary to maintain my progress toward graduation. I only did the amount of work necessary to maintain this simple goal. This meant that the amount of work I did outside of my classes was really kept to a minimum and I had the time to play bridge, sing in the choir and unsuccessfully pursue young women.

Each floor of Lawrinson was laid out with the rooms arranged in an inward facing square. Our rooms all opened onto a hallway that circumscribed a lounge area, the shared bathroom with its multiple shower stalls, a kitchen that nobody ever used and the bank of three elevators. One benefit of living on the fourth floor is that we could reasonably use the stairs to get home or go out. Put about 30 young men together on one floor of a dormitory and several pre-ordained outcomes can be expected. Pranks are one of those sure things. One favorite prank was to take the clothes or bathrobe and towel that hung next to an occupied shower stall and placing them in the hallway on the other side of the elevators as the unsuspecting mark showered. There was often a kind of meanness to the pranks but it didn't always target the same people. The pranks were played on various people at various times and didn't usually focus on one or two people although Joe, a blind student, was the victim more often than the rest of us. Sometimes the pranks did exhibit a certain amount of creativity and genuine affection. Joe was one of the young men in the group of bridge players. If he played, we needed to mark one corner of every card with braille. He had a special embossing machine for that purpose. In bridge, as one member of a team deals the cards, his partner mixes the cards for the next hand and then places the mixed deck on the corner of the table convenient to the next person to deal. At one sitting Joe sat and waited as my partner and I dealt and mixed the cards. Unknown to Joe, we had arranged a deck of cards for a prank that we snuck into action for that hand. As we dealt the cards, he picked up the cards one by one and felt the corner where the braille informed him of what he had been dealt. We all witnessed how his face changed from the normal Joe to a Joe that was absolutely in 7th heaven. A beaming smile and a giddy joy took over his countenance as his fingers read the corners of his cards. We had arranged the deck so that he would get something like 28 of the 40 high card points (an ace is worth 4 points, a king, 3, a queen 2 and a jack 1) that a deck contains with a 2, 2, 3, 6 distribution of cards per suit. His partner's hand had been fixed to insure that he would be able to bid and play to a grand slam (the best you can do in bridge). It was fun to experience.

As I mentioned earlier, I had decided that I would try out for the Hendrick's Chapel Choir before I arrived at Syracuse. When it came time for my audition, I went one afternoon to the chapel and I met the choir director, Brent. He sat at the piano on the stage of the chapel, and I stood next to him. He asked me to sing something for him out of the Methodist hymnal. He picked a popular hymn that I would know, and I sang it to his accompaniment. He asked me if I had had any experience in singing in a choir and I was obliged to admit, no, I hadn't. He noted that I had a tendency to croon which is a stye of singing that anyone who has ever heard Elvis Presley, Perry Como, Bing Crosby or Frank Sinatra would recognize. I didn't know that was a thing – I just thought that's how you sing! He noted that I tended to slide into the correct tone or note. I think he described it as "not hitting the note precisely". My response was, "Oh ...." He then asked me if I could read music. I had a year of guitar lessons where I learned to read the treble clefts where melodies are usually represented with notes that I had indeed learned to read and play. I also had the general idea of the annotation of notes to represent the length of notes. I knew the difference between, and the names of, whole notes, half notes, quarter notes and eighth notes. I knew that the pattern of printed notes going up the page meant that the notes in the passage represented sounds getting higher in pitch. What I never really had any experience in was the bass clef. As a guitar player, I had no use for the bass clef. For the next five years, I would get to know the bass clef well. So, Brent asked, "Can you sing these notes down here?" He pointed at the bass clef. I said, "Sure!" I thought it was just another treble clef. I had never taken a music theory class in my life – only guitar lessons and music lessons with the lady that brought a cart full of percussion instruments and recorders into the third-grade classroom. I started too high because it looked like the only clef that I knew. Brent, "lower." Then he explained the bass clef to me.

The Hendricks Chapel Choir is involved in most of the most memorable times of my Syracuse experience. The tradition of the first Thursday rehearsal for new members in September was to be introduced to the music that we had to sing on Sunday. We normally had to sing a piece for Sunday's church service and sing the musical parts of the liturgy. It was so much fun to sing with a bunch of other good singers! Brave new world. After our first rehearsal, we were taken on a tour of the Chapel. A guy named Bill took us around the chapel and told us various stories of the place. The pinnacle of the tour was from the roof looking over a brick wall onto the quadrangle of Syracuse University. A couple of years later the girl that stood next to me for the tour of the Chapel that evening, Joan Barris, would run around that quad naked except for the sneakers on her feet, taking part in a phenomenon called "streaking" with about 5000 other students. Streaking was a curiosity which appeared on college campuses in the fall of 1973 in the south of the US and spread to northern campuses in the spring of 1974. I never streaked.

Joan and I held hands as we walked into the lounge of the Hendricks Chapel, as we were instructed to do. I didn't know her, but I noticed her prettiness immediately. She to me, "When will this thing be over!" I, "dunno." She, "I missed the ice cream social for this!?" I didn't answer. Then they blindfolded us and led us into a room. We thought that all the other members of the choir were gone and only we, new members, were on this tour and Joan could go back to her dining hall and eat ice cream. I was happy to be with Joan a few minutes later as we were led into the cellar lounge, blindfolded. The older members were there, unseen by us behind our blindfolds. It was wonderful to hear, "The Lord bless you and keep you. The Lord lift his countenance upon you and give you peace and give you peace ....". They sang for us, and I felt truly blessed to be in that place, with those talented people, feeling less than deserving to be there but, nevertheless there and hearing this message of love, caring and the admonishment to accept peace in four glorious parts. Joan forgot about her ice cream social and a lifelong friendship began.

Joan and I would spend a lot of time together. We could actually walk along a pathway going from place to place and sing together without feeling silly. She is an alto – I, a bass-baritone. We talked about the deepest ideas of life, death, plans for our lives, the plight of the planet and how we would make our marks on the planet without damaging the environment. We were both idealistic in different ways and we both shared a love of music and musicals. Singing impromptu duets with Joan was a real treat. Her singing voice was rich and velvety – pure and clear but with a richness of texture that filled the air and lingered there before it left the world emptier than before. Our conversations touched on everything except on our own relationship and the relationships she had with boyfriends that came and went over the course of our four years together at Syracuse. (I stayed for one more year after she graduated). Joan wound up marrying the smartest Stumpie in the class of 1976. She got married about a month after her graduation and I played my guitar and sang at her wedding. We stayed in touch after college although we didn't have the opportunity to see each other nearly as often as those years in Syracuse. I probably spent more time with Joan in my first two years (until she started to spend more time with her future husband) than with anyone else. After college and as time passed, our conversation themes dwindled to the shallowest and most inane topics of being involved in growing young families. We each had children. I moved to Europe. Her marriage ended. For quite a while we didn't communicate at all. Now through the magic of Facebook, I am in touch with her and her family once again.

The HCC was my club in Syracuse. I loved being with these friends of mine there. The space of the Chapel was large and seemingly as high as it was deep and wide. It was dominated by a domed ceiling held up, in the front, by 6 large Corinthian columns. In the front of Hendricks Chapel, in bold gold letters, the message hung in the air to greet anyone entering the space from the Quadrangle, "Ye shall know the truth and the truth shall make you free!" The room is beautiful. Creamy white, tall, and spacious. The floor plan is in the form of a Greek cross with balconies along the rear and side walls (from which we sometimes stood to sing, bearing candles, during the Christmas concerts. The regular rows of pews waiting to be filled and a big sense of silence waiting to be banned by the incursion of music. Hendricks Chapel was the last remaining historical building directly on, and at the nominal "head" of the Syracuse University Quadrangle. A mixture of Federalist and neo-classsical architecture, the acoustics of the space was magical and we, in our choir, loved to hear our voices reflected back to us at the end of a piece. Sometimes the moment of that sound ebbing to silence had an astonishing effect on those who occupied that space. There were times when we finished a piece and there was nothing to do but grin at the wonder of what we had done as the echo died out to absolute silence.

I think that I was one of the few people in the choir who had no experience in a choir before joining the Hendricks Chapel Choir. Most of the people in the choir were veterans from High School Choirs, Church Choirs or were music majors who were immersed in the idea of music as an ensemble undertaking already before the HCC experience. For the first time in my life, I was face-to-face with people for whom music was a really important part of life. For me, it had always been a decoration for life. It had never held a central position in my life. Music accompanied my life, but it wasn't central to my being, nor was it involved in my dreams for my future or in any way came into question as a central pillar of life. Up until meeting the people that I met in the Hendricks Chapel Choir, I thought that the best expression of loving music was having a nice stereo system. Music was, in my life's experience, something to be listened to. Making music – committing oneself to the making of music as a central occupation of life, well ...that was simply unthought of. At Syracuse University and represented well in the Hendricks Chaper Choir, there were piano majors, organ majors, voice majors, music education majors as well as hobby musicians who played in orchestras and bands. There were those like me who just loved to sing and lucked into this ensemble and shared these student days together singing our hearts and souls out every Thursday during rehearsals, every Sunday during the worship services and at those concerts and concert tours where we could perform for the sheer joy of performing.

In any case my first two years of college passed without any progress on the romantic or sexual experience fronts. There were several crushes that I had on what I thought of as unattainable young women, several friendships with young women who might have had crushes on me (although there was no way I would have fathomed that possibility at the time) and mostly a day-to-day of life spent going to classes, playing cards with my buddies on our floor, playing sports like touch football, basketball or catch with a baseball or a frisbee and working at part-time jobs to help stem the constant outflow of money caused by going to college while owning a car. I spent Thursday evenings and Sunday mornings at Hendricks Chapel. I tried to have as much time as possible with Joan, but she didn't have as much time to spend with me because she was doing much better than I in the romantic experience department.

During the summer between my freshman and sophomore years, I was invited to come back to work for the "pots and pans" company, American Future. I was informed that I had been selected to be a sales manager in a new office that was being started in the Albany area of New York. A district manager, who had been a sales manager the previous summer named Lloyd Agnew, from Springfield, Massachusetts, was awarded a territory with two sales managers, a young lady named Carol, from Youngstown, Ohio and me. We became a team that talked to each other every day for that summer and saw each other at least two or three times a week. Our headquarters was the RPI (Rensselaer Polytechnic Institute) campus in Troy, New York.

The responsibility fell on a sales manager to recruit his own sales team for the summer. The company booked, at various times, meeting rooms at local hotels or college campus locations in the Albany, Troy, Schenectady area for several recruiting meetings prior to the beginning of the summer vacation and placed ads in the local newspapers exactly like the one I had seen the previous summer on Long Island. I took the role of the young woman who had recruited me the previous summer. For taking over that role, I had spent a two-day management training session in the

Philadelphia area earlier that spring. I did everything they told me to do and spoke the words they taught me to say to roomfuls of people that came to see what I had to offer. I offered an opportunity to learn what I had learned. I offered the fulfillment of the desire to be successful. I introduced the "marketing program" which would bring self-confidence, hone communication skills, promised success and guaranteed a minimum of $ 800 for 8 weeks of work to anyone who simply followed the program's instructions. (This at a time when the New York minimum wage was $ 1.85 per hour).

All the sales managers met on a college campus somewhere near Philadelphia just prior to the start of our summer sales campaign. There were about 20 district and sales managers there. We had each been tasked to go through the recruiting process, do follow up calls on the candidates that had come to our recruiting events, estimate how many candidates might show up to the training course and book an appropriate size training room to accommodate the sales group with which each of us would start our summer of work. My boss for the summer, Lloyd and my colleague Carol expected groups of about 10 to 12 which was the estimate for nearly every one of the other managers. My estimate was 20 to 25. I was advised by Ed Satell, the President of the company, to revise my number downward because I was: a- inexperienced, b-awfully young, c-nobody had ever started a summer with such a large group and who knows why else. In any case, 23 people showed up. I had the largest sales group that American Foresight or American Future ever had up to that time.

The thing with direct sales of any kind is that the first successes for most direct salespeople comes from them selling to their friends and family first. After our four-day training period was over and my team went out into the market and started selling, we sold an incredible number of pots and pans in our first week of real work. I was a star in the company, and I learned to make money by motivating other people to sell and make money. Unlike the previous summer where I was mostly traveling alone, as a sales manager, I went out with different members of my team every day. Whereas the compensation for a salesperson was 20% of whatever was sold, my compensation became an "over-ride" or a percentage of the sales that each salesman in my group made. The summer started with this huge success and then settled down into a summer of attrition. The members of the team sorted themselves out into successes or failures. The failing quit and the successful kept on going as long as the success lasted. At the end of the summer there were only five or six salespeople left in my group and only one bonified star salesperson, a young lady who drove this old red Volvo, and whose name I think to recall was Debbie. I learned from my experience of that summer that there is no way of judging how successful a person will be based on the impressions they made at the beginning of our acquaintance. The people I thought would be successful because of their likability or their looks or open, easy way about them turned out to be disappointments in terms of sales success whereas others who it took me more time to warm up to and who had their odd hard edges or funny ticks had the right combination of grit, desire to succeed, and the ability to accept, and take to heart, training and coaching became unexpected sales successes. By the end of the summer, I had earned more than $5,000 but had spent a good $1000 of it on living costs over the summer because I wasn't living with my sister but rather in a bachelor lifestyle along with the fellow management team members, Lloyd and Carol.

The summer ended with me having earned enough money to pay for another year of living in the Lawrinson dormitory and having a full meal plan at the cafeteria at Sadler Hall next door. I could still afford my car although unexpected repair costs were becoming more frequent and ever more expensive. Car insurance was becoming a burden and toward the end of my 2nd year at Syracuse, I began to see that I was running out of money. I was invited to return to American Foresight for a summer of pots and pans, this time as a district manager for Long Island. As a district manager, I would report directly to Ed Satell and have a group of sales managers. When they made the offer, I was 19 going on 20 years old and was told that I should be able to earn over $12,000 for the summer of 1974. I simply could not bring myself to accept the offer. My perspective at this point was that the previous two summers I had dedicated my life to earning money by selling young single working women over-priced pots and pans they didn't need. Although I was proud to have been successful at what I had done, I didn't feel any value in talking people into spending money in this way. I was beginning to feel it was a misuse of my talent and being a district manager for such an enterprise didn't seem attractive to me, except, of course, for the money that was being offered. Even at that, the money wasn't really being offered, it would have to be earned as commissions on the backs of the sales that the salespeople generated and the success of the sales managers as recruiters for the enterprise at the beginning of the summer. Although I came to the realization that I didn't have any money to sustain my life as I knew it, I turned down a job that promised to pay me over $1000 per week for a summer of simply silencing my conscience.

An Introduction to Industry

I sold my car for almost no money in the spring of 1974 and when I returned to my sister's (Barbara's) house for the summer between my 2nd and 3rd years of college, I bought a bicycle to get around. My poor college period began then. Barbara's husband, Harry arranged with a friend of his who was an electronics engineer, Bill Kitchener, that I would get a summer job at the factory where Bill was the engineering manager. I became a factory "assembly worker." I had no skills in the world of electronics. I didn't know how to solder components, populate printed circuits, or run wires from point to point. I really had no idea at all how electronics worked or how a factory functioned. The business where Bill was the "brains of the outfit" was called Artek, Inc. The President and, I suppose, major shareholder was a man named Charles Leonhardt. I remember him as a man, in his late fifties or early sixties, who wanted to be known for his quiet manner, successful aura, competence and for being smarter than he probably was – (kinda like me now, only I'm older and will never be known for my quiet manner.) Charlie, as everyone called him, was, besides the CEO (as he would be known today), the mechanical engineer in the outfit (although, like me, he had no credentials as an engineer). Bill Kitchener was the brains of the outfit. He designed all the circuits for the products Artek made. His designing was done on yellow legal pads. He would sit at a desk in a darkened office with oppressively dark blue painted walls with a pencil in his hand, sketch electronic schematics with squares, triangles, squiggles, parallel lines, other symbols all connected with a network of mostly horizontal or vertical lines. He was a good-looking man of my brother-in-law, Harry's, age (I suppose about 35 then). Harry and Bill had worked together at another company and became friendly before they'd both departed that company for better jobs or more money. I was fortunate enough that the friendship was good enough that Harry could call Bill and ask for help for me in my summer of need.

Bill arranged a job for me in the factory. The factory was a space that was about 10,000 square feet, the largest part of which was an electronics assembly area with four long work benches each of which could seat six or seven people next to each other. Each work space had good lighting, a magnifying glass with a ring illuminator, a soldering iron with ready spools of solder and solder wick, several contraptions to hold circuit boards, trays to hold components, several spools of small gauge wire in different colors, foot rests and, to the extent that the work station was occupied, a lady, usually at least a little overweight and usually as old as or older than my mother was at that time. Some of the workstations were occupied by someone assembling wires into cable harnesses onto big wooden boards (as large as a large movie poster). Glued onto these wooden boards were large diagrams with lines representing each wire. Each line was marked with matching numbers at each end. Each line was given a color which matched the color(s) of the wires on their various spools on the work bench. The diagram showed little dots where nails were hammered into the wooden board at various points to guide the harness assembler to bend each wire along its predefined route from its start point to its end point. A normal cable harness at this factory contained approximately 50 to 100 separate wires and was as long as four feet in length if it were to be stretched out to the length of its longest wires but when bent at the various angles that the harness was contorted into before actually being mounted into the final product for which it was designed, the harness made it easier to connect electrical contacts within an aluminum product housing which measured a couple of feet long about 18" high and about 12" wide. I didn't know it at the first introduction to these wire harnesses, I would become intimately involved in the problem of electrical connecting points for the rest of my life.

Another common pastime for the assembly ladies at Artek was assembling printed circuit boards. Printed circuit boards or PCBs are a two-dimensional version of a pre-manufactured wire harness that arranges wire connections on a flat piece of electrically isolating material (at that time a kind of material made of glass fabric reinforced epoxy resin called G10–today called FR4). Most of the circuit boards used at Artek were simple double-sided circuits which means that circuits occupied both the top and bottom surfaces of a circuit board. These boards were drilled with holes which were "plated through" with copper. The holes served a double purpose of holding the legs or leads of components which would anchor the electronic components to the circuits in proper position and making an electrical conduction between a line connected to the hole on one side of the circuit board to a line connected to the same hole on the opposite side of the circuit. Artek made a couple of simpler products which required only single sided PCBs but my work there would largely be on products using double sided PCBs.

The whole employee team at Artek was about 20 employees. When I came to work for my first day, there were: Charlie Leonhardt, two engineers, including Bill, a woman in the drafting room who was responsible for keeping the drawings in good order and making prints of the originals when necessary, a man who did purchasing, a secretary, a bookkeeper, a traveling salesman who came into the office infrequently, a foreman in the factory, two technicians who tested sub-assemblies and worked to complete functioning prototypes, a man named Tony who worked in a machine shop who's job was to make prototype machined parts or special parts required in a hurry. There were four assembly ladies who worked at the assembly stations either assembling circuit boards or assembling wire harnesses or assembling the completed machines (which involved assembling the harnesses into the machine chassis, mounting subassemblies into final assemblies and connecting controls and switches to the harness which would complete the functioning end product). There was a shipping/receiving clerk and a lady responsible for quality control and product inspections. Rounding out the team were two general helpers. I was a hired for the summer as a general helper and took my place at the very bottom of the social hierarchy of Artek in the summer of 1974.

On my first day, Bill met me and interviewed me and asked me to fill out an application for employment. I'm sure that he was just doing his friend, my brother-in-law, Harry, a favor by giving me a summer job when I needed one and he saw his duty fulfilled at the moment that I took my place next to the other general helpers on the factory floor after my interview and my introduction to the factory foreman. I was happy to be making $100 per week. It really didn't make me feel badly that I had given up a chance to make more than 10 times that much as a district manager for American Future peddling Wonder Ware. I was happy to have what I considered to be a solid job.

Artek had a so-called "piecework contract" to assemble industrial AC power distribution units. This sounds much more complicated than it is. Most of us know these as six plug extension units. The ones that Artek assembled contained a switch/circuit breaker unit and three duplex-three pronged-female replacement wall sockets connected by a total of six pre-stripped, pre-bent thick gauge wires of black and white all mounted to a pre-punched face-plate and then assembled to a long, box-like container along with a long six foot plug-in cable. An assembly line of three positions had been set up for this product. The first worker would take a face plate, mount it in a jig and bolt the three duplex units in place and snap the switch/circuit breaker into prepared holes and then pass the assembly to workstation 2. There the wires would be pressed into the proper holes to make the connections between the components and then passed along to position 3. At position 3 the cable and box were fitted, connected, and assembled and the whole assembly dropped into a cardboard collection box. The foreman would come by at irregular intervals take the parts from the box, plug each assembled unit into an electrical source and switch the units on as a kind of final assembly test.

For two weeks, I worked on the assembly of power distribution units with very few breaks where I would work on preparing wire ends for the harness makers or bend and trim components for the circuit board assembly ladies. It was mind-numbing, repetitive, and soulless work. The only way to survive an 8-hour shift was to set goals of improvement or play mind games related to how fast or efficiently the job might get done. If I sat in seat one, the guy in seat two hated me for going too fast. If I sat in seat two, the guys in seats one and two both hated me for going too fast. In the end I was confined to seat three and a purgatory of waiting. The cause of my banishment to seat three was that one of the assemblies blew a fuse and almost started a fire, during a period I occupied seat two and was responsible for the wiring of the units. I could not imagine that I could have made such a mistake and continue to feel that I was framed to look bad by one of the other two but the only one who could answer that would be the person who planted the bad part, if indeed I had not made that mistake. In any case, I felt awful and decided that the job was not for me and decided on that Thursday that I would call it quits the next day. I told my brother-in-law Harry of my plans over dinner, and he expressed some disappointment but he supported me in my decision and he told me that I might be able to help him out at his job, perhaps, in the coming week, if, at best it would only be temporarily.

The next morning, I went to work with the plan to go to Bill after lunch and tell him of my decision to quit. I never got a chance to though. Bill came out to the assembly area looking for me early in the day and asked me to follow him to his office. Bill didn't often go out to the assembly area. If he did, it was to work with the technicians on the solving of some kind of problem related to work on improvements of a product or work on the design of a new product. Having Bill come out to the factory floor and ask somebody to come with him to his office just never happened, but it happened on that day. I sat down and as he spoke to me, I concluded that he didn't sound nearly as smart as I knew he was. He spoke with a relatively thick New York accent. He spoke like a guy who says Pawl for Paul and Lawnguyland for Long Island. On this day he told me that he needed somebody who could draw to work in the drafting room.

Yes, indeed, I could draw. I would never consider myself capable of drawing like an artist, but one thing I knew I could do was draw well enough to get ideas across. During High School I had completed two years of an advertising design class in which we had to maintain a sketch book and had to become proficient in the advertising design process from layout to mechanical to separations and printing plates. For the forestry program at Syracuse, students studying Forest Resources Management were required to study surveying and drafting in their freshman and sophomore years. My drafting was related to architectural work and representing outdoor spaces, but I only needed a couple of hours of looking at the drawings that Artek already had to see what I needed to change to be able to draw for Artek. The discipline of technical drawing is the same for Architects, Landscape Architects, Civil Engineers and Mechanical Engineers. The units change. The tolerances are expressed in different ways and of course, the materials each use are different, but in the end, it is all the communication of wishes in clear and precise symbols and language that the reader understands without doubt or need of further clarification.

Bill told me that I would become Artek's draftsman from that moment on. He told me my pay would double to become $ 200 per week and that there was a stack of ECOs in the drafting room that could keep me busy into my old age if I wanted to stay and work instead of going back to school when fall came and gave me a wink that said not to take him too seriously. I went from a potential quitter to a person with a new perspective on life within one morning. My spirits lifted and soared and when I sat at my drawing board to get to work I had to ask the lady in the drafting room what an ECO was. An ECO, I came to learn, is the bane of every engineer's and draftsman's existence. Engineering Change Orders are the follow-up paperwork that must be done to document a change in a product so that all documents match the wish of the engineers responsible for a product. To give an example, let's consider the change of a drawer handle on a piece of furniture from a handle that was deemed to be too light or fragile to a more robust handle. The people responsible for purchasing must be informed to stop ordering the old handles and must be informed of the source of and the technical requirements of the new one (oftentimes the engineers or designers specified exactly where and from whom the product should be bought). The mounting holes in the drawer for the handle may now need to be another size or even worse, they might be in totally different places, different hardware might be required to hold the handle in position, etc. ECOs deal with what to do with already produced parts (modify, scrap, stock for possible future use, etc.). They deal with the modification of old or the creation of new drawings or purchase specifications as well as with the change of all documentation related to processes in production, assembly and testing of products both already in production or designed for future production. One of the first laws of engineering that I learned in my very first weeks of working in product engineering is that ECOs are always created much faster than they are carried out and tend to pile up. They are the perfect source of procrastination.

On that Friday, my first day in my apprenticeship in product engineering that I have now been in ever since, I looked through the ECOs, got the lady in the drafting room, Pattie, I think she was called, to get the drawings or specifications that the ECOs referred to out and I started a new life in industry. At the beginning it had to do with making the changes on each document that needed changing according to each ECO and then taking the stack of documents to Bill to have him sign off on each change. The pile of ECOs got smaller but never disappeared. I worked for Artek on and off for a little over four years but I am sure, that when I left, the stack of ECOs was bigger than when I started.

Taped to the drawing board that would become my work place for the next several years, was a drawing that Charlie had started. It was a design for the repackaging of a new version of Artek's most successful product, the Bacterial Colony Counter. Artek's products were sold to laboratories that worked in biological and medical research. Bill, as an electrical engineer, was the guy that designed these products but his mode of operation was to work with electrical schematics which showed the various elements of a circuit arranged in the way they were connected in order for the product to perform its intended function. Charlie fancied himself a mechanical expert and created the way the product would be mechanically put together and function. On that Friday, I not only took over Charlie's, the President of the company, role as the company's mechanical designer, but I took over his drawings and was made responsible for finishing them and creating all the necessary documentation to convert Bill's schematics into a working new model of the Artek Bacterial Colony Counter. The new version would be called the model 880 and, by the end of summer, the project was well on its way to becoming reality.

The first drawing was a large drawing that covered most of the drawing table. I would come to learn that it was an "E" size drawing. Engineering drawing sizes have names. Letter size drawings of 8-1/2" x 11" are called "A" size. Double that at 11" x 17" are "B" size. Double that at 17" x 22" are "C" size and so on. So this first drawing of the Artek model 880 was a drawing covering 34" x 44" and showed the side view, front views and rear views of the machine chassis in ¾ scale. Looking back on this project from nearly 50 years in the future as I am doing now, I am certain that Charlie's design was not the result of a good engineering mind making the best design decisions. If I were to design the chassis from scratch today, the design would certainly be more elegant, easier and cheaper to manufacture and easier to assemble. On the other hand, finishing Charlie's work and giving life to his ideas in the course of my first 8 weeks of industrial life gave me a certain value in Charlie's eyes and, although the design could have been better, I learned the processes of working sheets of metal into useful forms in a matter of weeks. This education would continue over several years to the point that I felt confident in working metal in uncountable ways to solve a wide array of problems in the design of instruments, machines and processes used in medicine, biological and materials research, electronic devices and all manner of production equipment. "Learning by doing" is how Germans describe my education in design – they say this in English although I can't recall learning that exact expression during my English-speaking life in America.

Bill worked mostly designing circuits on lined yellow legal pads. These he would give to me to redraw and combine on "C" size electronic schematics. These schematics would show the electrical connections between transformers, inductors, diodes, diode arrays, rectifiers, capacitors, resistors, thermistors, coils, amplifiers, integrated circuits, potentiometers, switches, fuses and connectors. For every line or segment on a schematic there was a corresponding line (or land) on a printed circuit board or a piece of wire in a harness or cable. For every connection of a line to a component there was a hole in a circuit board or a solder contact point on a circuit board or a solder or crimp connection to a wire which allowed an electrical connection to a component or connector in real life. My job at Artek became converting the electrical engineer's pencil diagrams into a product that had a mechanical reality. The ideas were transformed in a step-by-step process into physical pieces of assembled materials. The process began in Bill's office with ideas scribbled on legal pads, then scripted into engineering documents at my drawing board and then metamorphosed further into representations of physical reality in the design of various elements. Beyond and between the design of chassis, brackets, mechanical parts, assembly drawings and the layout of the wire harnesses came the design of the printed circuit boards that converted useful incoming signals into usable outgoing signals. Designing a printed circuit board (PCB) to match the schematics on those yellow legal pads became one of the more important jobs I would learn that summer of 1974.

My Introduction
to Printed Circuit Boards

Designing a PCB as your job is like being paid to solve puzzles the whole day. These days I play a game on my iPad called "Pipe Art." The goal of the game is to connect end points of the same colors with a pipe of that color without interfering with the connecting of any other end points in the game. Likewise, connecting components on a circuit, without making any unwanted connections or blocking off any connections that must be made, is the job of the PCB designer. The job can be made harder if your boss tells you to avoid unnecessary holes. If you recall, I wrote earlier that the holes have two functions. One as a holder for component leads or "legs" and the other as a way of connecting from one side of the board to the other. A hole which has the sole function of getting to the other side of the board to make a previously impossible connection possible was called a "stitch-through" by us at Artek and Bill didn't like me to use them because he thought that they cost money. This is one of those cases where I can say that Bill was probably wrong. I'm sure he spent more money on my time solving the puzzle of how to connect a dense circuit without stitch-throughs than we ever would have spend on a couple of extra holes per circuit. It is also a true statement to say that short connections between electrical connection points on a circuit board are generally better than long connections.

The process of designing a printed circuit started with a 4 to 1 representation of the borders of the board to be designed. A board, which was typical for us, of 6" x 4", would be designed in a larger scale and would have an outline of 24" x 16". Then the integrated circuits (IC) would be represented on a layout drawing, usually with die-cut stick-ons which were printed on the same 4:1 scale and purchased from a company called Bishop Graphics. When laying out the IC locations one tried to make certain to maintain the necessary space between IC packages to fit the discrete components associated with the input or output to the ICs nearby and all the tracks or connecting lines which had to be run along the surface of the board between the components and their attendant pads. Then, using the normal drawing tools of the draftsman, one draws the components into place and mark the locations of each hole to be drilled into the finished boards. Using a blue pencil for the traces or lines or lands on the top of the board and a red pencil for those on the bottom side of the board one connects all the hole positions and IC pad positions as they appear on the electrical engineer's schematic. Blue lines could not cross blue lines, nor could red lines cross red lines. When this layout was completed, Bill and I would check the layout line for line, component for component (against the catalogue details for each component), hole for hole and pad for pad. The next step was "taping". Taping was done on a fresh sheet of matte-finished polyester film (often called Mylar). One started by sticking the IC patterns in place, then progressed to sticking 4:1 scale pads in the places that holes for mounting components (and those dreaded "stitch-throughs") were planned on the layout. The sheet was now sent to a photographer who had a large horizontal reproduction camera to make one inverted copy (inverted so that the copy really represented the bottom of the original. The original was used for the "top-side" taping and the copy was used for bottom side taping. The tape for the taping was a black, crepe adhesive-backed, optically opaque tape also manufactured by Bishop Graphics. The designer would roll out the tape to match the blue or red lines on the layout and cut the ends at the terminating pads or holes with an X-Acto knife. The tapes I used at Artek were 0.125" for higher current carrying lines and 0.062" lines for signal lines. After the tapings were completed and checked, the tapings were sent out to the photographer again to reduce the artworks to their correct 1:1 scale to be used by the producer of the PCBs as the "artworks" for the production of the circuits. The lines that had been 0.125" were now 0.031" in width and the lines that had been 0.062 were now 0.015". By modern standards, such lines are thick. The lines I used then for our bacterial colony counter boards were like tractor trailers to today's formula one race cars! In any case, the entire process seemed, nevertheless, magical to me then and the PCB continues to fascinate me to this day.

For me, the usefulness of a bacterial colony counter can be summed up in its role as a teaching implement to introduce me to the world of how industry works to create or find problems and solve them whether or not the problem is indeed worthy of solving. Its role in my life, and Bill's and Charlie's and for all of us at Artek was unmistakably, good and was necessary to our success and emotional and professional fulfillment. At the time that the first bacterial colony counters (BCCs) were designed by 3M and Artek their usefulness was still in question. Whoever has tried to count the number of randomly arranged dots of various sizes in a sample of dots on a page or a piece of fabric can appreciate what a BCC is supposed to do. Bacteria grow in colonies in various shapes and forms. Some bacteria arrange themselves in colonies that appear to be round dots of various sizes and colors; others as stripes or elongated, comma-like shaped colonies; some fan-like and others blob-like. Important is that they always arrange themselves in colonies when grown in agar in Petri dishes. Reproductive success in bacterium can be measured by the relative number of colony development per unit area over time. Likewise, the success of antibodies against bacterium reproduction can be confirmed by the limiting of the growth of the relative number of colonies per unit area over time in a treated sample. Research labs have developed tests to measure success or failure of bacteria to reproduce by growing bacterium in prepared Petri dishes and then counting the number of colonies after a period of time during which they can reproduce and multiply. Historically, lab assistants outfitted with magnifying glasses, needle-pointed probes and illumination devices which either provided top lighting, through lighting or "dark-field" (illumination from the sides or top against a black background) counted the number of colonies by hand.

The advent of close circuit television (CCTV) technology and the availability of very high-resolution TV cameras built around ultra precise vidicon tubes with very fine resolution deflection circuits made it possible to consider manufacturing automatic BCCs. (The use of video cameras to solve industrial problems became a repeating theme throughout my working life). Artek's BCC contained a very high-resolution CCTV camera, a stage for mounting the Petri dish to be counted, various modes of illumination, various modes of adjustment and calibration, a button to push to get the machine to count and a display that showed a result. Between the camera output of the picture it saw of the Petri dish and the number displayed on the LED readout of the model 880 there were five printed circuit boards mounted in what we called a "bucket" or "card cage" with names like "Deflection Circuit", "Video Processor", "Edge Detection Board", "Counter Board", "Display Controller". It is interesting to note that the machine was an analogue machine without a computer or microprocessor in sight. Beginning about three or four years later, digital devices built around microprocessors would become the core of any such product designs and ten years later I would use semiconductor based CCTV cameras called CCD cameras in the design of a CCTV controlled machine used to make high technology printed circuit boards. The camera and vidicon we used were the last gasp of American CCTV technology leadership in the world. The basic technology we used was created by a General Electric site in Syracuse, New York that specialized in industrial camera technology to be used for high resolution applications, high accuracy/low distortion applications, low light level applications and sophisticated control requirement applications for general industrial, military, scientific and medical products. In a sign of the times, GE gave up CCTV technology at the site and sold the unit to the man who had managed the site at the end. The drum-beat of digital technology and Japanese competition caused the exit of many great American companies from this market sector. The CCD cameras I would later use in the 1984 development of my own design for a machine using CCTV would be manufactured by Sony, a famous Japanese consumer electronics manufacturer and an early adopter of CCD technology. CCD technology itself however, was invented in the USA in 1969 by two scientists, Willard Boyle and George E. Smith at Bell Labs. For their work on the initial CCD device (charge-coupled memory) Boyle and Smith received the Nobel Prize for Physics in 2009. The first optical CCD devices were a line array camera manufactured by Fairchild Semiconductor and an early two-dimensional array (100 x 100 pixel) CCD digital still camera was first manufactured by Kodak.

TV camera technology is a perfect example to examine how technology changes in electronics presaged winners and losers of the future and moved the center of gravity of the electronics industry from west to east in a matter of three decades. Industrial changes that occurred in the 1970s set the path to Asian dominance of the manufacture of electronic imaging devices (still and video cameras) and electronic display devices (monitors, TVs and projectors). The leading producers of vidicon tubes and their controlling deflection circuits in the 1970s were RCA, GE, Philips, Hitachi and Sony. As such, these leading producers, with the exception of Sony (who was the last entrant into the vidicon tube and deflection coil business) didn't take the steps necessary to enter the competition for mastery of the CCD or CMOS imaging device market. Today, of the 10 companies listed in a recent "Market Watch" report as the most important companies in the area of CCD and CMOS imaging devices:

- Teledyne Technologies Inc.
- Hamamatsu Photonics
- Panasonic Corporation
- Samsung Electronics Co., Ltd.
- Sharp Corporation
- Infineon Technologies Ag

- Axis Communications
- Sony
- Toshiba
- Agilent Technologies Inc.

Only four are western companies and only Sony remains of the companies that were leaders in the vidicon business (although Toshiba and Panasonic also made vidicon-based cameras up until the 1980s).

The likes of RCA, GE and Philips who had huge investments in the area of vidicon and deflection coil production throughout the industrialized world of the 1950s and 1960s, must have known about the weaknesses and disadvantages of their technology when compared to CCD devices in the 1970s and the CMOS devices that came in the 1990s but they decided to either sell what they had, in the cases of RCA and GE or milk out their cash cow until it dried out in the case of Philips. Although Kodak invented the digital still camera in the mid-1970s, they half-heartedly entered the market but struggled to make a profit on the manufacture of cameras because they were used to selling cameras as a "loss leader" and making their profits on film, paper and chemistry sales. One must juxtapose the development of digital photography in the 1990s with the success that Kodak had enjoyed in the 1980s and 1990s. Times had literally never been better for Kodak. If you recall, this was a time when cheap "point and shoot" cameras using 35 mm film existed alongside the more expensive single lens reflex (SLR) cameras favored by the photographer-hobbyist or professional. Most middle-class families in the US or Europe owned at least two film cameras in the 1970s and 1980s. My own family of five owned two SLRs, both Japanese, and a couple of point and shoot cameras that were always handy at parties or family gatherings (not to mention the old Polaroid "Land" camera that still collects dust in our basement). As the demand for film cameras plummeted and digital photography became popular, Kodak was simply not able to compete as a digital camera manufacturer. Kodak, at its core, was a chemical company used to manufacturing emulsions, coatings and chemistry at margins that allowed them to manufacture cameras at a loss with the knowledge that they would earn the money back (and much more) on film, developing chemistry and paper. Although they tried to compete with early digital cameras designs, they were not in a position to compete in this arena of electromechanical and high-tech manufacturing required to make CCD cameras. Their competitors were Canon, Sony, Olympus, Fujifilm, or Nikon in this game that they were doomed to lose. Of course, nobody could foresee in the 1980s that cellular phones would be coming in 20 years that remade the way that the world took and stored pictures or made videos.

RCA, GE and Philips were famous brand names in the area of radio, TV and the early electronics industry of the 1930s to 1960s. Along with their technological know-how they had the financial resources to build the factories required to build the glass vacuum tubes which were the early components required to build electronic products. Vacuum tubes acted as amplifiers, rectifiers, light collectors, imaging devices and display devices. These companies and their ability to manufacture the components which became the back-bone, muscle and brains of the electronics industry should have set them up for leadership in the electronics revolution which encircled the developed world in the last third of the twentieth century. Instead, 70 years after the introduction of the solid-state transistor, the center of gravity of the electronics industry lies in East Asia and with companies called TSMC, Samsung, Foxconn, and Huawei. Of all these top ten electronics companies in the world according to a ranking by a website called blog.bizvibe.com, only Intel manufactures a significant portion of their products in the west.

To win in the electronics manufacturing game, it seems to me that a company must be willing to live with low profits or even losses for a period of time which is longer than the patience of

Top ten electronics companies in the world

Rank (2020)	Company	Revenue (USD billions)	Headquarters
1	Apple Inc.	260.17	USA
2	Samsung Electronics	221.6	South Korea
3	Hon Hai Precision Industry	175.62	Taiwan
4	Huawei	122.97	China
5	Dell Technologies	90.62	USA
6	Hitachi	88.42	Japan
7	Sony	80.92	Japan
8	Panasonic	74.73	Japan
9	Intel	71.9	USA
10	LG Electronics	54.39	South Korea

many western investors. My personal theory is that Asians in the post World War II period saw electronics as an opportunity for growth exactly because American companies saw electronics as a disruption to its hegemony and fat margins. The hot "electronics" product of the 1960s for Americans like my father came from companies like Magnavox and RCA who produced large pieces of furniture that contained a color TV, AM/FM radio and a stereo system complete with turntable and optional external speakers. These "all-in-one" entertainment systems were made of wood and relatively thick, steel sub-chassis for holding the circuitry. These were largely made with vacuum tube technology and point to point wiring harnesses. The steel support for these devices needed to be relatively robust because the sockets that held the vacuum tubes in place required a considerable amount of insertion force so the contacts would be reliable. Japanese portable radios and portable cassette tape recorders made their debut in the US during the 1960s. The radios were small enough to fit into a shirt pocket, ran on batteries and were made by the millions. The cassette recorder from Panasonic that I received for a Christmas gift in 1969 was about the size of a carton of cigarettes, but a bit wider. With its microphone and two button record function, I could make my own recordings of music in the basement of my parents' house as a 14- and 15-year-old. I don't recall anyone other than me ever having heard any of those tapes after production, but the making of the recordings passed time and I was provided with hours and hours of entertainment. I recall trying to get the reverb effect so often used on the country western records I had at the time by placing the microphone in the bottom of a trash bin. The effect was to make me sound like I was singing from the bottom of a trash bin, and I needed to use my imagination to hear the reverb effect I was trying to get.

While I carried my transistor radio around everywhere I went, my father showed off his stereo system to friends and family with his Frank Sinatra records whenever a new guest came to visit. Although he had paid much more money for that entertainment system than my transistor radio or my cassette recorder, I do recall having to go the store with a handful of vacuum tubes every once in a while, to test the tubes on a diagnostic system at the store which indicated a tube as good or bad. He would then buy a replacement tube and (hopefully) carry out a repair. If that didn't work, he would ask my Opa to come over and take a look at the system. My grandfather was a technician at Sperry Univac and therefore better able to diagnose problems on the system than my father, but the solution was always the same: find out which vacuum tube was bad and change it out for a new one. I noticed that almost always, the offending part had a smoky gray haze somewhere to indicate that the tube had developed a leak and the vacuum had failed. Compare this to my portable radio and my cassette recorder which only ever needed to have the batteries replaced and never really failed. I do recall that the tuning indicator stopped working once. There was a little red line that moved left and right across two parallel scales of numbers which indicated the approximate frequencies of the radio stations that could be bidden to play. The radio continued to work but the indicator stayed in its place although turning the tuning dial worked to pull in the various stations in the same relative order it did before, when the indicating line used to move to show the proper frequency. I figured out how to take the radio apart to see what was going on and, for the first time, marveled at the clever electro-mechanical design the station indicator was. The red line was a little upside-down T shaped piece attached along its bottom to a piece of string, which was suspended between two pulleys (located on each side of the radio), one of which was connected to the tuning disc. The tuning disc had two functions: the first was to turn a potentiometer which did the actual tuning of the frequency of the radio receiver and the second to rotate the pulley which moved the line left and right to give an indication of which direction the tuner was scanning on the frequency scale and to show the approximate frequency at which the tuning scale was set at a particular moment. There were three failure modes for this indicator: lost friction, the string coming off a pulley or the string breaking. Besides the lesson in electro-mechanical assembly, this was my first experience with any printed circuit board. Six or seven years later, Bill Kitchener and Artek would introduce me to the world of designing with PCBs.

The Japanese entry into consumer electronics was the first major step for an East Asian country into the world of global consumer manufacturing. The Japanese would prove formidable competitors to the likes of RCA, GE, Magnavox, Zenith and Philco in the US and Philips, AEG, Telefunken, Grundig, Metz and Blaupunkt in Europe. I was a witness to the growth of world markets in general after World War II and the rise of East Asian manufacturing in particular, but the indications were subtle in my early years of PCB experience and best perceived with the 20/20 hindsight of what I would experience over the next 50 years of life experience that would follow. The house I grew up in was full of American made goods. The kitchen white goods and the washing machine and dryer were all American brands like Westinghouse, Frigidaire and GE. The radios and TVs were either GE, RCA or Magnavox. My father's cars were always Fords, until one time in the late 60s, he bought and, relatively quickly, sold, a used Austin Healey Sprite (a tiny British sports car with a floor that was so rusted out that I picture my Dad being able to propel the car with his feet, Fred Flintstone like) – it was the only foreign car he would ever own. As most of us know, the Asian invasion of American consumer markets began with transistor radios (my Panasonic cassette recorder) and cheap toys in the 1960s, progressed to cars (like the early Datsun 240 Z sport car driven by one of my college professors) and single reflex 35 mm film photo cameras in the 1970s and took full hold in the 1980s during the early years of my printed circuit board career with game arcade machines, TVs, Walkmen, CD players, Video Recorders and ultimately PC clone computers. There was a moment in the early 1990s, that we all thought that cellular phones would lead to a new renaissance in western electronics production as Motorola, Philips, Siemens, Nokia, Ericsson, Blackberry, Nortel, AT&T, and other western companies crowded into the production of handsets and network infrastructure required to build out the global wireless network. We didn't realize, this would be the beginning of the capitulation of electronic manufacture to low wage China because these cellular phones would represent production volumes seldom seen before in a newly globalized electronics consumer market.

The growth and arc of my career in electronics that began with the summer job at Artek in the summer of 1974 would progress and expand through the years of learning and the acquiring of the skills and tools of product and machine design through the 1970s. The pinnacle of my business and professional growth culminated in my arrival in Europe in the mid 1980s and lasted through the end of the 1990s. Over the next several years, I would be an unwitting audience member, occupying a front row seat, of the theater of economic realities as well as being a marionette-like character doing the bidding of an unseen master. Although I would be a contributor to progress, where the progress led, was beyond my control. It would take me, from the time I moved to Europe in 1987 until the late 20-teens to finally understand my place in the history of the PCBs through my initial and ultimate successes through the 1990s and then my failures that inexorably led to my present situation in 2024.

Had I gone to university to study mechanical engineering or industrial product design, I could not have sought a better learning vehicle to begin a career in machine design than that summer of 1974 at Artek and working on the design of the model 880 Bacterial Colony Counter and I could not have sought a better teacher than Bill Kitchener. At the end of that summer when I left after my last day of work to go back to Syracuse for my junior year, Bill told me that my drawing table would be there waiting for me to return on my winter break and that those ECOs still needed to get finished.

My introduction to PCB design in 1974 seemed like an interesting side-bar to the general education I was accumulating through my summer job at Artek. What I didn't realize at the time was how important these curious little green printed wiring devices would become to my life both professionally and personally.

In most of the sources of information that exist today, the birth of printed circuits is attributed to another immigrant named Paul – Paul Eisler – an Austrian Jew who, prevented from working as an engineer in his native Austria because of Nazi restrictions on Jews, emigrated first to Belgrade and then to the UK. While in the UK, in 1936, he is credited with the invention of the Printed Circuit Board although a search for a patent returns no satisfactory result. Eisler's experiences at the hands of the Nazis made him a pacifist. Although he could see the obvious benefits of PCBs to weapons design, he naively hoped that his invention would first be noted and used as a means of improving the reproduction of music or sound reproduction or used to improve broadcast technology. The first known and recorded use of PCBs, despite Eisler's idealistic hopes, was in allied explosive fuzes required to detonate munitions in proper proximity to its target during World War II.

Today, we find PCBs in anything with a source of power that can be converted into electricity. PCBs are there when converting any form of power into another form of power. To the extent that power is turned into communications by the manipulation of characters, sounds, images, words, light or tactile feedback, PCBs are necessary. Converting any source of information into any other source of information involves PCBs. No advancements in technology since the invention of PCBs can avoid using PCBs to advance because no advancement can exist today without electronics and digital communications. PCBs are literally and figuratively the basis on which electronics are built. I had the good fortune to get in the way of PCBs during a summer job because I had learned to draw.

Landscape Architecture Studies

I returned to the College of Forestry in September of 1974 but decided to change majors to Landscape Architecture from Forest Biology and Resources Management. In the School of Landscape Architecture, I imagined myself working toward a job that I could picture myself doing. I had always had a fuzzy idea of what a job in Forest Biology or Resource Management would entail and nobody could really make it clear to me what such a job would look like, feel like or be like. Had I come from a more educated family, I might have understood the role of graduate schools and research institutions as a further steppingstone in the search for a career in Forest Biology. Had I understood the role of paper companies and how the business of wood, pulp and paper fit into our industrial and commercial landscape, I might have seen a career path beyond simply 'working with trees and toward conservation of forests.' I didn't switch to Landscape Architecture because I had a clear vision of what a Landscape Architect did. I switched because I saw it as a place to prepare for life as a creative problem solver. I had a professor, Frank Maraviglia, from the School of Landscape Architecture (SLA) within the ES&F who had been my teacher in the drafting courses my Forestry curriculum had demanded. He also taught a course in creative problem solving. He and I knew I was very good at creative problem solving and in the end he was the one to convince me to switch. I suppose, in the end, I saw myself as a guy at a drawing board.

The first memory I have of my time as a Landscape Architecture student was the first day we were assigned to our LA-301 – "Introduction to LA Design (Studio)" – if my memory serves me well – studio space. We were the largest class ever. I think we were about 126 students that started the studio in the fall of 1974. By the spring of 1977, our numbers were reduced to around 40, I think. We 125 kids (young adults?) and one older lady, who came to get a college education late in life, gathered in a space comprised of a large room big enough for most of us and a neighboring smaller space for the rest of us. It was the first time I met most of them because I had transferred into the program over the summer. Our first project involved us forming into groups of between 4 and 6 students each. Each group was to design a portable home for a family who belonged to a tribe of sun-worshiping nomads in a post-apocalyptic world. I was put together with Rick Weber, Gary Hamilton and Steve Baumann. All three were upstate New York natives and I was meeting each of them for the first time. Gary and Steve knew each other, and I recall seeing them around campus before this first meeting. Rick had just transferred into the Forestry School from a private junior college called Paul Smith's in the Adirondack mountains of upstate New York. Rick grew up in Niskayuna, New York, a city not far from Schenectady and Albany. Gary grew up in Utica and Steve was from Glen Falls. Gary, Rick and I would become good life-long friends and Steve would be an acquaintance that we all maintained until college ended.

Our approach to the project was to focus on the practicality of the nomadic aspect of our "client," the sun-worshiping family in their community. Given that the family would have to carry everything with them without pack animals and given that they would be spending most of their time out-of-doors in their beloved sun, we designed them a roomy tent-structure which could be carried as three separate pieces or bundled together as one long package. Each modular section of what we designed was comprised of four poles (of about 8 feet in length lashed together). We cut into an appropriate form and heat-fused a heavy plastic material commonly used as "drop cloths" by house painters onto the poles to act as the walls of our structure. Each individual module folded together into a package of about 6 inches in diameter. Rick was a master at lashing the ends of each pair of poles together so that they folded together and opened as if hinged. The result was a modular structure that weighed about five pounds each, three of which formed an indoor space with three triangular spaces (sleeping areas) arranged as three points of what could be an incomplete four-pointed star and a more-or-less square floor area in the middle in a pyramid-shaped area that was the entry and family shared area.

At the end of the semester and before we were to receive our grades on the project, we were all invited to bring our structures to a farm field on the property of one our professors and build our structure. Altogether there were about 20 project groups who built various kinds of structures ranging from tent-like structures like ours that focused on the practical aspects of a nomadic civilization to those structures that took much of the morning to build and stressed the religious and cultural life of the people when they settled into their somewhat bulky and complicated homes. Our home was ready to inhabit in a few minutes and in fact, was the lightest and easiest-to-assemble structure of the designs presented that day. Although spartan and, admittedly, a bit small, it did afford shelter from the outdoors for a family of three or four. We explained that the design was indeed scalable to a much roomier size but our student-sized budget (we had to buy our own materials using our own money) limited the size we could build for the project and still afford to continue life in non-nomadic Syracuse.

We did not get a good grade on our efforts. According to the team of professors that were responsible for the evaluations we had focused too much on one aspect of the project (the practical) and hardly focused at all on the religious or spiritual aspect of these sun-worshipping post-apocalyptic nomads. Although our nomads didn't have sore backs from carrying their homes around and our nomad clients were able to build up their homes upon arriving at the destination after a long journey within five minutes, other student groups' designs received much better grades although they didn't have elegant designs that made life easy for their clients, but they did show more respect for the cultural imperatives of the civilization they were designing for. We were a bit stunned by the result, but we learned something. Know your client and find out what's most important to him. In this case, our clients were not our fictional nomads but rather our evaluating professor-team. The goal was not to make an elegant design for nomads. The goal was to get a good grade. The way to get to good grade was to find out the priorities of the evaluators.

The Nomadic Dwelling Project did bring me into contact with Gary and Rick and for that I am thankful. In one of those remarkable bits of coincidence and serendipity, I already knew Rick's girlfriend who was an alto in the Hendrick's Chapel Choir. When

I found out that Rick and Abby (we always called her Bos for some unknown reason) belonged together, I had one of those "what-a-small-world" moments. They had been high school sweethearts, and both grew up in Niskayuna.

That third year at Syracuse was the year that I began to feel like a poor student. Up until that time I had had savings from my entire teen years, when I spent nearly no money and the high earnings of selling pots and pans. In the fall of 1974, having money saved up and always at hand for a year or more looking forward was a relatively distant memory. The amount that I had earned and saved from a summer at Artek was a fraction of what I had earned the previous summers and so my future financial outlook became shorter. At that time, I had only a semester's worth of money if I were to live in a dormitory again and participate on the full meal plan at the university's dining hall. An acquaintance of mine from Lawrinson Hall and the Forestry School asked me at the end of the previous semester if I would be interested in taking a quarter share of an apartment about a mile away from our campus. The rent would be $75 per month compared to having to pay about $500 per semester for a shared room in the dormitory. I would save $500 for the year so I took the share of the apartment. The other three young men knew each other relatively well and I suppose they asked me because they viewed me as a reliable quiet Asian guy that would be good for the rent each month. I suppose they were right. I didn't have much interaction with my apartment mates that year. I recall that two of them were Forestry students and one a Syracuse University student who was on the swimming team. They were nice enough guys but there wasn't that much time that we actually spent together. Most of my time was spent at Marshall Hall, either at the studio or at my Landscape Architecture classes. Beyond that, I was still taking a course or two per semester at the University, spending time at Hendricks Chapel and trying to get a girl or woman interested in me, although I still had no idea how one went about doing that.

One cold night one of the altos from the choir called me and asked me if I was busy. If I was home in the evening at that apartment, chances were, I was reading, either to pass the time or because I had to for an assignment. But, even had I been, at that moment, close to solving all of mankind's problems, a call from this particular young woman would have caused me to drop what I was doing and allow mankind's problems plague us for at least another day. I supposed mankind might forgive me in this situation. She continued that she would really like it if I could come over and spend some time with her. I babbled and stammered like an idiot and said I'd gladly come – only probably not that graciously. She lived about a 10 minute-walk away. I recall, besides being chilled to the core of me by the weather, being totally confused that I was being summoned by her in her loneliness. I arrived at her place, and we began to talk about our days. This woman and I had known each other since my first week in Syracuse. She was pretty with a bubbly personality, somewhat too tall and a bit bigger than I to make a perfect picture with me if we were ever to be a couple. She was outgoing and friendly and had agreed to go out on dates with me at various times in the past, but I had never moved to kiss her, hug her or hold her hand because I just didn't know how to bring myself to do any of that. On that evening and night, through the talking and the words, all of which really had no meaning, she took me by the hand, kissed my face and led me through all the gestures and motions of seduction that I should have tried on her at some point in the years of our acquaintance. Wow! What a sensation that was. My head buzzed and my body floated. I didn't feel as if I had mass – I felt as if I were pure emotion and feeling. Unfortunately, although she had liked the sex (apparently), she couldn't take the cloying neediness of all that emotion and feeling I aimed in her direction over the next few days and she more-or-less banished me from her life for the next year and a half. Although it wasn't much more than a "two-night stand" the ice on my virginity was broken and I finally felt my age.

My second summer at Artek began a couple of months later. I worked full time there during those summer vacation months between the beginning of May and the end of August. During that summer I lived with the Montchal family – a family I knew from church. In that neighborhood (also in East Meadow) I met a man, Mr. Eichhorst, who worked a full-time job during the week as a delivery driver for a building supply business and was a shop steward in the New York City waiter's union. Through him, I worked Fridays, Saturdays and Sundays either at a restaurant called the Plattdeutsch, a catering hall type of restaurant where big parties were often celebrated with hundreds of guests or at other local catering halls or Jewish temples where weddings and Bar Mitzvah parties were frequently celebrated. Having had waiting experience from the time I spent in Richmond as a runaway, I fit perfectly into Mr. Eichhorst's weekend plans. I was often available, didn't need any real training and was willing to work whenever he needed someone to work. I was extremely happy to be working in this way for the union, especially with Mr. Eichhorst, who always provided me with a ride back and forth from the gigs. I only needed to walk about 50 meters from the Montchal's house to the Eichhorsts'. My responsibilities varied from party to party depending on the service that the partiers had chosen for their celebration. If it was a buffet for the Stuben Society of the NYC Police department, the most demanding job was "beer-runner." The qualifications for that job were speed, a friendly but slightly "wise-guy" attitude and keeping the tables straight in my memory so that the patter that one had at each table could be continued throughout the night. Every guest wants to have the feeling that he is being remembered and that one of the beers I was bringing was for him, just as he was draining the last one. If the party was a fancy wedding with French service, we needed to serve the food from terrines and platters to their plates one at a time and one couldn't really spend any time chatting because the concentration one needed to get the food safely and quickly onto the plates without dripping drops of soup or sauce onto the guests' backs or shoulders was absolute and mandatory. I enjoyed the rush, rush, rush of waiting tables for big parties and particularly liked to be the beer runner. Mr. Eichhorst had a principle when it came to picking his teams for parties. He wanted enough people to be able to do the work, but not too many because the earnings pot was limited to 15% of the cost of the party for all the workers plus whatever tips were taken in and split up among the team. I reliably earned about $85 to $100 per shift. There were very often two shifts to work on Saturdays, so the money for a weekend of work was often more than what I earned during the entire week of working at my drawing board at Artek at $5.00 per hour.

During our third year we had to take a course in "Land Use Planning". The Professor who taught us Land Use Planning was a man named Allen Lewis. His job was to make us knowledgeable about how to use the process of land use planning to create regulatory frameworks that allows sensible management of future land use so that the Sense-of-Place can be preserved, and a community can maintain a greater value for each landowner than if each landowner could do what he wanted with his own land. The tools at hand for Land Use Planners are water use restrictions, minimum property size restrictions, zoning laws, infrastructure plans and restrictions on infrastructure development, environmental restrictions and even restrictions on what color the houses in a community must be or the kinds of windows or roofs are allowed or the building materials that may, may not or must be used in the building of a structure. I wish that I could report that Allen made all this fascinating but, regrettably, his lectures were about as exciting as watching paint dry. Allen was well prepared for our lectures, but we all had the feeling that he had been reading from the same lecture notes for the entire time he worked at the college. He supplied us all with the necessary information about Land Use Planning we needed to know. Gary would become a protégé of his and wound up working at the same planning office in Bucks County Pennsylvania where Allen had worked. There are some professors who seek to inspire through their dynamism and some who fall back on their erudition – others use humor to hold interest. Allen was the perfect example that you don't need any of those to be a successful professor. Allen was unapologetic about being a good political "operator" and was a master of doing the necessary and sufficient. The lessons I learned best from Allen Lewis is that there are many ways to measure success and many ways to achieve what one considers success.

Allen had a good relationship with Steve Baumann, the fourth member of our team for the "nomadic shelter" project. Allen had bought a beautiful and well-appointed house near the college campus with five bedrooms. Steve had helped him renovate the house and had received free board at the house in return. Steve suggested to the other members of the "nomadic shelter" project group, Gary, Rick and me, that we could board at Allen's house for our fourth year of school as well. We would each pay a set amount per semester (I think to remember about $ 500) and we would each have our own rooms and meals included. Allen saw himself as a mentor to us young men in the sense of a "life coach." His idea for the year we were there was that we would live in a kind of a cooperative in which we split the chores of living in the house. Each of us, the four of us students plus Allen would take up a 20 % load of the responsibilities of keeping house and each of us would keep our rooms presentable. Each of us needed to plan one dinner each week and submit a grocery list of what was required for the meal we would prepare, and Allen would buy the food during his once-a-week grocery shopping trip. On the night that one cooked one was also responsible for cleaning the pots and pans, the dinner dishes, and the kitchen so that there could be no rebukes for how much mess someone else made while cooking. Allen was proud of the system he had devised for the house, and I must admit that it worked out quite well. We all had to learn to cook at least one thing each week and the house was always clean and presentable, and we all enjoyed calling the place home. Gary, Rick, and I saw each other every day and every night and our friendships flourished. Steve was always cordial with the rest of us but he didn't bond in the same way as Gary, Rick, and I did. Quite often Rick's girlfriend, Abby (or Bos – from the HCC) was over at our place in the evenings or on weekends. When they married after college, I was Rick's best man. When I married in 1982, Rick was my best man.

Through the four semesters of my third and fourth years at Syracuse my view of myself changed toward a realization that I was much more of a technical person interested in the nuts and bolts and the structure of things than how our thoughts and designs and creativity bend to the cultural imperatives of society. I witnessed this constant tension between the need to educate us students to be prepared for the technical demands of our futures and at the same time make us sensitive to feelings, the importance of culture as it is represented now and in the past and the importance of the environment. The landscape architect is ideally a professional possessing an impressive technical capability and a fine sense of cultural imperatives and respect for the environment into which his work fits.

Many of us students did not have a clear idea of what a landscape architect did, and I must admit, our professors didn't clear things up for us very well. I never worked a day in my life as a landscape architect, so I still don't know, but our professors gave us such a broad-brush picture, it was impossible to form an accurate image of, much less, understand the reality of actually being a Landscape Architect. Most of the students who started in the third year of the program were artistic types, nature types, hippy types or undecided types. I was one of very few in the program who could be called an engineering-problem-solving type. Gary was an undecided type and wound up opting to get a degree in Land Use Planning in four years and thereby foregoing his fifth year to get a landscape architecture degree. After graduation, he went on to graduate school at Texas A&M to get his master's degree in Land Use Planning. He had a successful career which took him first to

Pueblo, Colorado then to Bucks County Pennsylvania then back home to work for the Department of Transportation in Utica, NY. Rick was a nature type and went on to get a master's degree as well. His, in Landscape Architecture from the University of Michigan. He would work on designing a national park in Panama and would return to work at a Landscape Architects office in Saratoga Springs (not far from where he grew up) and ultimately work as the park administrator responsible for maintaining the natural legacy of the New York Adirondack State Park.

An Introduction to Computers and Computing

We all were required to take a course called Computers and Computer Programming. This was 1974 and computers were not yet fixtures in average offices. The personal computer would take another 10 years to become fixtures of home entertainment and office word processing and calculating tasks. Drawing on computers or designing on computers were ideas that were waiting to be real. Most of my classmates thought this Computer and Computer Programming course was a waste of time. It did not help that the teacher of this class probably held the same dim view of what he taught as his students and seemingly did his best to make the course as boring and densely opaque as possible. During the final exam, which was given in the same elegant theatre-like lecture hall in Marshall Hall the lectures for the course were given, one of the students, five minutes after we all settled in with our exam form to fill in our answers, ambled up to the stage with his exam in hand, set it upon the baby grand piano which occupied the center of the stage, sat down on the bench of the piano, opened the lid covering the keyboard and began to play "Moonlight Sonata". That act of civil disobedience and pure frustrated defiance was applauded by the other students and that poor student meekly walked out of the hall led gently by the arm by our course teacher. Most of the students failed that course and I don't know if they had to repeat it or if they were allowed to substitute another course for the requirement. I did well in the course and enjoyed the puzzle-like rigor that programming required and the creativity one needs to apply to express problems in lines of code into the computer such that a suitable solution can be extracted from the computer.

In a small room, which was not much bigger than a closet, on the floor of Marshall Hall where most of the professors had their offices, stood a small typewriter-sized programmable device called a Wang Programmable Calculator. The company Wang would become famous in the late 1970s and 1980s for office word processors, office computers and later mini-computers (which does not mean really small but rather medium-sized and not big). My introduction to this machine during the Computers and Computer Programming course was an absolute revelation. One would think that only having one machine would be a problem with 125 other students who might want to try this machine or work on it but it turned out not to be like that at all. I was the only one that ever touched the thing. Nobody knew how to use that machine except for me (and I include the department professors). Nobody else was interested. The machine had a keyboard, a series of nixie tubes (the original number displays which were embedded in vacuum tubes), a cassette tape to store programs and data and a small printer. The Wang machine was so little in demand for anybody else that that closet sized room became my office by default. I was always there when I didn't have to be anywhere else, and everyone knew after awhile that they could find me there. We had to take a basic civil engineering course where we needed to understand how to change the grade of the land by "cutting and filling." I wrote a program that contained an input mask that correlated to data points that matched an existing terrain and compared that data to another set of data points that represented the finished, graded landscape. The program would calculate the amount of fill (the volume of earth required to be added) and the amount of cut (the amount of earth required to be removed). The program would then give a number of inches to add or subtract to every data point to make cut equal fill for the entire data set. Making cut = fill, we were told, saves money by the project people neither having to pay for additional fill-earth nor paying to cart off excess cut-earth. Going deeper into the engineering course, we needed to learn how to grade the surface of the road in cross section to make sure the roadway drained. We learned to draw the profile of the center of the roadway onto the existing landscape so that the roadway would match the existing contour of the land but at the same time remain comfortably straight or curved to make driving safer and more comfortable. I wrote programs that would aid in those tasks and then calculate cut and fill for the road sections that resulted. It was a valuable lesson in how a user must communicate conditions in a real world to a device that can calculate and give numerical results and how those results must be put in a form that a user can understand, interpret and use.

I became the computer nerd of the School of Landscape Architecture – at least for my class year. We had a larger computer on the College of ES & F campus, but it wasn't nearly as fun to program and use as the Wang machine because the Wang machine was there, available and gave immediate feedback. The CDC (Control Data Corp) machine was a room sized machine used by many graduate students and professors in the forestry paper and chemistry departments (located in an entirely different building from our Landscape Architectural "domain" in Marshall Hall). There, the only access to the computer I had was to drop off a box of punched cards in the late afternoon and receive a printout with results the next morning. This kind of large computer and the way that a user interacted with it was, for me, something totally new and something that I had only read about in books. I had no personal experience. I had not learned any large computer programming languages and I knew no one who knew how to work with such a machine. However, because of my success as the only Landscape Architecture student in memory that had made use of the Wang Programmable Calculator to actually do anything, I became the group leader of a project that made use of a brand new graphical "drawing" application tool that the Landscape Architecture school had acquired for the big CDC machine. I had used xs and os to draw on the small printer of the Wang device (like printing on an adding machine) therefore, it was reasoned by one of our professors that I should be able to learn a Fortran IV graphical application program to make land use maps. Our advising professor had convinced a planning board that computer mapping could be used as a visualization tool. The county-wide area could be represented by a computer generated map which indicated where various land uses were planned. Furthermore, one could visualize how local areas would develop in reaction to specific planning decisions. The project foresaw inputs from the planning board such as what land-use planning biases could, theoretically affect a location within the county in the future. Land-use biases can be defined as points along a spectrum that can be defined in any number of ways. For example, from no development to intensive development (development density) or from zero residents per hectare to 1000 residents per hectare (resident density) or from zero vehicle kilometers per day per area to 100,000 vehicle km per day per area (traffic density).

We decided (or rather, our professor decided) that we would give the board a tool which could show incremental change over time to various "developmental biases." For our project, we asked the board to give us directions in development they would like to see for their county. The board settled on several developmental bias maps they would like to see over the future years. One was a nature conservatory bias. Another was a business development bias. Another, residential (bedroom community) bias. In today's world, with our knowledge of Google Maps and with games like Sim City or Forge of Empires, one can understand intuitively how a developing world might look on a graphical display or printout, but in the winter and spring of 1977, such graphical methods of representing possible future results of development were done the "old-fashioned" way. Such maps were drawn by hand and coded using various colors and/or density of color to represent what the presenter wanted to convey. These people on the board of the county planning commission would have been happy to have a set of maps that were hand-drawn and beautifully rendered by the group of students (six or seven of us, I think to recall) but our professor (who's name escapes me – Thomas Something-or-other) thought that an algorithm driven set of computer generated maps would yield more powerful, and perhaps, less refutable, results on what development models would be the "best" to pursue. I was told years later by a source who might have known the truth or not, that our professor, who had been an assistant professor who had not yet received his PhD, used our project as the basis of his doctoral dissertation. The source of this rumor (it was nothing to me but a rumor) told me I should have been insulted and angry for not getting any credit for my contributions to the project. I couldn't work up any feelings of anger or insult because, although I was proud of my work, I didn't see anything truly earth-shaking in what I had done. I was given a project with which to learn and I learned. That the professor used us to get ahead, if indeed he had, was not a big problem for me. I was in no position to complain and there was nothing that the credit would have done for me except give me the same pride of accomplishment that I am expressing here.

The very first part of the project involved organizing the group so that everybody would have something to do but since nobody else in the group had any interest in computers and/or programming, I became the de facto "chief cook and bottle washer." My role became doing anything related to computing, algorithm design or organizing data into usable form for our program and the assigned role of everyone else in the group was to do the time consuming and mindless work of coding maps with number codes and typing out computer cards that contained programming language or data – This turned out to be 10 s of thousands of cards with one line of data or one line of computer code per card. The next part of the project involved me learning Fortran IV well enough to write the program that sorted through input data, arranged it, applied an algorithm to the dataset which then output a dataset which could be represented in a map. For that part of the project, I referred to one of the books that we had been assigned to read in our Computers and Computing course, but, up until then were never really expected to read or internalize. Once I knew enough about organizing data for a Fortran program, we began creating datasets that represented our area-to-be-planned. This was done by taking several maps of the area and having the rest of the team assign codes to each pixel of the map (using transparent grids overlaid on the map in several iterations) that represented what was already there. We digitized several maps which showed transportation density and features, population density, economic development density and features, conserved and protected areas along with "conservation value indexes", etc. Once the team had digitized each map, I had to write the data into my program so that the graphical application would accurately print the map as desired. The program that managed and manipulated the data, applying factors to each map data point or pixel to yield a printed representation of the future land-use plan for each position on the map had to be written out as the lines of a program that expressed the algorithm. The algorithm had to be designed to allow the planning board to express their biases for how much area should be set aside for each future land-use and our algorithm would point out, by graphical means, where the best places for a particular future land-use might be located. The inputs into this decision had to be coded into the algorithm as "influences" such as present use, neighboring site use, access to transportation, water, municipal services, environmental influences such as soil types, geological limitations, and vegetation inventories as well as locational data and something called "special conditions".

Every influence had to be expressed in some kind of value along a spectrum of possible values. In the end, working on this project gave me a unique look into the world of exercising political will. The results that would be printed out by our program had to express the will and the biases of the planning board for whom we were doing the project and our job became simply to provide them with a tool that sorted through a great deal of data and pointed out where best to place which land-use. It was clear, however, from the start, that certain people had certain uses for certain locations already picked out in their own minds. In effect, these people had all the data they thought necessary to make the decisions they thought were the most sensible. I set the team working on coding the maps with "present use" data. For every influence that the planning board or we could think of, we needed to code a different map. This involved assigning a set of about 20 different "influence" data rankings to each point of the map. Unfortunately, the map printing program we had on the computer available to us was extremely low resolution. As I recall, it could only print pixels of a physical size of 1" x 1". This means that if we were going to print maps on the standard tractor feed printer we had available to us, we had to make some decisions early on in the project that made the project useless for anything other than a demonstration of what might be possible in the future. We made the decision early on to represent our planned area on four pages of width of the tractor-fed paper (we could only fit 13 one inch "pixels" on one page). This meant that the width of the map was 52 pixels wide. The area which we were planning contained about five or six villages and communities and occupied an area that was about 10 miles wide (east-west) by about 18 miles long. Each pixel represented a square which was about 1000 feet per side and therefore we needed to work with a total universe of data for about 4200 pixels for our somewhat rectangular but irregular shaped zoning area. My feeling was that the data set was far too coarse and represented an area so large that every data point was at best an approximation or average and at worst a useless midpoint between extremes so as to make the approximation meaningless. Better would have been a resolution five to ten times finer but even at five times finer, the dataset would have ballooned to 105,000 data points per influence (or over 2 million data points to type onto punch-cards for the "influence" data) and maps would have had to be made up of 20 stripes of paper each about 38 feet long. When taped together the map would have been 22 feet x 38 feet in size – or totally out of the realm of our possibility. As it was, when it came to run the program at the end of the project in order to generate the five or six planning maps we submitted as examples to the planning board, the program and data took up several boxes of typed punch-cards for each set of maps we printed.

The project progressed from the first meetings of the group in January well into March before we were ready to place a box of punched cards onto the "Inbox" tray at the computing center to see if we could coax a map out of the room-sized machine. I submitted a box of cards of about three or four hundred cards that only contained my program and a set of dummy data just to see if the program ran with a uniform set of data as "influence" data. (The team was still hard at work coding the maps and had not begun to type the data onto the cards). I was told by the computer operator that one entered the programs with data by 4:00 pm and received the corresponding printout the next morning. I waited anxiously for the result only to receive a singe line printout the next morning. It said, "Syntax error in line 1". This meant that I had to find what was wrong with the syntax of line 1 of my program, correct it, type out a new card and then go through the program line for line for similar errors, correct those, type out new cards for each of those lines, check the order of the cards and put them in the "in" basket to the computer room and hope that the program would run and I'd have a successful printout with the required results the next day. The big problem was, I couldn't find a syntax error in line one. I went through all the cards and did find some errors of typing (spelling, punctuation or other errors that might fall under the category of syntax) and corrected them. These cards were about the size of normal business-type envelopes and were printed with columns and lines. If my memory serves me correctly, there were about 16 rows of 80 spaces wide arranged on each card. Some of the columns were separated by darker or thicker lines – for example a line, that looked like a very important separating line went vertically down the card separating column 10 from column 11. The next day? Syntax error in line 1. Another day of the same before I somehow found out that Fortran Program instructions run on our computer were not to be started on column 11 as we had done on all the cards. Fortran looks for input at column 7. I went back to the group and told them the bad news of my terrible mistake, borne of ignorance, which would force them to type all the program cards again from the beginning. I felt terrible, but at the very moment of chastising myself in front of the group, we had an idea: we would cut four columns off of all the cards with a paper cutter which we would fixture with a mechanical stop in the form of strip of tape on the table of the paper cutter. We then submitted the stack again. Success – or a kind, any way: "Syntax Error in Line 7"! The next day it was Format Error in Line 19. So it went, day after day – an error statement until about one week later the program ran properly and I had a printed map in my hands. At this point I began to uncover the logical errors in the algorithm of the program but I was now in a position that I could deliver cards and expect an output. We completed the project and the planning board was happy to receive the documentation we submitted to them. I learned Fortran, data formatting, Do loops, the importance of if/then statements, variables, constants, true factors and fudge factors (like knowing how to place a finger on a scale to get to the right weight) but never programmed a large computer again in my life.

The Semester in Bremen

It was a requirement at the School of Landscape Architecture at Syracuse to spend the first semester of the fifth year of study off-campus and, generally, outside of the USA doing an independent study. The thinking behind such a requirement has to do with how we perceive our environment when it is not a familiar one, how we react to the social context of a strange environment and how our perceptions of space, social context and local environment are created. We were welcomed to explore what was unique in us that made the perceptions we had and the experiences of new environments good, bad, exciting, difficult, fulfilling or whatever else might have been evoked. I had originally planned on going to Korea between September and December of 1976 to do an independent study of traditional Korean garden and park design. Rather late in the process of getting my proposal approved for the project, I found it impossible to get a visa which would allow me to stay there for the slightly over three months that I needed to stay. I wanted to take my chances with a three month visa and just overstay my stay a few weeks, but my project advisor wouldn't accept that. I needed another plan for the semester that started in September and had only about 8 weeks times to write another proposal, have it approved by my faculty and make the travel and living arrangements for the semester.

During the month of May in 1976, the Hendricks Chapel Choir had had a tour of Europe during which we sang concerts from Copenhagen to Rome over the course of 30 days. Although we gave about 15 concerts in the month that we traveled our route from Copenhagen, through Hamburg to Bremen by train and then by bus to Amsterdam, Brussels, Paris, Rouen, Strasbourg, Geneva and Rome, the only place we really got into contact with local people was in Bremen. One of the members of our choir had an uncle in Bremen who was the conductor of the "Bremer Jugendchor" and through that contact, a joint concert was arranged which had the two choirs sharing billing at a wonderful venue in Bremen (the famous Obere Rathaushalle in Bremen's historical Rathaus or City Hall). I needed to get a new destination approved for my coming off-campus semester project. I needed a new topic because traditional Korean gardens and parks design only would have worked in Korea. No four-month visa, no Korea. To make it easy on myself to sort out the logistics of the trip, I asked, through long-distance air-mail post, newly made acquaintances I made in Bremen during a concert stop there if I could possibly stay with them for the following semester. One of the people I asked consented. We agreed on a rate of room and board that I would pay for the semester and I booked a flight to Dusseldorf which would get me to Germany and I decided to take the train from there to Bremen which would be about a two and a half hour journey. During the rest of the summer I put the finishing touches on my new study proposal entitled "Developing the Elements of a Sense of Place".

Arriving in Dusseldorf several weeks later, I took the train to Bremen where I was met by Herr Vogel, Erich, the father of the family that would become my "German family". At the point that we met, Erich could speak no English and my school-boy German was so rudimentary as to be practically useless. I could form basic questions and statements from the vocabulary of words I knew but had done so little reading and conversing in German that I could not understand most responses to what I said. Of course, part of my confusion might have been caused by me. Chances are that what I stated or asked was not understandable to the person who was responding to me in the first place! Hr. Vogel picked me up at the train station and I remember our drive to his house as being awkwardly quiet. I would grow to love and respect Erich, but that ride to the Vogel's suburban home was about 15 minutes of silence punctuated by short bursts of trying, but failing to communicate. When we got to the house, it was evident that Erich had left the house (to pick me up at the station) in the middle of a day reserved for the plum harvest in their garden. I was happy to help in the harvest and learned on that afternoon that two or three trees can yield what seemed like tons of plums. I also learned that these plums were not the over-ripe sweet, juicy fruits I remembered from having eaten a few in my life (when the pit would kind of separate from the fruit automatically and the juice would leak out of the corners of one's mouth). These plums had pits that were stuck to the fibrous mass of fruit and were relatively sour to eat. Erich's wife, Wilma ruled the roost in the home. She said that these fruits were all to be picked that day because she wanted to stock the pantry with plum preserves and make plum cake that day. Erich agreed and that's what we did!

The plum cake we had that afternoon for our afternoon coffee (a weekend tradition in the Vogel home) was different than any cake I'd ever had in America. It looked like a Sicilian style pizza. A dough with sliced plum wedges arranged in neat geometric rows. I had never had a cake that I could ever remember being so, well, unsweet. The whipped cream that adorned the cake was also not sweet. Despite the strangeness of it all, I praised the cake and said I'd never had cake like that before (which was true!) and asked for more ...twice. From that time on, whenever I came for a visit to the Vogel family, I was served plum cake and if the Vogels were still alive today, I would still praise it to the skies and enjoy it in memory of that special day of the plum harvest on my first day at the Vogel family house.

Erich (I called him Herr Vogel during those months) was, generally, a passive presence in the house allowing the family dynamics to run as they did without intervening much. He worked as a printer in a box and packaging factory in the city. He was a staunch union man but was trusted and valued both by the working members of the union and the management of the company. Although Erich was very dedicated to his work and enjoyed his own work as well as having a role in training new apprentices in the factory what really lit up Erich's life was music. He was an extremely accomplished flautist who specialized in Baroque music. The composers he most admired and most often played were Bach, Telemann, Handel, and Vivaldi. He often played concerts in the region bounded by the cities of Hamburg,

Bremen, Oldenburg and Hannover. Most Sundays he either played in the chamber orchestra or sang in the choir that accompanied the [radio] broadcast church service of the St. Martini-Kirche. Wilma and the two older children participated in music as choir singers as well. Wilma was a full-time homemaker and a part-time teaching assistant at a local school. There were three children in the family, Antje (who was 19 at the time and my "pen pal" through whom I had made all the arrangements during that summer), Norbert, who was, I believe, 14 or 15 at that time and Thomas, who was, I think, 12. Antje had a boyfriend at the time, Holger, who would later become her husband. During the time that I was there, Holger was a conscript in the Army. One very sharp cultural difference between the kind of family I came from and the kind of family that the Vogel family was became evident when Holger had a weekend off from military service and he came to spend the time with Antje. He stayed with Antje and slept in the same room – something that would never have happened in my family with any of my sisters. Sleeping together was only for married people in my family and most of the families that I knew of from my working-class Long Island upbringing.

Most weekdays for me started with breakfast together with Wilma and Thomas. I remember that they had a family dining room table that was positioned on the wall that adjoined the kitchen. A rectangular hole in the wall allowed dishes, food and the other materials of meals to be passed from kitchen to table and back again. Weekday breakfasts of my youth, at the home of my parents, were always a bowl of canned fruit, a bowl of cereal and a glass of milk. Breakfast at the Vogels was always buttered bread or rolls with cheese or cold-cuts and juice, milk, tea or coffee. I learned that such a breakfast is what a typical German eats – For us Americans, it resembles more what we would have for lunch. Erich had usually left for work and Norbert and Antje had more going on as teenagers and weren't always still there or not yet up and about when it was breakfast time for Wilma and

Thomas, who often left for school together. I would spend my days wandering around the downtown area of Bremen which was a bus ride of about 20 minutes from the suburban edge of Bremen (past the "Gartenstadtvahr", across the street from the "Galopprennbahn") where the Vogel's house was.

My days would always begin with a visit to the public library where I could read the "International Herald Tribune" without having to buy it. To this day, I still start my days with an American newspaper. The International Herald Tribune was eventually bought by the New York Times, which was fine with me because I had grown up with the New York Times Sunday edition lying around our living room all week. Later on, in my international traveling business days, I would always seek out the Herald Tribune, either at the hotel I stayed in or a café. Often, I found a stand full of local magazines and/or foreign magazines and newspapers mounted on long wooden binders which would also act as hangers to keep the pages flat. In some cases, particularly in five-star hotels, someone had gone through the trouble of ironing the pages free of the creases that were normally there. In the Bremen library, the papers were mounted but remained creased as delivered. The five-star newspaper treatment would have to wait for later in life.

During my time in Bremen, I fancied myself a city planner in the making. I thought I was gathering the knowledge I would need to make urban centers more livable than I knew them to be from my limited experience of cities. At that time, my goal was to work to help create, recreate, or maintain urban spaces as human scale spaces that were practical, beautiful and livable. This was 1976. I had migrated from a suburban tree hugger to a city lover.

East Meadow (where I grew up) is a village in the Town of Hempstead on Long Island that occupies a territory of about 16 square kilometers which translates to an area of about 6 square miles.

One quarter of the area of East Meadow is occupied by a Nassau County Park called Eisenhower Park. The Park represents the only truly "green space" in East Meadow. To imagine the size and character of East Meadow (without the park), imagine a square area of about 2 miles per side (or 10.4 sq. kilometers) in which about 12,000 single family houses are built on building-lots of more-or-less uniform size of ¼ to ⅓ of an acre each. About 40,000 people live there. That represents a population density of nearly 4000 people per sq. kilometer. East Meadow is representative of the character of much of the two Long Island non-New York City counties of Nassau County and Suffolk County. Nassau and Suffolk Counties contain about 1,000,000 single family dwellings with a population of roughly 3 million people covering roughly 1200 square miles. Green spaces on Long Island represent about ⅓ if the area of Long Island (20% of Nassau County and 40% of Suffolk County). Given that 3,000,000 people live in the developed 2000 square kilometers of Nassau and Suffolk the population density of all Long Island is markedly less than the population density of the developed part of East Meadow. Bremen on the other hand occupies an area of only 1/10 the size of Nassau and Suffolk and has a population of about 600,000. 68% of Bremen is "green space" which means that only 32% of Bremen is covered by housing, businesses and institutional development. This means a density of population in Bremen in its built-up areas is about 6000 people per square kilometer or 33% denser than East Meadow and four times denser than Long Island as a whole. Only about ⅓ of the people in Bremen live in single family dwellings whereas over 85 % of people on Long Island live in single family dwellings. The character of Long Island is defined by single standing houses on small building lots for mile after mile. The American Dream is on view on Long Island, the fulfillment of which is the house, two or more cars, an expanse of front lawn and a back yard with a wooden deck or patio equipped with a gas grill. Other views of what we should aspire to were seldom entertained. Most of us just grew into the dream without ever realizing that other dreams could exist. For many of the people who grew up there and stayed, it seemed inevitable that we would do exactly what our parents did before us. My semester in Bremen gave me a new view of what was possible.

For the first time I was living in an urban setting. Although my time at Syracuse had introduced me to another way of living during my on-campus life, all my friends there, with very few exceptions, had come from suburban neighborhoods from upstate or western New York, Long Island or New Jersey, with a few from Ohio or Pennsylvania. I could count on one hand the friends who went home to families that lived in apartment buildings in cities or to a house on a farm when it was time to head back home during holiday or summer breaks.

My time in Bremen was marked by cultural awakening and loneliness. I lived with a family that was very different from my own. I learned to rely on public transportation to get around. I was moving around an urban environment in which I was constantly near people I didn't know. My German, at least at the beginning, was only good enough for me to get myself misunderstood or in a situation where I could prompt an incomprehensible response. Each day, after consuming the newspaper at the library, I took walks around the city with a sketch pad and note pads to soak in the "sense of the place" and try to analyze what caused my emotional responses to the physical spaces I was experiencing. Bremen's downtown area was a patch work of neighborhood development projects which, during the mid-1970s broke the city up into small physical vignettes with little in the way of a unifying sense of place. A walk from the main train station to the "Neustadt" on the other side of the Weser River was, at that time, a series of sharp borders between neighborhoods. Crossing a street back then in 1976, particularly passing under the raised portion of the Rembertiring and the street-level Breitenweg from the large open expanse of the train station's plaza, gave the impression of leaving one place, experiencing a somewhat menacing "no-man's" land and coming into another place entirely. I learned then that only when one came to the unique paving areas of the "Altstadt" did one begin to feel what Bremen wanted to project about its history and what the history of Bremen said about what the place meant to its residents. Through my wanderings through the neighborhoods of downtown Bremen, I learned how the place was recreated to evoke emotional responses from people passing through. Some of the design elements worked well but I always felt during my walks through the city then, that Bremen could have been done better, in particular, in making the city feel more cohesive despite its hodge-podge post war development. Post war planners needed to respond to the destruction that took place during the second World War and the very real needs that the city had to provide economic growth to the local population, in particular to provide affordable housing to a city that was a target of bombing for 5 years of war. Approximately 62 % of the housing stock of Bremen was destroyed by bombings during the war. My semester there was 31 years after the war had ended so reconstruction and rebuilding was largely done but I am certain that if so much had not been destroyed through bombings, the city would have had a much more cohesive "sense of place". Having said that though, many cities that were more completely destroyed were able to rebuild with far more cohesive city plans than Bremen was able to do because there was still much of Bremen that survived the bombings that remained integrated in the city's landscape. Gdansk, Berlin, Dresden and Hamburg suffered much more damage during the war and were able to rebuild with less of the "herky-jerky" nature of city district transitions that Bremen displayed during my semester in 1976.

The further development of Bremen over the last 46 years since I did my study there (as I write this in 2022) has improved the transition from district-to-district in downtown Bremen and the general sense-of-place there. The waterfront along the Weser river is being slowly developed into an entertainment and restaurant area. During the 1960s and 1970s, it seemed that the city had turned its back on the river as if to hold its nose against the smell of the coffee processing facilities on the river then. Now, it seems the city is happy to turn its face to the river and people are finding the river to be a valued part of the city.

Each day I went into the city and roamed around and observed, mostly from the walkways and streets as I didn't have enough money to spend my time in cafes, pubs or restaurants. If I had to do such a project today, I probably would have engaged more with people who lived in the city, but the me of 22 years old was more interested in the spaces that the people occupied than the people themselves. The 68 year old version of me is more interested in how the locals use and perceive the spaces they occupy and move about in. I recorded what I saw with photos and sketches. It was an extremely solitary undertaking. I was an observer of spaces and the elements of space (paving materials, lanterns, public seating, plantings, signs, green spaces, statues, storefronts, walkways, water features, uninterrupted vistas, small alleyways, busy streets, traffic and people as fillers of space, etc., etc.).

My German improved over the time that I was there but I never got to the kind of fluidity of speech and fluency in the expression of ideas that one needs to have in order to have discussions about feelings. Although Wilma, Antje and Norbert could speak some English, I began to feel extremely lonely and isolated with the coming of the short gray days of November. Bremen weather is not unlike London weather with its constant overcast and unrelenting cold grayness. I spent nearly every evening writing letters to my friends and family in the US. The thing with writing letters is that it is an outlet for your own thoughts but the back and forth of conversation is often missing. I very much enjoyed getting mail in response to my letters, but I missed just being in communication with people who I could understand completely and could understand me completely. I hit bottom after receiving a letter from my sister who simply described the content of her day and made no mention of anything of the things I had written about in my previous letter to her. It was as if what I had poured out in three or four tightly written pages had not touched her. She simply acknowledged receipt of the letter and described her day. Her letter, far from making me feel connected to her, made me feel disconnected from her and any other anchors I had in life. I felt so alone I simply locked myself in my bedroom, sat down on the edge of my bed and cried.

The only respite from the loneliness came in the form of letters from my friend, Gary Hamilton. He and I were both good and conscientious letter writers. We always allowed the letters to serve as the back and forth of conversation and not just as a means of maintaining a protocol of our days. Getting letters from him was a joy and writing the response relieved my loneliness. He had had a similar off-campus experience in the spring semester of that year. After we had met in the design studio project of designing the "nomadic shelter" our friendship strengthened into something special. We could talk about anything even though we often disagreed. After he had completed his semester in London, Gary traveled through much of western Europe by train. We kept in touch and arranged to meet in Paris during the Hendricks Chapel Choir tour. He had only planned to stay in Paris one evening and the next day and then he wanted to make his way to Rome. The one evening we had we walked the streets of Paris from Montparnasse in a zig-zag path that took us past the Eiffel Tower, the Champs Elysees, the Tuileries, the Notre Dame, through the streets of Montmartre and Pigalle to the Sacre Coeur and then on to the hotel we stayed in near the Gare Du Nord. It rained on and off for much of our walk and we got soaked but we had a walk to remember for a lifetime that evening. We talked about his time in London, my last semester at Syracuse, our recent concert tour concerts in Copenhagen, Bremen and Amsterdam, our plans for the near future and far future, how all the prostitutes we saw underway had a reason to have their umbrellas that evening, etc., etc., etc. We simply walked, talked and gawked.

Toward the end of the semester, I started a friendship and developed a crush on a young girl, named Anja, I had met in the St. Martini Church choir and finally spent time with on that choir's tour to France and Switzerland. She was only 17 at the time and we realized we liked each other about a week before it was time for me to leave to go back to America. She wound up in a hospital to have an operation to correct scoliosis of the spine just before it was time for me to go. I visited her in the hospital and took some flowers and was pleasantly surprised when she pulled a wrapped gift out from a space next to her bed and gave it to me as a farewell gift – it was a picture book of Bremen that I treasure to this day.

The next day, I boarded the train to Duesseldorf. Erich dropped me off at the station and we shook hands as we'd done three and a half months earlier at our meeting. This time we could talk, and we had memories to share. It was gray and cold. The train pulled out of the station – Erich and I waving at each other. The snow started to fall around mid-morning. The landscape between Bremen and Hanover is flat and uninteresting except for the utter flatness. The grass in the fields stays green all through the winter. The fields are punctuated with hedgerows and canals or streams with birch and poplar trees marking their passing. The snow started collecting on the green fields as the train did its high speed, muted clacking until the landscape streaming by was a sugar-coated winterwonderland scene. Bittersweet is the very definition of that trip home and all I could think of was Anja and why hadn't she made a bigger dent in my life a month or two earlier?

From College to Full-time Working Life

When I returned for my final semester at Syracuse in January of 1977, I learned what it was to be truly poor. I had gone through all the money I had in my semester abroad. In fact, I had to sell the single lens reflex camera I had used to record my experiences during my time in Germany to pay for the flight home from Germany. I had bought the camera used in one of those camera shops on 32nd Street in New York City just before my trip. I was able to get all my money back on the sale of the camera in Bremen. It was one of the few times in my life that I could claim having made a good purchase and a good sale of a personal item. I worked as a teaching assistant for one of Frank Maraviglia's drafting courses and was reduced to living on $ 100 per month (including rent, food and one date a month – if I could convince anyone to go out with me!)

One Friday evening in early March of 1977, having just completed a design project for a Residential Architecture course I took that semester, I took a walk around campus just to get some air and enjoy the outdoor warmth of coming spring. I met a young woman who was a freshman in my technical drawing class and stopped to exchange some small talk with her. She introduced me to her roommate who was standing next to her. The roommate was a young lady called Sarah, a theatre student, and the first thing I thought when I set my eyes on her was that she was the most beautiful thing I had ever seen. It was a case of love at first sight. I tried to convince the two of them to accompany me to the bakery I was headed toward to get some cake or cookies and perhaps a cup of coffee, but they declined saying that they were headed for a dining hall right then for an early dinner before heading out on a double date to go square dancing at a local suburban Syracuse country dance hall called the Ozark Inn. They said they'd take a "rain check" on a visit to the bakery, meaning they would be glad to do it another day. I took them up on their offer to accompany me the very next day at about the same time. I simply went to their room at the co-op they lived in and told them I was there to cash in my "rain check" and they consented to go with me to the bakery. There was a little confusion on their part at the beginning of who, between them, exactly it was that I was pursuing. We cleared that up after the bakery when I asked Sarah if we could meet the following day. She said she'd be happy to. We were a couple from that time on. There was no period of pursuit or needs for me to strategize how to get together or closer. There were no doubts about how she felt about me and no questioning of my motives in wanting to be with her. All my doubt-filled impressions of myself (concerning my desirability as a partner) as a result of all those past unsuccessful attempts to own the heart of a woman suddenly disappeared and were replaced by the sense of confidence I had because I was in love with Sarah, and she was in love with me.

Over the course of the next two and half years I would get to know her family well. The Christmases of 1977 and 1978 were spent together with Sarah and her family in Delmar. I would travel to Syracuse or Delmar to be with her as often as I could. I would spend vacation days or saved up, already worked over-time hours (or promised, to-be-worked-in-the-future-extra hours) to cobble together three-day weekends with a tacked on Friday or Monday so that I could spend as much time as I could with her. Once I had my own car, I won another evening per trip with her. I could leave at 4:00 am from Syracuse or 6:00 am from Delmar and have a chance at getting to work at 9:00 am on the Monday or Tuesday I left her. It often took me until as late as 10:00 am to get to the office, but my bosses had an understanding about my situation, and they seemed to like the idea of having a love-smitten young man as an employee. I even managed to keep my job after the time it took me until Thursday to get to the office when a Sunday night freak snowstorm awarded me three wonderful extra snow days locked up with Sarah at her co-op.

From the time we met, we pictured a future living in New York City while she pursued an acting career while I kept on working at my job or, perhaps, find a job in the city. Everything built up to the advent season of 1978 in the middle of her junior year when we actively pursued discussions of our planned futures together. She had another 17 months to go until graduation. She was planning on going to London for a semester-long off-campus experience in the weeks following that Christmas so we would be separated by an even greater distance for the coming semester. Our relationship was rock-solid. No doubts about how the future would develop were visible. I was happy with my working life. I loved and I was loved. Life was delicious!

From the time I left college, my working life was developing into a constant learning experience in which new projects introduced me to new knowledge of how the industrial world works and my tool chest of solutions to design problems became bigger and fuller. My confidence grew and I was comfortable with my place at Artek, the company that I started at during the summer of 1974 and that had hired me while I was still in college for a full-time job. This saved me the insecurity of not having a job upon graduation and the considerable effort that so many of my friends were expending to find jobs in Landscape Architecture upon graduation in 1977. The friends who had the backing of families that would continue to support them in college went on to graduate schools or took low paying but educationally enriching internships which might lead to more secure employment. For some friends, job hunting became a major project covering several months and sometimes longer. Then, if they were lucky, quite a few got offers for jobs as draftsmen in Landscape Architectural offices for $7000 to $8000 per year. Artek offered me $15,000 per year to stay with them as their "Chief Mechanical Designer".

I stayed with the Montchal family again directly after leaving college, but shortly thereafter found a tiny apartment (about 20 sq meters in size) that would cost me $165 per month in rent. The apartment was in Wantagh, about 8 miles away from my job and not too far from East Meadow where I had grown up and where the Montchals were and close to my sisters – who lived in Hicksville and Westbury – we were all within a five-mile radius of each other. I still had my bicycle to get me either back and forth to work or back and forth to someone who lived near-by (with whom I could ride back and forth to work from their home). My expenses were low – I could pay my rent with less than one week's pay and still have enough money to buy food for that week. My food was mostly Chinese take-out, Italian meals, half consumed at the local pizzeria and half brought home as leftovers and food purchased from the "coffee-truck" that came by the factory back door two or three times per day. Several factories in our neighborhood could be served from the parking lot by the alley way behind our backdoor. Besides freshly brewed coffee, the truck offered sandwiches, pastries, sweet and salty snacks, ice cold soft drinks as well as participation in sports pools (a form of illegal, but widely participated-in petty gambling). My apartment was so tiny, it didn't come with a kitchen. It had a two burner portable electric stovetop, a toaster oven and a refrigerator (which only ever held eggs and some soda, a six pack of beer in case I had a visitor who wanted one – I was pretty much a tee-totaler). It came furnished with a sofa-bed

I couldn't afford to buy a car when I finished at Syracuse and returned to Long Island. I rode a bicycle to work from the apartment in Wantagh to Farmingdale where my drawing board beckoned every day. One early morning – it must have been about 7:30 – as I crossed over the Southern State Parkway on an overpass on Carman's Road (on the border of Farmingdale and Amityville or Massapequa – I suppose), I heard a small dog yapping on the other side of a fence that separated the Parkway side of the overpass from the road. The fence was a chain link fence with a small gap underneath that could be made big enough to let the dog pass under by simply pulling on the bottom of the fence. The dog was fully grown but young. She was a brown mixture of some kind of wire-haired terrier and dachshund. Picture a dachshund on long legs with tufts of wiry terrier hair sprouting out the top of her head and along her abdomen and having a small beard. This was a dog with character! I inquired around the neighborhood if anyone had ever seen the dog or knew where she might have come from but was greeted with caring concern from a number of people in bathrobes and morning-just-out-of-bed hair, but no recognition of my newly found canine friend. I used the telephone of one of these kind souls to call the office and ask them to send a van with a driver to pick me up along with my bicycle and this funny-looking dog.

From the office, I called what we used to call the "dog pound" – what they probably call the animal shelter these days. They sent a van to come and pick up the dog and they told me that they would call whether or not anyone claimed her over the next week and took my telephone number at the office and at my home. She had slipped from my mind when the call came late that week with the message that no one had claimed her. If I didn't come and get her, they would "put her to sleep". I often wonder what the success rate was with this method of making a person feel culpable in the death of a dog that one has come to know in saving found-dogs' lives. In any case, they were successful with me. I took the dog. When I got home with the dog on the day we went to get her with my other sister's car, Sherry, who was living with me at the time, thought that she was so sweet and cute and wanted to name her "Fifi". "Fifi?" I remarked, is a French dog's name. This dog is obviously not French. If this dog was anything, she was German. We came up with the name Sauerbraten, which was one of our favorite German meals. This name has the charm of being both German and representing something that we both liked, but it is unusual for a dog to be named after an ethnic meal. Even the more so if one comes to reside in the country of that meals origin which Sauerbraten would do for the last 8 years of her life. We seldom used her full name when calling her or referring to her, she became "Braten". Although the analogy and translation is not one-for-one, imagine an English bulldog named Roastbeef and being called "Roast" for short. Sauerbraten would accompany me from those transition years from young single man building a career to the height of success as a family man with a successful business. Now that I think of it, if I were a superstitious man, I'd have to say that Sauerbraten was as close to a well-functioning good luck charm as anyone could have wished to possess.

Even after I could afford to buy my first car about ten months after starting full time work, with Sarah always at least 3 hours drive away during that time, I didn't really have any local social life except my family, my participation in the local church and my involvement with a few families that had come to become friends through church. The center of my Long Island life became Artek. I was a salaried employee which meant that I was never paid for overtime work, but because I was always trying to collect as many hours of work as possible to offset against free Fridays and/ or Mondays (that I could use to extend weekends with Sarah), I was often working from early in the morning into the late evening hours. I didn't have much time during those first two years of my career to build a social life on Long Island. My time on Long Island was completely consumed at work – otherwise I was visiting Sarah wherever she happened to be. She was usually either at Syracuse or home for winter or summer vacation in Delmar. One summer a former High School teacher of mine, a chemistry teacher, Mr. Gelobter, had an opening for her to be a camp counselor at a summer camp for elementary school age children in the Poconos in Pennsylvania. She was delighted not to be home that summer, but she wasn't happy to be trapped in this idyllic setting with a biweekly rotation of 9- and 10-year-old girls from New York City, Long Island and North Jersey. I would visit her there for her free days and we would play at being mature lovers having a secret tryst at a local hotel. I was happy, productive, and fulfilled. It seemed that my life was made. I had a life laid out before me with Sarah and my work providing all that I needed in my life. I was all set until I wasn't anymore.

After I had been at Artek for a year, in the spring of 1978, I asked my boss, Bill, for a raise in salary as I was told is normal practice by everyone I knew. I knew that I was valued and well liked at Artek so I really did not expect to have any problems getting a raise in pay. Bill said, "yeah, yeah; I'll take care of it" when I asked and "yeah, yeah; I'm working on it" whenever I reminded him of my request throughout that summer. After waiting for three months and always getting the same answer, I simply lost my patience and decided to find another job. I went to one single job interview and was offered a job to start immediately at a company called Theta Instruments that made laboratory equipment for testing the effect of temperature on materials. The machines had names like Dilatometers, Flash Diffusivity Instruments, Thermal Conductivity Meters and High Temperature Viscometers. The company was in Port Washington, a town along the "gold coast" on the north of Long Island – a bit closer into the city than where I lived which meant a longer commute to work than the commute I had had to Farmingdale which was along the same south shore of Long Island where I lived and a bit east.

A Journeyman Mechanical Designer

On my last day at Artek, something in me was regretting what I was doing. Bill Kitchener had been so good to me when I needed a mentor. He had taught me so much of what became the basis of my working life that I was feeling badly about leaving. The company had just been sold and would become a "Dynatech" company. The project that I had started while I was still a student, the ELISA reader, became the most valuable thing that Artek had done. On the last day of work at Artek, I was introduced to an engineer, Lew Levy, who was a brand-new hire. He would work on the ELISA reader project, and we would somehow remain in contact with each other, but I can't remember exactly how!

My new boss, Gerald (Jerry) Clusener, was an immigrant from Germany who still had a noticeable accent. Jerry was the business man and President, but the brains of the outfit was another German named Karl-Heinz Raffalski. Karl-Heinz was the Bill Kitchener of Theta Industries. Nothing happened there without him and all the technology that Theta put into their products was put there because Karl-Heinz could figure out how to make it all work. This business was a bit smaller than Artek with only 7 or 8 employees. But the brainpower per worker was definitely higher, if only because Karl-Heinz figured prominently into the average! During my job interview, Jerry asked me what I'd done, about my education, and what I wanted to earn. He was happy with all my answers and offered me the job with immediate effect at the rate of pay I'd asked for. I probably should have asked for more! I'd asked for $ 20,000 per year which he translated to $ 9.62 per hour. Everybody at Theta Industries, including Karl-Heinz, punched a timecard "in" when he arrived and punched a timecard "out" when he left. It was the only job that I ever had where that was demanded of me. The work was demanding and fulfilling to do but the spirit of the place was stale and cold. There was no emotional connection between people at that place and I can't say that I was happy there. I can still remember Jerry sitting at his desk in a pensive position – deep in his own thoughts and concerns. He would always sit up and brighten when he realized I was there, but his normal, unobserved, condition was of a man carrying responsibilities that he was concerned about bearing up under. I understand him completely now in this stage of my life and business but was a bit oblivious to his concerns in those days. Now that I think of it, I never had the feeling that we had too much to do at Theta, as was normally the case with Artek and other businesses I've experienced since Theta Industries (at least when we were doing well). There was the same stalwart solidness to Jerry as there was with my first boss, Nicky. The same sense of loyalty to those committed to, and the same quietness of purpose (when things were slow) infused both personalities. Only Nicky smiled more.

I learned about achieving temperatures as high as 1600 °C in atmospheric conditions using resistive heating elements like platinum wire. Higher temperatures were achievable but usually needed to be done in non-oxygen containing environments or in a vacuum. I learned that cooling could be done by directing liquid nitrogen through blown glass (quartz) tubes that surrounded a tested sample of material. We built an apparatus that needed to achieve near perfect vacuum using a set of vacuum pumps which started with a simple vane pump, then a "roughing" pump, then a diffusion pump with a cold filter which used liquid nitrogen to cool the remaining gas molecules (not evacuated by any of the previous methods or pumps) into lethargy. We built a bell jar out of a double wall of stainless steel that formed the bounds of this near-perfect vacuum. Through the double walls of stainless steel, we had arranged a labyrinth of metal vanes to direct circulating cooling water to protect the polymer seal of the bell jar from melting when a laser pulse raised the temperature of the sample inside of the bell jar to over 3000 degrees C in an instant. We feared that the reflected energy of the pulsed beam might raise the temperature of the bell jar. We also feared for the consequences of a poorly maintained vacuum which would result in the case of a damaged polymer seal: An atmosphere of expanding gas which would raise the pressure inside the bell jar that might cause it to jump up and down with a startling bang. Building such instruments which measured energy changes in millijoules per micron or differences in length and thickness in microns per degree per millisecond demanded a balancing between applying energy to (or extracting from) a sample while keeping everything else as close to nominal as possible. Whereas much of the work that I did at Artek was related to electronic packaging, at Theta Industries, I was stretched much more in the direction of solving basic mechanical problems and problems of thermodynamics using blocks of glass, ceramics, insulating materials, stainless steel, aluminum or brass.

The work was demanding, required creativity applied in a step-by-step fashion and carried out in an environment where everybody did their work with their heads down and their noses firmly pointed at their drawing boards, work benches or lab tables. The atmosphere at Artek had been much more open and collegial. At Artek, we often spent time talking about what came to mind beyond the work we were doing. We took breaks together. Sometimes we'd arrange for a game of tennis on our lunch break, or we'd play some handball against the wall at the back of the factory. Such social engagement simply did not take place at Theta. The extra money and the interesting work were positive compared to Artek. Everything else, including the relatively long commute was negative compared to the experience of Artek. If I had it to do over again, it would be hard for me to decide what I would do with my hindsight. The work experience was truly a great experience and the knowledge that I was worth so much more in an area of work for which I had no formal education was also a positive life experience for me, but the people at Artek and the work environment that I had enjoyed was missing in my life.

It was while I was working at Theta that I became engaged to be married with Sarah. I bought the ring without asking her beforehand, but I was so sure of her love that I just jumped in and bought it. I spent all the money I had and though it wasn't the two months salary that the salesman told me that "most men in my position" spring for, it did set me back about $ 1200! She, thankfully, and as expected, consented to marry me and we were as happy as a couple could be – or at least I was as happy as a young man could be. A week or two later, she was off to London for her semester abroad. We wrote each other letters – or rather, I wrote her letters and she answered with little cards in which she wrote little messages of love and "missing you" and such. She wasn't a writer! We would talk on the phone each week, but the expense of intercontinental phone-talking was such in those days that it felt as if you were throwing dollar bills into the ether with each sentence spoken or listened to. I much preferred letters (or failing that, getting at least a silly card). The thing with the phone calls was that after hanging up, I was lonelier than before spending all of that money to talk. With a letter or card, I had something of her in my hand.

On one of our weekly phone calls, she told me that she didn't want to marry me any longer. She just didn't love me anymore "in that way." We went around and around on the phone, with me saying that I was seeking reasons, when, in fact, I just wanted to have what she was saying remain unsaid. No, it wasn't somebody else. No, it wasn't anything I had said or done. No, she hadn't been play-acting about what she said she had felt before. Yes, what she felt for me now was different than before. We spoke for hours (I soon learned, $ 700 worth) and the message remained the same – she not only didn't want to marry me anymore, but she also wanted to break up with me and set me "free." I asked her to please re-consider until I could come and visit her in London, and we could work it out. There was no way for me to understand whatever it was that had led to such a drastic change of heart in a matter of months. I worked out with my boss to get a week free from work and I flew to London to try to save the relationship. It was my first visit to London. At the beginning of my visit, it seemed as if, per-haps, my coming might have helped. She seemed happy to see me and we spent some time being tourists. She showed me her neighborhood – I can't remember anymore which district it was, but I do remember that it wasn't an affluent area. We attended a concert at the Royal Albert Hall and went to dinner at a nice sea-food restaurant. I remember sitting across from her at the window of that restaurant and chit-chatting. A good-looking, well-dressed version of what must have been an Englishman – probably our age or slightly older – passing by outside the window, looked in at her, caught her eye and winked at her and smiled in an overt flirt. She was delighted and giggled. I seethed inwardly and showed her my best understanding grin. That moment, had it happened before our long telephone conversation, would have meant noth-ing. Sarah was a very attractive young woman, and I was used to men looking at her. In our pre-breakup days, I was secure in our relationship. In that moment, I should have known, that what we had was gone – not because she giggled, but because I seethed. I suppose 45 years of passing time does add something in the end.

The week of breaking up in person is a bit of a blur in my mem-ory. What isn't blurred is her steadfastness in her decision to dump me. She did have a "friend", Alan, who, I think to recall, was south Asian – from India. She insisted it wasn't anything like our relationship and wasn't the reason for breaking up. We did a lot of walking and talking. There is a song that I have learned (and love to play and sing accompanied by my guitar) since that experience called the "Streets of London". Whenever I hear or sing that song, I recall a moment from that trip with Sarah. We were walking and window shopping in the evening on a street lit mostly by the light of shop windows. She was holding onto my right arm as women do when couples stroll. There are shops (camera and jewelry shops come to mind) where the door is set deep into an outdoor foyer and wares are shown in a lighted display window which invite people to enter the foyer to look at the display before entering the shop. We were just about to enter the foyer of one shop as we continued to peruse the display window. As we turned the corner, an old man in an old and worn-out soldier's uniform, complete with medals, raged at us. He scared the living daylight out of both of us. Sarah screamed and I hustled her protectively away:

"Have you seen the old man
Outside the seaman's mission
Memory fading with
The medal ribbons that he wears?
In our winter city
The rain cries a little pity
For one more forgotten hero
And a world that doesn't care
So, how can you tell me you're lonely
And say for you that the sun don't shine?
Let me take you by the hand
And lead you through the streets of London
I'll show you something to make you change your mind"

(Ralph McTell 1969)

Other memories swarmed: Sarah on my arm walking in a sun-lit scene at a park in Syracuse. I could see the stripes and specs of blue, green and brown in the iris of her eyes. The arm-in-arm walk up the darkness of a Syracuse street, she slightly taller than me in her high-heels and a bit tipsy from a champagne reception at a theatre event; the two of us walking our way to bed and into a future that would always contain the two of us. The stolen moments at her home hoping no one would walk in on us. The day we made love in her sun-drenched room on campus not realizing until it was too late that a sizable crowd of people in the dormitory across the street had gathered at their windows to watch. The moments are still etched in my mind, but when we stopped making memories together on that London trip, we were over. I left her in her apartment in London, the engagement ring in my pocket, and walked away alone. The Sarah phase of my life ended almost as suddenly as it had started.

When I came back from London I realized I had never felt so empty in my entire life. I felt as miserable and as forlorn and worthless as I had ever felt. Nothing in my life prepared me for the depth of the loneliness I had descended into. I went from the security of knowing I was loved into the certain knowledge that I was not. Even worse, I questioned if Sarah's love had ever existed at all. I took the ring back to the store to ask how much they would give me for the ring. They suggested that it was worth $280. I told them that their own insurance adjustor had appraised the ring for $1400 after I had paid $1200 for it. Silence. I took the ring with me and put it away in a drawer. Sometime, several months later, I was in a conversation with my father for the first time in a couple of years. He told me that he was getting married for a third time. I asked him if he'd be interested in giving his new wife, Ada, a nice engagement ring. He said yes, so I gave him Sarah's ring for Ada. I hope it's floating around Ada's family now making somebody happy to have it.

I went back to work. In the months that Sarah had been away in London, I found myself, for the first time since being back on Long Island, at a loss for things to do. For most of the previous two years, I always had Sarah to occupy my mind and my free, non-working time. I started singing in a couple of secular community choirs. One, a local group that mostly sang popular music or standards from the 1940s and 1950s as well as choral arrangements of music from musicals and the other associated with Hofstra University that sang ancient music; madrigals and music of the pre-baroque period accompanied by an ensemble made up of musicians playing instruments from the Middle Ages. I took ballet lessons at a local adult education program. I was the only male in the class, but it was something I wanted to learn, and it gave me something to do on another night of the week.

Through college friends, I came into two separate cliques of women friends who lived in New York City. I started to drive into the city on the weekends and spend time with one clique or the other. The friendships were strictly platonic but did provide a spot on the floor or on a sofa to crash, so that I didn't have to drive back to Long Island every evening. My landlord made sure that Sauerbraten, the dog, left alone in my apartment, was fed. Nowadays one must only pay a toll for the Midtown Tunnel in the direction of driving into the city. In those days, one had to pay a toll in both directions. The 59th Street Bridge was always without a toll but was less convenient, so I always paid the toll and drove into the city on those Friday evenings or Saturday afternoons via the Midtown Tunnel. There were quite a few times that I needed to drive home via the 59th Street Bridge simply because I could not afford to pay the toll for the Midtown Tunnel after a weekend with my friends in New York. Sometimes I needed to survive on what I had at home and the leftovers from my weekend until I got paid on Friday again.

And so it was that I had already begun to fill my life with non-Sarah activities before our breakup. The difference after the breakup was that everything I did that used to make my life full now made my life feel empty. It all felt so meaningless. My over-arching emotional state-of-being was lonely. I had weekly res-pites from my loneliness at church on the Sundays that I didn't go into the city, where I often saw the Montchal family and/or one or the other of my sisters and members of their families. The traditions of the church, the music, the camaraderie of wor-shipers gathered together on a Sunday, the quiet reflection on the message of the sermon and the Bible readings, the old hab-its of the cyclical routines of standing, sitting, praying, reciting, chanting and singing in unison were the basis of blocking the loneliness out for an hour or two. There was also Thursday eve-nings (I think to recall), when I would visit my sister with my laundry. I didn't have access to a washer and dryer for my clothes, so my sister, Nancy, and I came to an accommodation whereby I paid her $20 per week to do my washing and ironing and she would invite me to have dinner (for no extra charge) on laundry delivery and pickup day – Thursdays. These evenings stand out in my memory as a reminder to myself that I never really had a very good reason to feel lonely. My sisters were there for me (not to mention their children) and there were so many other people like the Eichhorsts and the Montchals to whom I could always go to be welcomed and spend some time. My friend, Gary Hamilton, from college days, was always a letter or a telephone call away. But as fulfilled and "made" my life felt with Sarah in it, without her, it felt empty, and I felt miserable.

I tried to get myself into situations where I could meet women, but frankly, I wasn't in any kind of mental state to be a suitable "partner" or "boy-friend" material. I had never been the type of person to go out and spend time at bars, pubs, restaurants, or clubs. This will come as a surprise to those who know me these days. My reputation in my present hometown is one of a person who is always to be found at a bar, pub, restaurant, or club with a beer, wine, or whiskey in front of me and a willingness to engage in a conversation as a means of passing the time. I was different then. I recall going past a bar full of people called "Serendipity" not far from where I lived in Wantagh during a very lonely phase of life then. I was impressed by its name as serendipity is one of my favorite obscure English words. Serendipity means "fortunate coincidence" or "unexpected good luck." I found it a perfect name for a pub that I should just stumble across at a time when I truly felt in need of serendipity. I entered the pub with a sense of anticipation of meeting someone, if not to spend the rest of my life with, then at least to have a nice evening of conversation. "I'm an interesting guy" I told myself. "This place is full of people. There'll certainly be somebody to meet and talk to!" I walked up to the bar, ordered a soft drink, stood there like a "bump on a log," looked around at all the people in animated conversations with one another, drank my drink, and left. I felt totally like a fish out of water or a stranger in a strange land or a little Asian guy in a pub full of Long Islanders that looked and sounded like Long Islanders. That was the last attempt I made at going into a pub by myself until I started drinking and travelling on business about seven or eight years later.

In those days there were personal ads in the classified section of the newspapers. I wasn't up to spending money for my own personal ad, but I did get up the courage to answer an ad that read "young, cultured sww, [single white woman], 25, 5'-2", petite, attractive – seeking sm – non-smokers only – Port Washington." Here was a woman who didn't write that she was seeking a swm (single white man), and she didn't stipulate a tall-Cary-Grant-look-alike, so it seemed to me that I fit the bill pretty well. I didn't smoke. I was a single male and I worked in Port Washington. I sent a message to the newspaper with my telephone number, and after a day or two, she called me at my office at Theta. We arranged to meet at a bar in Port Washington after work the next day. After our meeting, I stopped answering personal ads. It wasn't that the meeting was a catastrophe or that she wasn't what she said she was that put me off of this particular way of meeting people. It was the feeling that I was being measured, rated, compared to a world of possibilities within the half hour it took to have a drink and a conversation. I knew that no matter what I said, she wasn't going to give me a chance at a date because I simply wasn't what she was looking for. To be honest, I don't think she was what I was looking for either, but I really wasn't as certain as she was. She, being the person who wrote the ad, made the decision that I wouldn't get her telephone number so there was no way to carry on a conversation that could lead to us getting to know each other better in any case. The experience wasn't exactly bad, but it wasn't one that I was anxious to repeat.

After the experiences of "Serendipity" and the personal ad, I not only felt lonely and unloved, but I also felt unlovable! I stopped searching for "Miss Right" and started to take up a more transactional approach to women. I went through a phase where I took advantage of the convenience of what was offered in the way of companionship or sex without committing anything of myself. If a woman wanted to spend time with me and was happy to keep it platonic, then I did that, and we became friends. If a woman wanted to have sex, then we did that, but none of those encounters led to anything deeper or more meaningful. I didn't feel good about myself in any of these physical encounters because there was nothing of value that followed. I had learned the difference between exchanging love and giving and taking pleasure. The latter was all I could get. The former was out of my reach and relegated to memory.

A few months after my return from London, I decided to leave the sterile and somewhat stifling atmosphere of Theta Industries and took a job which would place me squarely back into the world of electronics and printed circuit design. I joined a company called Venus Scientific which was located only a few blocks away from where Artek had been earlier when I worked there. The main business of Venus Scientific was high voltage DC power supplies for military applications. I was hired to work on a project to design low-light level closed circuit television (CCTV) cameras. As it was in Artek, electrical engineers drew their schematics on legal pads and gave them to draftsmen or designers to draw onto vellum. Once the schematics were completed, a rough mechanical design followed (for which the electrical engineer had something in mind, but usually didn't have the means to represent in a drawing). My role was to listen to the engineer's description of how he understood the product's look, feel and essence and return to him some drawings or illustrations of various versions of how the product might look, be operated, or be put together. I was teamed up with an engineer named Art Brady who became a lifelong friend. We made a good team, the work was fulfilling and, as it turned out Venus was exactly the kind of company I needed to find and belong to in my precarious mental state.

Venus was a very social company. It was bigger than I had been used to with a couple of hundred employees. The front offices were full of men in suits who worked in purchasing, sales, marketing, account management or contracts administration and well-dressed women, mostly single, who were assistants or secretaries. There was an engineering department of about six or seven electrical engineers and a group of application engineers and technicians who worked to design new products as well as trouble-shoot problems that always seemed to crop up in the production of already existing products. The drafting and designing department was a group of about 10 people. I was the only one in the department that had no fixed day-to-day product responsibility. I was lucky to be working on projects that were truly product development projects for which success was not guaranteed and progress and applied creativity were easily noticed. People took an interest in the development of the drawings that took shape over time on my drawing board. I worked in an office with three "older men". At that time, and for another couple of decades to come, it seemed I was always the youngest in the settings I found myself in. The exact opposite of what I am experiencing now. The other three men in the office were all in their 50s, I suppose. Two, Maury and Joe, worked on high voltage power supplies used in

CRT displays (cathode ray tubes) and the third, Bob, was, during the time I spent at Venus, working on low light level goggles for soldiers to wear. Such goggles are often seen on TV these days (worn by soldiers in total darkness, guided by the green images only they can see through their helmet mounted goggles), but in 1979, they were the subject of Research & Development projects at numerous companies throughout the world. I sometimes helped Bob on his projects, but I had almost nothing to do, except private conversations, with Maury or Joe who exclusively worked on high voltage power supplies.

Most of my daily work interactions were with Art Brady. We became friends when he started to include me in a group of people who would play tennis together. Art worked in a big room with a series of long work benches on which circuits and mechanical assemblies were put together. He had a desk nestled at the end of two rows of work benches. There, technicians and assembly people worked on prototypes and development projects. One of the benches contained power supply carcasses. They were there to be analyzed for failures. Strewn among the chaos of those long workbenches in that room were the prototypes for power supplies that would light up displays on F15, F16 and F-18 fighter jets. This room was where new products were built and tested and where new ideas became real. Although Art had a desk, he seldom used it, he was most often found at the side of a technician at one of the workbenches or sitting in front of a newly delivered or assembled prototype (also at one of those workbenches) to decide what went wrong and what went right. He would spend time with me mostly to check my work in the re-drawing of electronic schematics or the taping of printed circuit boards.

An early experience with Art comes to mind largely because, for many years thereafter, he never let me forget. A set of new circuit designs were required for a low light level camera we were working on. The prototype had worked, and we had an order to build 10 pieces of this newly designed CCTV camera which was meant to be used with very long focal length (1,200 mm or more) lenses. Among the other design requirements mandated by the receipt of the first production order for such a product, we had to redesign a set of three printed circuit boards. These boards connected to and controlled the image intensifiers, the yoke around the vidicon tube, and properly synchronized the output of the vidicon tube, processing the pulsating stream of electrons into a standard NTSC video output signal that would represent moving pictures of what the lens saw (sometimes miles away). I didn't know how to do any of that, but Art did. My job was to:

1. Design the look of the product, with its outlines, size, shape, textures and feel.
2. Provide mounting and connecting means for the various elements of the product. In this case:
   a. A vidicon tube that created a two-dimensional moving image from light focused on the face of the leading image intensifiers face-plate.
   b. Three image intensifiers placed end to end which created a multiplication of light to the vidicon (which was mounted on the output of the last of the image intensifiers.)
   c. Three printed circuit boards that controlled everything.
   d. A mechanical means to ensure that 30 pounds of force pushed the face of the vidicon into the face-plate at the exit of the last image intensifier.
   e. The interconnection means between all the elements including connectors, fasteners, brackets, mechanical parts and sheet metal or plastic housings.
3. Design the outline of the printed circuit boards so that the boards fit properly in the housing. and all the connections between the various components that comprised the three circuits were properly made.
4. Create documents to make sure that all the wishes of the engineers were known to the technicians, assemblers, and users of the product for the life of the product.

Art's job and my job intersected at 2a through 2c, 3 and 4. When a printed circuit is taped, the taping must be checked; connection for connection. Today, the process of circuit design is largely relegated to computers and software and checking is also relegated to computers and software. In 1979 Art and I stood side by side at my drawing board with a copy of the taped circuits and we used blue pencils to follow and mark tracks that were good, used red to indicate tracks that were missing and yellow to indicate tracks that had to be removed. We did this for the three circuit boards in several iterations. Eventually, everything checked out. We then ordered the PCBs and sent out our taped artworks, knowing we had checked every interconnection point.

The day that a design team receives the PCBs for a new design is a special day. We were excited and we put the first of the three PCB circuits into the prototype assembly area and had to wait a couple of days for them to be assembled and then sent them to the technicians to make the "in-circuit" tests before mounting them into the mechanical housings. All the other assembly work for all the other parts can be done when the necessary parts have trickled in over what is always an interminable time. The anticipation of success mixed with the fear of having overlooked something or done something wrong is both exquisite and heavy to bear. Something turned out to be wrong with one of the circuits. It took Art a few minutes to find out that, despite our careful controls a very short connection between two integrated circuit pads was missing. I ran back to our control copies and saw the connection there. I went to the original taping and checked it. The connection wasn't there. Sometime between the checking and the making of the circuits, the little piece of black adhesive tape had fallen off! I was just lucky it didn't stick somewhere else where it could have been an unwanted connection! For the next 10 years at least, Art would, when he felt he needed to take me down a peg or two, tell me, "It must have just fallen off!" We had to fix those ten boards with two drilled holes and a jumper which meant an embarrassing set of ECRs and ECOs (engineering change requests and engineering change orders.)

The demographic and social dynamics of Venus Scientific is a microcosm of how the working world worked in the 1970s and 80s. There were two centers of power and privilege in the company, dominated by white men in the front offices (where the well-dressed attractive women worked) and in the engineering offices, located in a separate part of the building. The engineering department had its own attractive, well-dressed secretary. The president and majority owner of the company was a man named Phillipe Galuppi, who's over 80-year-old father would regularly visit. I once heard that Phillipe's father had been a son of the mayor of Rome. I had the impression the father had started the company, because I recall, one time, when I was up front, Vicki (the engineering department's attractive secretary) took me by the arm and showed me the father, sitting at what I thought was his desk, sound asleep (and whispering how sweet she thought it was). I assumed it was his office. I also recall him coming into the office with his wife once (I got the impression that they had been married for over 50 years – perhaps he told us once) – Vicki or Ray, one of the important suits from the front office – told me the story that Phillipe's father, probably around 1925, was visiting from Italy and staying at the Plaza Hotel, when he saw, and was fully smitten by, a young, beautiful woman there at the lobby of the hotel. He got into conversation with her and explained to her that he was visiting from Rome and wasn't planning to stay in New York much longer. He told her that his father was prominent in Rome (I've since checked and a Gallupi was never mayor of Rome between the late 19th century and the early 20th) and that he was well connected to the Cardinal who resided at St. Patrick's Cathedral. He proposed to meet this newly-met love-of-his-life the next weekend at St. Patrick's at such-and-such a time and he would arrange to have the Cardinal marry them. The woman replied that they had just met and that he must be crazy. He replied, "Signorina, non sono pazzo. Sono innamorato." – Miss, I am not crazy. I am in love. I'll be there and I hope you will also be there. – "Io ci sarò e spero ci sarà anche lei."

It's one of the most romantic stories I've ever heard attached to someone I've actually met. I suppose some or most is not true as I heard it and perhaps my memory has polished the story to glow more than the actual events, but I still tell the story of Phillipe Galuppi's father's romantic soul. As a man who has fallen in love at first sight twice and can always imagine possibilities at the sight of a beautiful woman, I could actually believe a man doing this if he had the means.

There was a group of people at Venus Scientific who were single – both never-marrieds and formerly marrieds – who sometimes planned to go out after work together. Not very far from where Venus had its factory, a new office park, called the Huntington Quadrangle, had been built where banks, insurance companies, trading companies, law and accounting firms moved in. This was a relatively new phenomenon on Long Island in the 1970s. In the middle of this office park, a night club and event venue hoped to capitalize on this ready access to upwardly mobile young professionals by hosting "Corporate Mixers". These were events for which flyers were sent to the companies in the area and were scheduled to start on a weekday directly after work. Vicki or one of the other secretaries at Venus decided to get a group of office people and engineering department singles to attend a "mixer" one Wednesday evening. I was asked to join and having nothing else to do, I went. It started off much like my experience at "Serendipity": me, standing alone amid a crowd of people and feeling out of place and lonely while it seemed that everyone else belonged and were enjoying each other's company. As if by magic, and out of nowhere, a blonde woman appeared at my side and started to chat with me. I had seen this woman walking between the front office and the engineering areas at the back of the building; walking briskly by my workstation – always seemingly in a hurry to get where she needed to be, pretty, bright-eyed, smiling and always perky, [thankfully] shorter than I, she had made an impression on me as way above the level of humans at Venus that I had the possibility to know well and have in my social circle. She was always very well dressed and she was always with the other well-dressed, front-office types at Venus. I suppose that I was aware of the caste system that existed in my consciousness in those times, in that place. In spite of my own feelings of being out-classed by this woman, here she was introducing herself to me as Barbara, a contracts administrator, who had started working at Venus relatively recently. We separated ourselves from the crowd we were surrounded by and wound up sitting on the steps leading to a largely empty raised area of the club. There, we spent the evening in conversation about how our lives had led us to that place together on those steps. She was recently divorced, still living in the house that her ex-husband had left to her and their two daughters, Kathy and Nancy (who were 9 and 12). Her ex-husband's family had owned a well-known furniture business in Hempstead, the larger town which East Meadow actually belonged to. The bankruptcy and subsequent closure of the business had led to stresses in their marriage, and she was dealing with the transition from being a housewife and mother to becoming a single, working mother.

One thing was clear. We really liked each other and felt totally comfortable in each other's company in spite of the difference in our ages. She was 36. I was 25. As I recall, when it came time to leave the party, I followed her home in my car and we took advantage of the freedom she had that evening of having left her daughters at a friends or sister's house so that she didn't have to come home early that evening. That evening (and night) of love-making was the first time since the first time (from college days) that I felt led and guided into a world of feminine desire and pleasure. In Barbara, I was being introduced to the world of her sexual pleasure by someone, not only with more experience, but who was willing and able to communicate what she wanted. Very early in the morning, I left Barbara's for home to tend to Sauerbraten, my dog, who was probably truly sour for having been left alone so long. She was "paper" trained, which meant she relieved herself on newspapers left on a plastic sheet on the floor, but she was hungry. I cleaned up after her, fed her, then slept deeply for an hour or two. At seven, I showered and dressed for my next day at Venus and was off to work. When Barbara came by my cubicle, whooshing by, doing her rounds between the front office and the engineering offices, she was as pretty and well dressed as ever, bubbly, and absolutely beaming. I was probably smiling like an idiot too. One thing was certain to us, and was soon certain to everyone that saw us. We made each other very happy.

We were soon spending all of our time together. We went to lunch together every day. When we could arrange it, we would spend some time after work and before she needed to go home to tend to and feed her girls and I needed to tend to and feed Sauerbraten. I'd go to visit her on weekends. Sometimes I took the dog. My weekends going into the city stopped abruptly and I was now headed in the other direction to her house farther east on Long Island. Her daughters and I became friendly. I never played an adult in the house with the girls. I tried to just be a guest in the house and can't recall ever getting into any conflicts with them. They were just great kids. I liked them and appreciated the time I spent with them. Often, they weren't there on the weekends because they spent time with their father, but not always. It wasn't long before Sauerbraten and I more-or-less moved in with Barbara and her girls. My apartment remained empty and I would rarely go there. I recall that my sister, Sherry, moved in for a time when she and my mother weren't getting along. I would visit at the beginning of each month to pay my rent. The rest of my life was subsumed into Barbara's life and work at Venus.

Our life experiences were totally different. She was fully mature and I was this thing becoming what I was to become. Her friends were also mothers and fathers of kids her kids' ages who all had homes and established careers and the lives and problems of people of that age – pushing 40. Her friends were all nice to me and seemed to accept that I was a part of her life but I was totally exotic in this setting, I suppose. There is this description of people describing a young man like I was together with an older woman as a "toy-boy" but I really don't think our relationship was ever anything like that. We never declared love to each other, but we were totally committed to each other's happiness.

My family, as represented by my two older sisters, were not happy that I was living with an older woman and her children. All during our time together, I felt the disapproval. It wasn't anything that broke out into the open in any way and caused any open friction. We didn't really talk about it, but it was there as only family disappointment and disapproval can be there without being openly discussed. My younger sister Sherry was happy that I was happy and didn't make any judgements about my judgement concerning Barbara. As it turned out, several years later, she would marry someone who was a good fifteen or more years older than she was. We all know though, a younger woman with an older man doesn't raise eyebrows nearly as high as a younger man with an older woman.

Barbara lived in Kings Park, a town which was just east of Huntington near the north shore of Long Island. The homes in her neighborhood were bigger than the homes I was used to from my youth. Her ex-husband had come from a relatively well-to-do family that had owned a well-known store, so my assumption was always that he was paying for the house and child support of some kind, but that Barbara was working because she needed to and wanted to. I tried to pay my part of the groceries and always paid our way when we went out together, whereby she always tried to contribute when we were doing "family stuff". We never had any conflicts when it came to money (or anything else, for that matter). Our relationship was just a series of falling, sliding, or stumbling from one step of emotional commitment to the next.

I met her siblings one-by-one and we would enjoy the day or dinner or the outing with no big explanations that I knew of. Her ex came to pick up the girls for the weekend when I happened to be there, and we were introduced with no great fanfare. I was there when the girls came back. There was a lightness of being and a bubbly, take-life-as-it-comes character to Barbara that was simply so easy to go along with and totally strange to my life among any women that I had met up to that point. We floated along.

During the fall of that year, as November's Thanksgiving season opened the way to the Christmas season, I became restless in my situation. Barbara and I hadn't declared to have loved each other although we clearly liked being together and had clearly committed ourselves to each other. I suppose we could have continued like we had but at some point, I found my interest wandering to the possibilities of other women and it seemed like it was the right thing to do to break up with Barbara. So, I did. It was one of the more difficult conversations of my life. I blamed it on the pressure of my family, but that was only partially true. The truth was, I had cold feet about going forward with or deeper into a truly loving relationship with the rest of our lives together as the goal. After having our time of life together with Barbara and sharing her home and family with her and through no fault at all of hers, I was afraid of missing the life that was mine. I suppose that I felt like I was living in Barbara's life at the expense of living in my own. My apartment was still waiting for me to come and occupy it again and I did. I recall that after I made the decision and moved out, I felt terrible and wondered if I shouldn't just go ahead and ask her to marry and commit fully. I talked to her and told her of my feelings. She rejected any entreaties on my part to get back together again. It was over. Sauerbraten and I went back home to the tiny apartment, leaving Barbara, Nancy and Kathy behind. By that time, I had moved on to another job, so the daily buzz-bys of Barbara, bopping from the front office to the engineering offices remained only a very pleasant memory.

I had largely abandoned my commitment to church, religion and faith during the post-Sarah and through my Barbara chapters of life. First out of anger at God and then just being unwilling to commit the time on Sundays to going to church as I had always done. One of the first changes in my life after Barbara was to return to my church-going habits. Why? I suppose it was the pull of tradition and a lack of intellectual maturity or emotional backbone to give my doubts about God and Christianity their full head. Ever since the beginnings of consuming books as an 8-year-old, the inconsistencies of what life was feeding me about religion, philosophy, science and truth niggled at the edges of my mind. Spending so much of my time, not only among Christians, but with Christians at a Lutheran School trained me to keep my doubts to myself and just go with the flow. Besides: I loved the music. I found comfort and genuine value in the ever-repeated Old Testament and Gospel stories. There were the poetic ways that my namesake, Paul, put his advice about life and faith through his letters to the early Christian churches. There was a sense of stepping outside of daily life into a vessel that was the church on a Sunday morning where we contemplated life through quiet thought, loud singing, standing up and sitting down in what is the essence of the tradition of worship.

My sister Nancy had changed churches from the church of our youth to a church nearer her home called Trinity Lutheran Church and I started to attend that church. Before long, I was singing in the Choir as the newest voice in their bass section. By this time, I was an experienced choir singer and always sang with confidence. After my time in the Hendricks Chapel Choir, choir directors generally welcomed me with open arms because I could read music and, although I did listen and generally blended in, I was assertive enough in singing my part that the rest of basses around me followed along (which was usually good, although there were times I led the section to make unabashed mistakes!). It was in that new Choir experience that I met Anita, with whom I would share an immigration experience.

Entering Adulthood, Lenkeit Industries and Multiline Technology

My meeting Anita coincided with an interesting time in my working life. During the fall of 1980, I felt that I was at an impasse at my job at Venus. There really wasn't anywhere for me to improve my outlook at Venus and the only way that I was going to earn more money than the $24,000 I was making at the time was to get into a company where I might get a chance of getting into a management role. I had confidence in my ability to design and solve technical problems but I had to convince someone who could give me suitable problems to solve that were worth paying me more than I was making to solve. In the fall of that year I began looking for another job. I interviewed at a company called Lenkeit Industries who were looking for a machine designer or mechanical engineer for a new division they were contemplating starting. Lenkeit Industries was a company that made dies for stamping metal parts. Throughout the post war period they had been a successful service provider who made tools to stamp electrical connector parts and sheet metal parts for the automobile industry. The owner of the company, Fred Angelo, was in the process of bringing the next generation into the company and had recently installed his oldest son, Michael, in the role as President of his company. Fred still came into the office and obviously still held onto the levers of power at his company, but he was happy to have his son take over the day-to-day management of his businesses. Fred owned another business that stamped out metal parts that were used in large volumes by the automobile industry called, Royal Button. Tools and dies that were built at Lenkeit Industries were used in the stamping and punching machines of Royal Button to make thousands, hundreds of thousands and sometimes millions of parts that found themselves into the upholstery, door panels or dashboards of Chevrolets, Fords, Buicks, Chryslers, Cadillacs and Oldsmobiles.

At my interview, Michael told me that Lenkeit had the plan to start an equipment manufacturing business that would make machines which would be used in the printed circuit board industry. Through the manufacture of punching tools that were used to pierce the holes and profile the circuits used in increasing volumes by companies like Atari, Commodore and Radio Shack for cartridges that carried the software for early personal computers and game consoles, Lenkeit came to learn of requirements for machines which might solve other problems now encountered by a growing industry of fabricators of printed circuit boards. This was the time of the growth of the computer industry. With the growth of the computer industry, more complex printed circuits (particularly multilayered PCBs) were required in ever expanding quantities. Michael had the idea for a series of machines that would be sold to PCB fabricators in sets. These sets would be used to punch a pattern of holes into the innerlayer panels, which would then be made into the finished innerlayer circuits. The same pattern of holes would be punched into the artwork films that carried the image of the circuits—remember that film with the little piece of tape that fell off with Art? These films were copies of films like that which were reduced to the size of the circuits, panelized and then used in the photolithographic process used in the production of the etched innerlayer circuits that are then sandwiched together with other innerlayers to form what will become a finished multilayer. In any case, Michael wanted to hire me on the spot but I was asking too much money. He told me that perhaps after they had achieved a certain level of success with the first sales of the machines that they could consider hiring me or someone with my "level" to help with the development of the machines and the new company.

I thanked Michael for his time and we were headed through his outer office on the way to the exit when we passed a little table holding a closed circuit TV camera on a stand looking down at a section of a PCB. Visible on the monitor next to the stand, one could see the round pad on a PCB artwork represented on the screen with a dark and rather thick crosshair superimposed upon it. I asked what they were doing. Michael explained that they were trying to replace a pair of optical projection devices with CCTV cameras. The machine for which the cameras were foreseen was to use two points on a film to align to references in the optical path of the cameras before punching holes into the film. Those holes, once punched, were to be in proper position with respect to the two points represented by the crosshairs in the cameras. The operator of the machine would align the artwork into position using the cameras by manipulating the table that the film was mounted on, until the film aligned to the two points, then activate the punches to form the holes. Lenkeit had already built a machine for this purpose using two optical magnifying projectors instead of the CCTV cameras he was trying out on that test stand. The problem with using two optical projectors (with their finely etched crosshairs) to look at two points separated by 24 inches or more is that it is impossible for an operator to see both of them at the same time while making judgments about the position of the film before making the decision to punch. Michael had cleverly seen that using CCTV cameras over each of the two widely separated pads on the films to show images on two monitors that can be placed directly next to each other in front of the operator would make it easier for the operator to keep track of two targets and pads on the film without having to constantly move his head to look from one place on the film to the other place on the film. In fact, the CCTV cameras were the difference between a machine which could be easily used to a machine which was accurate, expensive to build, full of great ideas but practically unusable. I learned much later that they had invested a considerable amount of money to build the projector populated machine – had sold it and been paid – but they had lost money on the machine and were now in the stage of redesigning before building a "beta-version" of the machine which they were hoping to introduce at a trade fair at the beginning of 1981.

We had now spent about as much time standing next to that test stand holding its CCTV camera as we had spent in the office for my actual interview. While still standing there and just before I intended to leave, I told Michael that at the job I was just leaving (at Venus), my job had been designing CCTV cameras. I told him that the way I would solve his problem was to create electronically generated crosshairs and superimpose those over the pictures delivered by the CCTV cameras and then deliver both images through a video processing system that displayed the pictures of both cameras side-by-side in a single monitor (TV screen) which would help the operator be able to see both images simultaneously. Bringing the images so close together would allow the operator to better judge the position of the images from the two cameras and ease his decision-making process. Aligning the artwork precisely would become easier and less subject to error if it were possible to simulate two optical projector images on one screen with the use of an electronic solution to scribing lines onto the imaging device of the CCTV cameras and by combining two images on one screen. Michael was now very interested, and we sat down in his office again. I made a sketch of how I would design the machine so that the operator's nose (and more importantly, his eyes) could be positioned about a foot from the TV screen. The operator could manipulate the table of the machine along with the film to be aligned while watching the progress of his manipulations on the monitor as both images moved closer to alignment with the crosshairs. Michael was sold on my idea. He and I made a deal which would set me on a new road into the future.

So, in the fall of 1980, Michael and I shook hands on a small moon-lighting job for me that was to be completed before Christmas of that year. The job was for $ 5,000. Half of which he would pay in $ 500 installments every week as I delivered him sketches, updates and progress reports, with the other half promised upon completion of the job. I was to design him the machine I had sketched for him in that meeting. Lenkeit would pay for any parts that needed to be made or purchased to make the machine, but I was to deliver a package of mechanical sketches – only sketches – his people would convert the sketches into drawings. In addition, I would deliver a package of two cameras and lenses, necessary illumination, a "black box" containing the crosshair generating electronics and video combining circuit and a CCTV monitor with all the necessary cables to replace his present optical projectors. For all the electronics, here again, he committed to pay all costs for purchased components and parts and any manufacturing costs related to PCB fabrication, cables and electronic component housings and control features. Michael told me that they were up against a hard deadline of an upcoming trade fair in early February where they wanted to introduce the new machine. If I met the deadline, he would hire me for my asked-for salary, and I could start my job with them as the engineering manager of the "equipment division" of Lenkeit Industries in February.

The day I got the first $ 500 check from Lenkeit, I went to the bank and cashed it. With $ 250, I went to Art Brady at Venus, gave him the money, explained the meeting I had had with Michael and asked him to do the electronic design for the crosshair generators and the video combining system with the promise to split with him the rest of the money 50-50 as it came in. He agreed and set off working on his part of the project. I went to work on the structure of the new machine. First, I worked on the sketches for Lenkeit to make the tooling components to fit the new design. I greatly simplified the design from what they had before. I created a new way of holding the film using a vacuum table manufactured from a three-layered structure of aluminum and a rubbery vinyl. I then had to work on the structure of the machine. I designed and had built a rather bulky structure to hold the monitor in the proper position in space but then needed to design a significantly heavy cantilevered steel frame to hold the monitor and Art Brady's control box so that the operator could easily manipulate all the controls. I created covers for the machine that made it look heavy and substantial although, in fact it was filled with air and didn't need to be nearly as bulky as it seemed. The design of the machine was pleasing and looked properly "high-tech" but it was a bit "boxy". My only over-riding design goal was to get that TV screen about 12" from an average operator's nose (and eyes) and to make the machine look like it was worth the $ 50,000 that Michael was hoping to price it at (although our goal for the cost of the machine was to keep it under $ 20,000 to build). I called on all the sheet metal manufacturers, quick turn machine shops and finishing businesses that I had come to know over the years to get parts done as quickly as possible and introduced Lenkeit to a whole series of suppliers that they never needed before because they were tool and die builders that made nearly everything they ever needed by themselves. Through my jobs at Artek, Theta and Venus, I had become plugged into an ecosystem of such suppliers as well as PCB fabricators, electronic component suppliers, cable suppliers and now, through this project I was becoming acquainted with suppliers of pneumatic controls, cylinders and suppliers of tool-and-die supplies.

The project for Lenkeit was a very fulfilling project and I enjoyed the constant intellectual stimulation of solving problems on the fly and keeping things moving relentlessly forward but it was just a moon-lighting gig. I still had decided to leave Venus for more money and more of an ability to move up a corporate ladder. Although I was hopeful to have a job at Lenkeit that would offer both in February if all went according to plan, I couldn't count on it all working out according to plan in October. In October, I took a job as "Chief Mechanical Designer" at a company called Republic Electronics. They manufactured radar simulators. Such devices are used to broadcast signals meant to mimic either reflected or direct radar signals. Republic's devices broadcast signals meant to be detected by actual radar receivers for testing and calibration in military or civilian applications. The luster of this job to me was the pay and the title. It was a good company located near Venus, Artek and Lenkeit and they were very happy to hire me and were tickled that I was able to work without supervision of any kind. To be honest, I was an odd fish at Republic. I was a completely mechanical person at a company that was comprised only of electronics engineers. I was not only the "Chief" Mechanical Designer, by the time I got there, two weeks after the interview at which I was hired, I was the only mechanical designer. The other one, who wanted to become the "Chief" had quit. As it turned out, they didn't need two mechanical designers. I entered in October and there were no new projects in the works because, apparently, new designs for radar simulators are (or at least were, at that time in this company) designed practically 100 % electronically with very little in variability of the mechanical part of the design. A housing, once designed for one radar simulator, can hold any number of other models of radar simulators. I did have a very nice big office where I worked alone and had a huge stack of hundreds of ECOs and ECNs to work on. If you recall, these are the bane of every draftsman, designer and engineer in the world! Giving a self-proclaimed creative person nothing to do but to work on Engineering Change Orders and Engineering Change Notices is like asking a novelist to correct sixth grade spelling tests or asking a composer to tune pianos or asking a landscape architect to pull the weeds in the garden. After about two months, I was done with the stack of ECOs and ECNs and I more-or-less ran out of things to do. I roamed the production floor for signs of problems that might be solved by improvements to design. I asked the electronic engineers if they had anything for me. This company saw value in me and wanted to keep me, but I wasn't sure why. I knew that I would not be able to hold out at this job for very long despite the pay, but I also knew that it would not look good to go looking for another job until I knew what would happen with Lenkeit and my moon-lighting project.

By Christmastime, my part of the project was largely done. The parts were flowing into Lenkeit's factory and the machine was coming together for the trade fair. I would stop by on my way to or on the way back home from Republic Electronics each day to follow progress and give instructions on details. Art Brady's part was also completed and worked as expected. Michael was happy with our work and was astonished that his idea of scratching crosshairs on the imaging surface of a CCTV camera had morphed into this embodiment of his product vision. He liked the boxy, robust look of the finished machine even though some of the more conservative of his tool-and-die makers were curious at the way that the cantilevered design could be made to bounce up and down like the roadway of a suspension bridge in the wind. All I could do was grimace, shrug my shoulders and give instructions on how to support the structure so that it would survive shipment across the country to California where the machine would be introduced at the trade fair. In the middle of January, when the machine was completed, had been trussed, packed, boxed and sent on its cross-country truck ride from New York to Anaheim, California (where the annual Trade Fair, NEPCON West took place) I was informed that Michael had already made the decision to hire me. On the morning I went to check on the progress of the packaging of the machine and its shipment, Michael gave me the news and introduced me to the other people in the front office and we did a walk around to the more important of the tool-and-die makers and machinists in the factory. They all had seen me coming and going and some of them had had to deal with my sketches and transform my ideas into drawings or even finished pieces of shaped metal, but now I was being introduced as a new member of a new team. I was to start at the beginning of February. I was to be the Engineering Manager of the newly started equipment division of Lenkeit Industries. There was a woman draftsman, named Amy, who had already been working on equipment projects as a draftswoman before I had come along, who would be reassigned from the "normal" drafting room working for the tool-and-die business to the equipment division and work under my supervision. There was a tiny office space next to the larger tool-and-die engineering area that would be my working space. It would be a space I shared with Amy and it was the first time that my work space was comprised of a desk with a telephone along with a wheeled office chair and not just a high stool at a drawing board. As I recall, there was a drawing board for Amy to work at and an additional one that I could use, but I had a desk, an office chair – and a phone – and it was there that I was expected to work. I felt like I had taken a step up in the world.

I drove on from Lenkeit, up the road to Republic Electronics to start my workday there. I immediately informed them of my intentions to leave. I was happy and relieved to quit my job there and give them the customary two weeks' notice before leaving a company. They were sad to see me go but understood my motivation. They knew that there was nothing there that could hold me and that the work that they could offer me was never going to fulfill that part of me that needed to apply creativity to solving problems or building something new.

At about the same time, a member of the church choir invited me to dinner at their home and I was happy to accept the invitation. These people had previously invited me to come to them during the Christmas season but because I had traveled to Europe during the holiday period, I had missed the Christmas season at the church and couldn't make it to their party. The family wanted to catch up with me, hear about my travels and, I suspect, wanted me to meet a young woman from the choir that I had seen but not yet been formally introduced to. As it turned out, the woman was Anita.

Anita and I had the time and opportunity to get to know each other that evening. As she spoke, I had the impression of a serious person (and attractive) who was trying to understand how different some people were from the kind of people she was used to and whether the differences made them good people, bad people, or something in between. I also had the impression that she was feeling overwhelmed by her work but never-the-less enjoyed the high energy of her days and the interactions of the various characters of her work world. She and my hosts were interested to hear of my trip to Europe and were impressed with the ease and familiarity with which I referred to the places that I had visited (Hamburg, Bremen, and Amsterdam). Anita hadn't been to Europe up to that point, although she had a step-grand-father who had come from Switzerland and returned there after the death of her grandmother. She told me that her parents had been to visit him there, but now that he had died, she didn't feel the link to Europe that she had felt while he lived. (Later, when I visited her at her home, I noticed a painting I recognized as being of the Chillon Castle, of Lord Byron fame, near Montreux, on the Lake of Geneva. She told me her [step] grandfather had painted it).

As the evening wound down, she told me that she was going to take the following Monday off from work and perhaps enjoy a day in New York City. It was a reward she was giving herself for working so hard and for such long hours. I suggested that we go together because I could be a good guide and at least show her a little bit of what I knew in the city. I explained that the following Monday was the 2nd of February, and I was supposed to start a new job, but I supposed it wouldn't matter much if I started one day later. So, we made it a date! We planned to do a round of museums on that Monday. I called Michael and told him that I was sorry, but I'd need to start Tuesday instead of Monday. What could he say? He agreed and Anita and I went on our first date on Monday. We wound up going to a movie matinee instead of the museums, because, we learned, most museums in New York

City are closed on Mondays! Other than that, seen from the perspective of my life, it was a very successful day.

Anita grew up in outward terms, very much like I did. She attended Lutheran school like I. She was active in the life of her church and attended regularly. In fact we both knew, through our lifelong "Lutheranness," many of the same people who crossed our paths through being part of the same Lutheran community in nominally neighboring towns. We both had similar experiences outside of our homes but very different experiences inside our homes. Inside her home was a home of four girls growing up in a loving family; all four quite close in age and all four enjoying coming home every day. Upon meeting them for the first time, I felt like I was transported away to a 50s family situation comedy like "Father Knows Best" or "Leave it to Beaver" only with all girls in the family and a working-class father. Frank Schultz was a union plumber in New York City. He was, simply put, a good man. He worked hard. He was a quiet, kind and patient man. He probably had to be with five females to come home to every night. He rode the train into Manhattan to work everyday. He was a plumber on big projects like the building of the World Trade Center or the renovation of the Woolworth Building. When I met him in 1981 he was, I believe, 63 or so. His second oldest daughter had brought home an Asian kid as her boy-friend. I was probably one of the first Asian "kids" (I was 26) that had ever stepped into his house. He, and his wife, Doris, were as warm and kind as anyone has ever been to me. They welcomed me with open arms both figuratively and actually. In the years preceding them, I hadn't had a lot of experience with parents of girls that I liked welcoming me with open arms. There had been parents of the white-collar families that welcomed me nicely enough, but with a reserve and a bit of curiosity that was nowhere to be felt from Doris and Frank. I'd had the experience of working class parents of one girl that I liked, who forbade her from ever bringing me around to their house again. It was a reminder of racism in working class America. In any case, Anita brought me home with her to meet Frank and Doris for dinner one evening. The house was in a nice Westbury neighborhood in the East Meadow school district not too far from where my sister, Barbara, lived with a welcoming, well-kept green lawn. We went into the side door into the kitchen where Doris, a buxom, pretty, blue-eyed, warm, bundle-of-energy woman looked at us as if we were the only thing that was required to make her day complete. She said to me, "It's good that Anita has finally brought you home!" They knew me from church. I met Frank in the living room, which was across the way, on the other side of the dining room table. He stood up and we shook hands, and he asked if I'd like a beer. In those days, I didn't drink alcohol very much – that's another story. I asked for a Coke I suppose, and we sat down and talked about our days as if I were there every day. There was no judgement in him or Doris. There were no penetrating questions, just conversation about our days and a nice dinner – beef roulade, I think. I had impressed their daughter about the trip I had made to Germany just before we had had our first extended conversation on that January day just before I was supposed to start the job at Lenkeit. The conversation ran to my trips to Europe and their experiences of Europe and Europeans. Frank had his first trip to Europe paid for by the US government as a soldier in 1943. He spent his time in the UK until D-day (the 6th of June 1944.) He was assigned as a technical sergeant on a plane that was carrying paratroopers on their way to their "insertion point" in Normandy. The plane was struck by German anti-aircraft fire and, after disgorging the paratroopers in an early jump, crash-landed with its crew of four. All were unhurt although their plane lost its wings as the fuselage settled in among the trees of a fairly densely treed area about halfway between Cherbourg and Utah beach. Somehow, magically, all were unhurt. They split up into pairs, two would reunite with allied troops and returned to their bases to carry on with the war. The other two, including Frank, spent a couple of weeks trying to stay free in France and then, eventually being found by enemy soldiers and captured, spent the rest of the war in a POW camp in Germany.

The first day after my first date (the one without museums) with Anita, I started work at Lenkeit. I threw myself into my work as the Engineering Manager of Lenkeit Industries Equipment Division which soon got a new name; Multiline Technology. My first job was to create a structure for the company. A tool and die business needs little in the way of corporate structure and one could see that in the way that Lenkeit was organized. After an order was received by Lenkeit, the order got a "folder". This folder then received a document which described the nature of the tool that was to be built. The folder described the drawings that were required to be made and a description of the part that the tool was going to cut-out, punch, bend, shape and/or form. The drafting department would then get this folder and the folder would receive drawings generated by the draftsmen and lists of materials, parts and manufacturing tools required to be purchased for the making of the tool to-be-built. The folder would then be awarded to a die-maker who worked together with the various machine operators that made the necessary parts which would ultimately be mounted together to make the ordered tool or die. The die maker would place work order documents into the folder which kept track of the time and money spent in the design, fabrication, assembly and testing of the tool as it was completed. Once the job was done, the folder's documents would be examined and evaluated so that material costs, working hours, machine usage and other details important to maintaining profitability and measuring worker and factory utilization could be known and recorded. An equipment manufacturer's demands on documentation are both more and less than the requirements of a tool maker's business. More, in the sense that a machine has far more parts and processes to be documented than a single tool or die. Less, in the sense that the requirements of specialty input by a tool-maker is practically non-existent. Fewer decisions are made by people on the production floor and more pre-thought is done by engineers that goes into the documentation for parts used in the machine.

When I came to Lenkeit they had no system of cataloguing drawings for various parts. There was no system for naming drawings. The concept of a Bill of Materials was new for them. (A Bill of Materials is a document that lists the parts that are required to make a machine.) Normally, Bills of Materials are organized according to subassemblies and assemblies. For example: a Bill of Materials for a product might comprise 8 assemblies and 75 separate parts required to put those 8 assemblies together into the delivered product. That Bill of Materials would have 83 lines – one each for the 75 parts and one each for the 8 assemblies. Each assembly would have its own Bill of Materials:

1. Assembly one might have two sub-assemblies and 38 parts
   a. Sub-assembly A might have 45 parts
   b. Sub-assembly B might have 6 parts
2. Assembly two might have three sub-assemblies and 25 parts
   a. Sub-assembly C might have 60 parts
   b. Sub-assembly D might have 22 parts
   c. Sub-assembly E might have 11 parts
3. Assembly three might have 6 parts
4. Assembly four might have one sub-assembly and 45 parts
   a. Sub-assembly F might have 3 parts
5. Assembly five might have 350 parts
6. Assembly six might have two sub-assemblies and 12 parts
   a. Sub-assembly G might have 27 parts
   b. Sub-assembly H might have 4 parts
7. Assembly seven might have 6 parts
8. Assembly eight might have two sub-assemblies and 30 parts.
   a. Sub-assembly J might have 14 parts
   b. Sub-assembly K might have 8 parts

In all, (if my counts and additions in this hypothetical example are correct) such a Bill of Materials for a completed machine would have 808 line items of which 18 are assemblies and sub-assemblies and 790 are parts which need to be made or purchased. Lenkeit and Michael would soon learn that manufacturing equipment was a far more complicated logistical undertaking than tool and die making, requiring a far more complex organizational capability.

Parts flowing into sub-assemblies which themselves flowed into assemblies which then were combined at a higher level of assembly were all previously done by the tool maker, but not kept track of by office people. The purchasing function was distributed among and handled by the bookkeeper, the tool-makers or the draftsmen. A system of purchase requisitioning didn't exist yet because the number of parts needed to be kept track of per job was in the 10s and 20s and not in the hundreds. The logistical complexity would increase by two orders of magnitude within the next 5 years. Engineering change orders and engineering change notices were not yet implemented because the tool-maker had always been the final authority on everything and he relied on his memory and whatever notations were made in the folder. A job folder was a universe unto itself without the need to relate that folder to any folders that had come before or were to come later.

The trade fair where Michael had introduced the new machine (called the Optiline Artwork Punch) was a great success. Eventually, we would be booking orders for the Optiline at a rate of two per month. To understand the full meaning of this success, one must first realize that the Optiline machine was seldom sold alone. It was the linchpin in a "system-sale" that involved several machines, tooling plates and accessories. Although the average sale of an Optiline machine was about $ 50,000. The average sale of the system was almost always more than $ 100,000. The Optiline was a machine used to punch the artwork films to manufacture innerlayers for multilayer PCBs. The Optiline was always sold along with a laminate punch (called the Acculine) which punched slots into the innerlayer panels prior to a photolithographic process. This process of bringing artworks and inner-layers into contact with each other and shining a light through the film onto a chemically prepared and UV light activated etch resist to form the image of circuits on the copper-clad surfaces of the innerlayers, called "exposure", was well known from the manufacture of simple PCBs. Photolithographic processing or the use of exposure to image PCBs was an improvement in technical capability compared to the process of serigraphy (silk screening of etch resist through an imaged silk screen, like the technology of imaging tee-shirts) which preceded it. After imaging, the chemical surface was developed to create areas of hardened resist (where the film had been clear and light transmitting). Where resist remained, it blocked etchant from removing copper (where the conductive copper traces were formed – or rather, left behind). The black areas of the film blocked the light from activating the resist thereby causing the resist to be removed from the copper surface during development of the resist. Where no resist covered the copper, the copper was etched away by the action of the aggressive etching chemistry. The formed slots in the layers (punched by the Acculine) and the corresponding slots in the artworks (punched by the Optiline) were used to align the artworks to the panels in exact position so that the position of the circuits that were formed on each layer would align to the designed position of the circuits on all the other layers. The shorthand for the system would become "the Multiline 4-slot registration system." When all the different layers that were created independently were properly aligned and bonded together into a multilayer board, a hole drilled through a pad on an outerlayer image would pierce all the aligned pads in every innerlayer at that position with very little variation. The holes acted as the electrical connecting means between layers, so that the layers could be electrically connected using an electro-plating process called "plated-through copper". Within a couple of months of the NEPCON fair we had five or six orders for sets of the Acculine and Optiline machines. Michael's dream of becoming an equipment manufacturer came true in an explosion of orders and interest in special projects for new machines and accessories to help solve the problems that all the PCB companies in the world were discovering they had as each company approached the problem of fabricating high layer count circuits one after the other.

This period in the PCB industry was an incredibly robust time for developments in capability and capacity. Today the market is mostly comprised of "job shops." PCB job shops are companies who make PCBs to order for third parties who purchase boards to their own designs and then assemble them into the products that they sell. In today's electronics world, few people make their own PCBs. Samsung has their own PCB manufacturing capacity some of which they use to produce circuits which go into their own products, but Samsung also purchases a great deal of PCBs from job shops in China, Taiwan, Vietnam and Korea. Among all the famous companies in the world that make electronics products, Samsung, of South Korea, is the only company that continues to make a large commitment to PCB manufacturing for their own use in their own products. From the 1960s through the 1990s, many large manufacturers of electronics made their own PCBs.

At the same time I was experiencing all this growth at Multiline, Anita was experiencing the same kind of growth of the automobile leasing business at Manny Hanny (how most people referred to the cumbersomely named Manufacturers Hanover Trust Bank). As a result, she didn't have much time for me, which was a good thing, because had she had more time for me she probably would have thought I wasn't interested in her because I didn't have a lot of time for her. I was happily immersed in the projects of designing new machines, special machines, developing long-term relationships with our suppliers and customers and with building Multiline Technology with Mike. I would see Anita every Thursday evening at choir practice at the church and of course, as time went on, we'd spend more of our weekends together. A rite of passage for us was spending the first weekend together with her family and her Uncle Henry at her family's Hampton Bays summer house. Because Anita came from a family of four girls, to be invited by the family as a boyfriend and sleep on one of those fold out sofas that has a thin enough mattress to feel the steel support frame below was the signal to the family of the seriousness of the relationship. All three of my future brothers-in-law had had similar sleepless nights in Hampton Bays (HB). The nights were not sleepless only because of the discomfort of the sofa bed. The location of the bed in the all-purpose room/kitchen with the only connections to the bathrooms or WC combined with the detail that so many man-evenings at HB were spent, indeed, dedicated to, consuming beer made for a constant nocturnal parade of people needing to pee. I began to think my predecessors married into the family just to get into one of the more comfortable beds in one of the peaceful-at-night bedrooms!

Hampton Bays played an important role in our courtship, that phase of our life when we were building our adult identities, and in our young family life once the children came. Frank and Doris were the motivating force behind Doris's siblings and Frank's in-laws that got them involved together to build the place. They were all going to move from the Bronx to Long Island in the late 40s – but while living in the Bronx, it was Frank and Doris that drove out to the Hamptons one weekend and looked around. They saw a piece of property not far from Peconic Bay and inquired about the price. The answer was $2000 for four contiguous building plots, roughly 1 ½ acres! Frank talked to his brothers-in-law – Frank and Doris probably thought it would be perfect for Doris' siblings and their spouses to purchase it together. Two couples agreed, and they, with Frank's leadership built a summer place. They, together, put up a house in the front of the plot with three bedrooms and an all-purpose room that was a combination of a big kitchen and a big dining room. Each bedroom is 15' x 15' with a door that opened out onto an outside porch that was about eight or nine feet deep. The front end of the porch about 5 to 6 feet deep, built perpendicular and behind the "all purpose room", commonly called the kitchen. The kitchen had two kitchen tables, two refrigerators, a stove and sink from the 1940s. It had an odd paint job that had started out in the sixties as an attempt to have a Mexican hacienda feel and just abruptly stopped at one corner to segue suddenly into 1960s pragmatism – apparently an alcohol fueled project that ran out of energy and will at exactly where the green paint and yellow trim met the white wall. The overall effect of the house was that of a motel. To complete the motel effect we always parked on the lawn in front of the porch.

So, Gus, Henry and Frank (sometimes helped by Bill) worked on building the house for a couple of summers. It was a family project that cemented a family together for most of the 33 years until I met them. Uncle Henry, Aunt Anne, Uncle Bill, Aunt Grace, Frank, Doris and all their kids would gather on most summer weekends in Hampton Bays at the house that Frank, Henry, Gus and Bill built with their own hands. I, along with the children that Anita and I would have and their cousins were the last people who were added to the Hampton Bays (HB) experience. In my case, from 1981, and in the case of each child (or cousin), from the first summer of their lives and every summer following for all the intervening years up until about 2010.

The HB experience was the experience of being together in a place without television, poor access to radio and few of the creature comforts of the modern age of the 80s, 90s or the turn of the 21st century. There were no comfortable places to lounge around except in one of the many beds distributed around the three bedrooms and one wrought iron sofa with old musty cushions which was dragged out onto the porch every summer. We would normally arrive at the house late on a Friday evening and stay until Sunday afternoons on summer weekends. Oftentimes we would spend weeks at a time there during our summer vacations. The house has a porch with patio furniture arrayed under the porch roof and against the outside wall of the bedrooms. Each of the bedrooms has a window as well as the door that opened out onto the porch. The "lawn" is made up of a course, rather broad-leaf grass that can survive in sandy soil, but to call it a lawn is an insult to lawns the world over. It needed to be cut three or four times a year during the time of the summer that we actually visited and used the place. In later years, we would have the lawn cut once a year, just before we would come from Germany to use the house.

Anita loved the house at Hampton Bays when we met and was eager to have me love it as well as our relationship strengthened and grew. She loved being at the water either on the Peconic Bay which was a few hundred meters walk away or at the Atlantic Ocean beach which was on a barrier island reachable by a bridge a couple of miles away. I never liked the beach. To me, the sand is uncomfortable, the sun too hot, the insects a constant bother and the water itself held no further charm for me except for forming an endless horizontal plane that extended into the unseeable distance (as in, "a nice view"). Although I know how to swim, I can't swim well or for any extended distance (I tire after about 50 meters and feel as if I might drown unless I roll over onto my back and relax a bit.) I am happy to come out of the water after cooling off for about two minutes on a hot summer day. At the beginning, when Anita went to the beach, I went too. Once we became a secure couple, I admitted how much I detested being at the beach and received a reprieve from beach duty. I eventually bought a hammock with a hammock stand that could be dragged from shade to shade as the sun marched across the sky and read books or the weekend newspapers while everyone else went to the beach. Eventually, I discovered fishing. I would go with one of the brothers-in-law or with Anita's Uncle Henry and Frank to the canal that joined the Peconic Bay with the Shinnecock Bay, which was about a half mile from the house and try to catch fish. I remember fishing with them there or at the inlet between the Shinnecock Bay and the Ocean or off of the bridge that joined the barrier Island with Long Island, but I cannot actually recall catching anything except the odd eel which we always threw back because none of us knew how to clean, prepare or eat an eel that we didn't buy from someone who had already smoked it. We did see a lot of boats go by and they always seemed to be more successful at catching fish from those boats than we were at catching fish wherever we were. Eventually, I bought a boat and Hampton Bays became a fishing place for me. Anita was happy because I had a reason to love HB and I was happy because I didn't have to go to the beach and I could finally catch some fish. One of the business lessons I learned from fishing and the role the boat had in my fishing success was this: If you want to be successful, it's good to go to where success is possible.

Anita and I became a committed couple. Everyone who knew us was now expecting us to get married. Everyone who experienced us together told us we were perfect for each other, and I suppose we were. Neither one of us was very good at communicating feelings of discomfort, doubt, or insecurity. I found it strange for anyone truly in love to be so willing to forego love-making and the physical abandon and total release of good sex with a loving partner, but rules are rules. We started out and remained through our entire relationship (up until quite recently) an old-fashioned non-communicating couple. The scars that Sarah had left on my psyche and spirit were mostly healed although I still had the recurring dream of her being just outside of my cognizant reach in the dreamed time and place. I could feel her presence in a space or time nearby but found it impossible to get to that time or place and she never once appeared in a dream of mine – choosing to stay outside of recognition and remaining a hope of recognizable memory. The relationship with Anita strengthened within the bounds that it could strengthen. We declared love for one another about a year after meeting and became engaged to marry in the spring of 1982. We married on September 5th 1982.

A few months after later, Frank, Anita's father, would be diagnosed with lung cancer, at the relatively young age of 65. He was operated on to remove one lobe of his lungs and we were hoping for a full recovery when he spent some time with us in Hampton Bays that spring of 1983, but he died that summer. He reached the age of 66 (I'm three years older now). He did not live to meet any of our children. It was, in fact, his death which hastened our decision to start having the children. His death in the same year as his retirement moved us to abandon our caution about being ready for parenthood and precipitated an attitude in us to simply get on with what we both wanted out of life, which resulted in the birth of our first child, Laura, in April of 1984 after a long night of labor for Anita. Laura, newly born, and placed into my arms, looked into my eyes with her dark eyes and seemed to be the embodiment of peace and satisfaction. I was a father and this child, my daughter, endowed in me a sense of completeness of being I'd never felt before. We were bound together in that moment and connected through a family bond that seemed boundless and timeless.

When we took Laura home, Anita's Mom, Doris, came to help. Doris seemed to have a nice way with Laura but at some point she went home and we were left to deal with Laura on our own. I recall feeling totally unprepared for fatherhood. Laura was not always a happy child. There were times that she just didn't want to go to sleep and she fussed and cried when we put her in her crib to sleep. There were other times when she would fall asleep while sitting in a mechanical wind-up swing she liked to sit in, but we found it impossible to get her out of the swing and into her bed without waking her and causing her to scream as if we were intent on harming her. There were times that I wanted to literally tie Anita down into the bed so that she wouldn't go to pick Laura up and hold her when she fussed at night. I also recall putting Laura in the car and driving her around until she fell asleep in the car. She always fell asleep when we used this strategy, but she didn't always stay asleep once we were back at the house and carried her in again. So many memories of father-hood had to do with cars and the kids in their seats in the back. At about the time that Laura was taking her first steps and begin-ning to express herself in words as well as actions, we thought it a good time to have another child. We both agreed at that time that we would have four kids, two of our own and two adopted children who would be the youngest in the family. It was the only way that I could think of to truly pay back to life, God or nature, the luck, blessings and good fortunes that I had had in my life.

When Anita and I tried to have babies, we got babies. Very soon after deciding to have another child we discovered that we would be having two children. What I remember most about the experience of hearing that we were going to have twins was my walking out to a brand new car we had just bought a couple months earlier for about $9,000 (a small navy blue, four-door sedan called a Ford Tempo) and measuring the width of Laura's car seat and comparing the width to the width of the back seat of the car. I came to the conclusion that two and a half car seats would fit in the car if we occupied the two seats in the front. We wound up selling the car for $6,000 to a very happy engi-neer who worked in my group at Multiline and spending about $14,000 for a Chevy Astro mini-van that could seat up to eight passengers and who's bench seat could accommodate three baby seats across. After the announcement of the twins, we were afraid to try the exercise of having kids again! The first real dis-appointment of the whole situation was that Anita lost all the will to have any more kids, adopted or otherwise. It felt like a betrayal but it was one that I had to accept because she was the one who bore most of the load of parenthood as was the case of so many of us who had "traditional marriages" in those days.

As the twin's pregnancy (pregnancies?) progressed the doc-tor asked if we would like to know the genders of the coming children. Anita said no. I said yes. I asked Anita why she didn't want to know. She said they were often wrong if they didn't do amniocentesis and, in any case, she wanted to be surprised. We felt that amniocentesis, purely to determine the sex/gender of the twins was wasteful and an unnecessary risk. I didn't understand how the doctors could be wrong, but I accepted her wish and kept what I knew from her. We picked out four names to be prepared for every outcome and we assigned priorities to the names. Of course, I knew we only needed two of the names we had picked out. I remember that the first two boys names were Francis (after my father-in-law) and Chris or Christopher. I can't remember the second girl's name we picked out anymore, but the first was Julie. When Julie came out, Anita asked me if the doctor had been right or not. I answered that I wasn't sure yet. I was terribly distracted in the moment because Julie was a blonde! I am Asian, I never heard of an Asian having a blonde child! What I meant in answer to Anita was that I knew now that the doctor was at least half wrong and I wasn't sure if he was completely wrong yet. When it came to Julie, he must have mistaken her umbilical cord for something else! So (according to the doctor's predictions) Francis came out as Julie and Christopher...didn't come out! Julie was a big baby, coming out at one ounce less than 8 pounds. She had stretched Anita to her limit and beyond. Julie's umbilical cord still lay in the birth canal taking up some of the 8 to 9 cm (three and a half inches maximum) that Anita's dilation was. Francis (Christopher?) was projected as heavier than Julie (Francis?) because his bone-structure had been estimated to be bigger and they had expected him to be a half a pound bigger than Julie. They were a little concerned about him fitting through the birth passage with his round head which had not been formed into the "conehead" that Julie exhibited. Anita is a small woman of about 5 feet one inch tall and normally about 110 to 115 pounds in weight. Her pre-birth weight with the twins was about 130 pounds but one saw very little evidence of more of Anita in that weight! Francis was (and remains), in any case, a laid back and patient character – he made absolutely no indication that he wanted to escape Anita's womb. The doctor made the decision to do a Caesar's section (ein Kaiserschnitt or "emperor's cut" in German). I stood at the side of the bed with Anita's hand in mine speaking to her, Julie being tended to by nurses, Laura at home with Anita's sister waiting to hear news while they carefully cut a slit into Anita's abdomen and carefully removed "Frankie" from his dark warm world and he followed his sister into the world of the breathing 40 minutes after Julie. Frank looked kind of Asian – he had dark hair, thoughts of the milkman or postman dissolved into a realization of one of those little curiosities of life that genetics brings us.

The house that we had bought in Wantagh was what Germans call a bungalow and what Americans call a ranch house. I specifically wanted a ranch house because I felt it would be safer for our children than a house with steps, staircases and multiple levels. Anita and I loved our house. At the point that we knew twins were coming, the three bedrooms we had with the one bathroom seemed too small. The house had a big basement which was the same size as the house itself and I had the experience of finishing the basement of my parent's house, but we wanted to continue to have a house where all indoor life would take place on one level with no stairs for our children to stumble and fall down. One bedroom had become my office, Laura occupied one and the third, with the connection to the bathroom, was ours. Besides that, there was a good size eat-in kitchen, and a large living room space with an arch into a dining space which connected to the kitchen. The backyard was big enough for us to build out into it and still leave enough space for a sizable yard for the children to be able to eventually play in. We designed an extension to the house which would add a new bedroom for us and a large family room with double arches into the already existing dining area of the house. The extension also boasted an additional bathroom and a small space for a washing machine and dryer. The family room connected to the outdoors through a new rear door that opened out onto a new wooden deck. We had central air-conditioning installed and connected the control system and thermostats to the existing baseboard heating system that the house already had when we moved in. The house was perfectly setup for our life of suburban family paradise when we moved out and changed our lives and I became an immigrant again. This time, I took the whole family including Sauerbraten with me.

PCB Technology, Multilayers and Machines

The market-size of PCBs in the world was about $ 5 billion in 1974 when Bill Kitchener taught me about double-sided PCBs and the US led the world with about 50 % of the world market. In the intervening years between my start in designing PCBs to the point in the early 1980s that I was first exposed to PCBs as an industry, the structure of the industry had not changed much except that that the world PCB industry had grown to between $ 6 and $ 7 billion and the US market share had shrunk to 40 % with Europe, Japan and the rest-of-the-world (ROW) each having about 20 % shares of the world markets. At that time, multilayer circuits were generally manufactured by large telecommunication companies and large manufacturers of computers. It is estimated that the US produced about $ 700 million worth of multilayer printed circuit boards in 1980 – mostly in captive shops or shops owned and operated by large OEMs (original equipment manufacturers). Such manufacturers needed more layers than the two available to them on double-sided circuits to deal with the complexity of connecting an ever-growing number of integrated circuits, each with an ever-greater number of interconnections. My experience of interconnecting integrated circuits on any single board was largely limited to arranging the position of several 14-pin, 16-pin and 24-pin dual-inline (DIP) packages and then connecting them with the necessary connections to various discrete components like resistors, capacitors, diodes, power transistors, trimming potentiometers and board mounted connectors. A board containing up to 10 or 12 of these ICs was commonplace at Artek, Venus

175

and Republic Electronics in my days of designing circuits in the 1970s and all of them would fit on a double-sided circuit. My experience was shared by the 10s of thousands of designers throughout North America and Europe who were designing circuits for industrial, military, electronic instruments, and laboratory equipment in the 1970s. Only people designing for large companies like IBM, RCA, TI, AT&T, Motorola and some of the most advanced national laboratories in North America and companies like Siemens, Philips, Honeywell-Bull, Alcatel and Bell in Europe were designing multilayer PCBs and most of those circuits were being made in the factories of these large companies.

As the 1980s began, I had bought my first home, so I had a pretty good idea of which electronics products people wanted to install in their homes. Our taste for Magnavox or RCA TVs had been replaced for a desire for the latest model of Japanese TVs from Sony. Sony had made their Trinitron technology desired technology throughout the western world . Panasonic (National) became a respected name in home entertainment as well. The Japanese consumer electronics companies maintained a reputation for technical competence, good design and, for what was for Americans until then unprecedented, absolute product reliability in consumer products. A 1976 article that appeared in the German technical journal "Galvanotechnik" gave us a taste of how the regions stacked up against each other in TV production reliability and quality. The article states that:

1. US production of color TVs resulted in more than one defect per TV in "normal production" and a defect rate in finished TVs around 60 % to 100 % in "good" circumstances. This means that most of the TVs produced in the US and sold as new to consumers had already been repaired to correct defects before shipping.

2. Completed color TVs produced in Japan, on the other hand, exhibited defect rates of between 0.7 % (7 defective TVs in 1000 produced) to 3 %
3. German production of color TVs resulted in initial defect rates ranging between 30 % to 80 %.

The western world was slowly coming to the realization, already in the 1970s, at the start of my career in electronics, that the Japanese not only made products that the world wanted, but they made them for lower costs, produced them to yield better quality and sold them for better value than their American and European competitors. The electronics products that people bought for the home increasingly came from Japan. First, in the 1960s, there were transistor radios and portable cassette recorders, then TVs and Hi Fi components in the 1970s. In the 1980s came CD players both portable and stationary, Video recorders, cameras and, in the most humbling and bitter to accept aspect of Japanese export success (particularly to North America), cars.

My first couple of years at Multiline were largely occupied with the needs of domestic US customers. The initial orders for multilayer registration equipment came to Lenkeit Industries, before my time, from our distributor in New England, a guy named Larry Lyons. Larry was a distributor of the raw materials PCB fabricating companies needed to produce the boards they sold. Lenkeit industries had found the electronics industry through making tooling used to manufacture the metal components in wall sockets and wall switches for the leading manufacturer of such components called Leviton, a New York City company. Those tools would punch the contacts which were assembled into the wall sockets that made contact to the blades of the plug connectors for all our US 110 V electrical devices. Through their contacts to Leviton and to a producer of Printed Circuits called Photocircuits, a division of the Kollmorgen Corporation in Glen Cove, Lenkeit had early access to the electronics industry.

Photocircuits began in the business of making printed circuits for manufacturers of electronics such as RCA, GE and Delco (a manufacturer of automobile radios) in 1951. In these early days of the electronics industry, the components were largely still vacuum tubes and the material used to manufacture PCBs was single-sided copper-clad plastics like Bakelite. In fact, one of our earliest Japanese customers at Multiline for a registration system was called Sumitomo Bakelite. Early printed circuit boards were simple devices with circuits on the bottom surface and diagrams on the top which represented where an assembly worker should mount the sockets into which each vacuum tube was inserted. Discrete components such as resistors and capacitors could be directly soldered to the PCB by inserting the bare-wire-like leads into holes drilled through the plastic, which pierced directly through a pad on the reverse side of the board, which was, in turn, connected to an etched circuit which electrically connected that "leg" of the device to another device in the circuit. The insertion and extraction forces of vacuum tubes meant that the circuit boards were either rather thick to be able to withstand these forces without bending too far or breaking. Alternatively, the boards were reinforced and stiffened by attachment to a sheet metal stiffener. With the invention of much more reliable and far smaller and lighter solid state components like transistors and later, integrated circuits, the circuit board was freed from much of the insertion and extraction forces associated with vacuum tubes, the materials could become thinner. Throughout the sixties and seventies, the world went through a process of development of substrate materials which went from simple plastics to paper reinforced phenolic, to glass reinforced phenolic to glass reinforced epoxy. At the same time, the development of integrated circuits as a business throughout the world diversified the business of manufacturing PCBs. When I started at Artek in 1974, the world would take the step from glass reinforced epoxy material called G10 to glass reinforced material called FR4. The FR standing for "fire retardant". Since then, not much has happened to the material specifications of the dielectric materials of about 80 % of the PCBs in the world except for constant incremental improvements. FR2 and FR4 are the leading materials used in circuit boards throughout the world and represent over 80 % of the value of PCBs in the world and, probably, according to my own "guesstimate" about 95 % of the produced square meters of PCBs manufactured in the world. When flexibility of the circuit was required for either assembly or product requirements early materials were treated paper, various polymers including Teflon, acrylic, polyethylene and polyester. Today's flexible circuits are manufactured mostly on polyimide or polyester.

Photocircuits, together with IBM developed processes for making double-sided circuit boards which were required by the US Army for a missile defense radar system called SAGE (Semi Automatic Ground Environment) beginning in 1952. Although this sounds like an incredibly advanced project, in my view, it was the last gasp of the post-World War II industrial age and first steps into the information age we occupy today. SAGE was a network of radar receivers, networked computers, secure communications networks and ground-to-air missile and aircraft-supported defense systems that was supposed to protect North America from nuclear attack by aircraft flying into North American airspace from the Soviet Union. The project, besides solidifying Photocircuits' position as the leading independent PCB supplier in the world during the building of the project, also made IBM into the leading computer manufacturer in the world. The conception and building of the project spanned a time between 1949 when the requirement for such a project was recognized (because of the first initial test of a hydrogen bomb by the Soviets in August of that year) and 1958. The system did not become fully functional until 1963. SAGE cost about $ 10 billion which makes it about five times more expensive than the Manhattan Project which gave us the bomb (in 1945) we were trying to protect ourselves from. The SAGE project only protected North American cities from aircraft-carried atomic bombs (if it worked

– some doubt the efficacy of the system, with some critics of the system claiming that it would have been as low as 25 % effective in preventing a bomb from reaching one of our US population centers.) To put the cost and scale of this project into perspective: Note that $ 10 billion spent in the 1950s is like spending 105 billion dollars in 2023. The only modern military projects that are more expensive are the F-35 acquisitions program which is slated to cost $ 400 billion and our anti-ballistic missile system which has a current cost of $ 300 billion and counting. As a result of this project, the Lincoln Laboratory was founded at MIT in Cambridge, Massachusetts and funded by the US government initially to do the research and development for the SAGE project. An anti-ballistic missile system became necessary when the Soviet Union first deployed ICBMs (Inter-Continental-Ballistic Missiles) in 1958! (The very year that SAGE came on line). Obviously the SAGE project was a boondoggle for IBM who would become not only the biggest producer of computers (until its hegemony in large mainframe machines was challenged by the success of open-source UNIX based mini-computers in the 1980s led by the design of DEC's VAX machine) but also one of the biggest producer of printed circuits boards in the world over the following 50 years. IBM operated PCB factories in the US, Japan, Germany and France until the last factories were either closed or sold in the early years of the 21st century.

Photocircuits was a part of the SAGE project and was given a big boost by its association with IBM and the military purchasing office mandating that Photocircuits and IBM were to both maintain capability to produce all the necessary circuits required for the 56 computers required. The circuits needed were robust, simple and had to be extremely reliable. The function of the printed circuits was to provide mounting platforms and electrical connections to the vacuum tubes that acted as diodes and various other valves (triodes, tetrodes, pentodes, etc.) in these massive machines! In the two decades that intervened between the beginnings of the PCB industry and my entry into it, one technical truth prevailed; if the military were involved in specifying the project, leading edge interconnect technology was seldom the issue. Reliability was. If a little was good, more was better. If a unit of five was necessary, then a unit of 10 was specified and the product was tested to a unit of 20. The SAGE computers ushered IBM and Photocircuits into a world where the interconnection between components had to function flawlessly. The 56 SAGE computers were distributed across North America in pairs. The pairs were logically arranged into parallel "tops" and "bottoms" for the simple purpose of having redundancy. Every top or bottom only existed to cover the possibility of the other "side" failing. This redundancy didn't come cheap. Each "machine" (top or bottom) covered the area of one acre or roughly the area of a football field and contained over 49,000 vacuum tubes.

We didn't know it at the time, but we, at Multiline had a front row seat to witness the development of the PCB industry from a small, niche industry that entered homes through telephones, radios and TVs, as it was broadening its footprint through inclusion in dishwashers, refrigerators, washing machines and dryers and through the expansion of electrical control devices in the automobile which would increase the use of PCBs from the initial car radio and work their way into central locking systems, window and seat controls and into battery, starter and engine management systems. During the 1980s, the PCB industry would literally form the basis of the communications revolution that has, to date, enabled the world to be connected constantly through each individual person carrying a smart phone with them; connects cars to a string of satellites that guides them to their destinations; networks our computers during our working days: connecting us to social networks as well as entertaining us through our smart TVs, and smartphones in our free time.

In the early years of Multiline Technology, the companies that drove our growth were a mixture of OEM (Original Equipment

Manufacturing) companies that made their own PCBs (called "captive" shops) and job shops. Companies that we dealt with on a very regular basis in the early 1980s were Hughes Aircraft, Data General, Hewlett Packard, DEC, IBM, Western Electric, Prime, Boeing, John Fluke, Tektronix and Wang. The technology that was driving interest in high layer count multilayer PCBs (and in turn interest in Multiline's machines) initially were large computers, communications and networking computers, mini-computers and defense networking systems. Such circuits were large (often meant to populate standard electronic cabinets which were made to accept circuits that were somewhat smaller than 19" or approximately 48 cm in width). These large PCBs were densely populated with circuits that needed to handle huge amounts of incoming data and redirect that data to millions of possible destinations. Multiline was in the right place at the right time. The back-bone infrastructure of the digital age was being formed throughout the western world. At every node of this infrastructure – at every point that data was generated and sent or received and deciphered – refrigerator sized machines did the work of sorting, processing, parsing, encoding, sending, receiving, decoding, aggregating, processing, and targeting the data stream from sender to receiver. The sender and receiver could be in the same building or at different locations of the same enterprise, in which case the machine was a local data processing center (supplied by companies like IBM, DEC, Data General, Hitachi or Siemens or Honeywell or ICL). The sender and receiver could be the same person and the machine might have been a word processing system used by an entire enterprise (supplied by the likes of Prime, Wang, Nixdorf or Olivetti). The sender and receiver could have been separated by half the world, in which case the machines near sender and receiver were network communication machines (supplied by AT&T, IBM, Nortel, Marconi, Ericsson or Nokia, among others). The data processing machines of the late 1960s would evolve into the personal computers, servers, tablets, cellular phones, WLAN routers, mobile and fixed network hubs of today but the technology they ushered into being would be the structure on which the coming, instant global communications revolution would be built.

The global communications infrastructure started out as a global data processing infrastructure and was built almost entirely on the transmission of analogue signals on telephone lines. At the beginning of my career, small manufacturing businesses still had typewriters, secretaries carrying their stenography pads (most often dressed nicely and in high heels), dictating machines and normal telephones with lots of buttons. The sign of a senior manager was a person (most likely, a man over 40) with nothing but a telephone and perhaps, a Dictaphone on his desk. From the time I started my career in 1974 by taping PCB artworks to be photographed and reduced in size in a large horizontal reducing camera, to the time in the mid to late 1980s when a set of Gerber data made on a computer in a design center of an electronics products manufacturer could be sent via a telephone modem to a company that had a plotter that could plot the PCB image on film without the help of mail delivery, Federal Express or UPS; the global communications infrastructure was being built by the manufacturers of large computers (curiously called "mini" computers because they took up the same space as refrigerators and not the same space as apartments, houses or warehouses, like the computers that had preceded them). From typewriters to desktop word processing would take an additional five or six years at Multiline. (As I recall, my business plan for the opening of our coming European business would be dictated to a very attractive young secretary who took shorthand into a steno pad and typed out my words on an IBM Selectric. It was 17 pages long and done in 1986.) I bought the company's first personal computer for myself in 1984 but would not use a computer for word processing until well after I arrived in Germany in 1987. I used the computer, a Compaq "portable" computer" to use Lotus 1,2,3, a spreadsheet and precursor to Microsoft's Excel. I wrote several small spreadsheets for calculating sales prices from purchase prices, helping to keep track of incoming orders and tracking costs of new product developments. Unlike today, the computer wasn't primarily a communications tool, but rather a calculation and memory sorting tool. Most of what I typed, calculated, or kept track of in the computer would be printed out and passed on to others in the office or sent by fax or printed out and sent by post, Fed Ex or UPS overnight service.

The first indication to me that there was a data revolution underway was the expanding use of faxes in the mid to late 1980s. Up until that time instant communications was only possible with a telephone or a telex (which was like having a personal or corporate telegram machine). The telephone was expensive across national borders and long distance calling in the US was also something that private people avoided, but businesses didn't shy away from calling "long-distance" because the cost of the instant communication to clarify unknowns or have answers to simple questions was well worth the cost of calling. Of course, it was hard to convey pictures via telephone. Having said that, I must admit that Lenkeit was the most progressive company I knew of, up to the point of joining, because they had an Exxon "Qwip" that I had never previously seen or known about. This little desktop machine had a rotating cylinder on which a piece of paper containing a message or drawing was mounted for scanning for transmission or a piece of thermally sensitive paper was mounted to print out an incoming message or drawing. In this way, Lenkeit received preliminary sketches of parts for which tools were to be quoted or made. When people speak of the impact on our lives of new technologies, I must report from my view that the advent and broad use of faxes made the biggest difference to the way I sorted my day-to-day priorities. Prior to faxes, one had day-to-day priorities and we had control of what our plan was because the timing of inquiries and the response time of our answers had a tolerance measured in days. We had a minimum time of a day-and-a-half for requests that came by courier or "FedEx". For post, our tolerance for providing an answer was plus two days from the time they landed on our desks because one could never know if the post had taken one day to get there or three. After faxes, we were put into reaction mode to provide immediate feedback, particularly if someone called immediately after sending the fax to make sure we "had received it". The sender knew we received it because he had the answer in his hands – there was no shirking, no hiding, no procrastinating except to admit that this particular fax was not going to be on the top of pile on my desk. This is a very difficult position to be in when one's entire life is based on being there for everybody!

I worked for six years in Multiline Technology in Farmingdale. I started with Amy, Mike and me being the whole Multiline team. The Acculine had been built and designed as a pneumatically powered machine before I came by the designers of Lenkeit's engineering department. One of my first projects to finish was to finish the building of a heavy duty version of the Acculine that would be powered by a hydraulic power supply and make the Acculine capable of punching thicker panels and more holes. The Optiline had been designed by Lenkeit but redesigned into its present state the previous fall by Art Brady and me as a moonlighting project. Art's and my contribution to the company could be easily seen because a great deal of the value of the Optiline machine came from the way it looked and the way it functioned with the use of electronics and ergonomic design principles to solve the problem of making it easy for an operator to make a decision about aligning before punching. Art built up a business in his home to supply us with the CCTV camera systems, the control boxes that generated the crosshairs and displayed the two images close to each other on the single monitor he delivered for each Optiline we built. I developed a base of suppliers who made the frames, sheet metal and machined aluminum parts we needed to build our machines. Many of the precision parts made of cast iron or tool steel were made for Multiline by Lenkeit. Lenkeit, who generally made precision tools in quantities of one, two, three or five was now receiving orders from Multiline for twenty, thirty and fifty parts at a time.

When I came to Multiline, there was a power and management structure in place at Lenkeit which had existed for a period of time unknown to me then and still unknown to me today. The General Manager of Lenkeit Industries was a man named Don who ruled Lenkeit and brooked no challenges to his authority. In principle, when I came, he was third in the management chain and should have reported directly to Michael. Don was defacto, my boss, but Mike insisted that I worked directly for Mike. This caused a tension between Don my boss and Don the General Manager of Lenkeit who didn't really have responsibility for Multiline which was "Mike's baby". Don had worked his way up in Lenkeit as a tool and die maker. He was an intelligent man, although not an educated person. I always assumed but was unsure if I was correct in my assumption that Don had Fred, Mike's father, to thank for being the General Manager. In any case, when I came along, there was Don, a guy that seemed to have been a sidekick and protégé of Don's called John, who was the chief of the engineering and drafting area, a production manager, Pete; a core of old time tool-and-die makers called Dick, Hans, Kurt, John, a second generation of tool makers including Dick's son, Rick and a guy named Mike L. There were also a group of four or five machinists who were generally scheduled to work on parts by Pete. In the Lenkeit engineering area I think to recall that four or five people worked at drawing boards. There was a bookkeeper in the front office named Lou and two women who worked as secretaries and administrative assistants. My recollection says that there were about 30 to 35 people there at Lenkeit in the early 1980s and that the work-force was split in three groups: front office, engineering and factory. The men among the front office people wore ties everyday and the tool makers wore blue smocks which resembled lab coats and the machinists wore smocks that more closely resembled aprons. I found the rigidness of the dress code at Lenkeit odd. It also seemed to have happened organically and not chiseled into any official dress code. I was not in the habit of wearing ties to work and never got in the habit of dressing up for work except when it was time to meet customers. If customers came to visit or if I went to visit customers, then I put on a tie and often wore a jacket. Later on in life, when I suspected that most of the people I would be seeing already knew me, I shed the jacket in favor of sweaters (jumpers) with a dress shirt and tie. I have always been more comfortable working in polo shirts in summer or plaid or striped leisure shirts of comfortable cotton or flannel in winter. I started coming into the office from the beginning of my time at Lenkeit/Multiline in my normal mode of dressing for work. The Multiline engineering team followed my lead for as long as I stayed in Farmingdale. It is interesting to note though, that after I left Farmingdale behind, and I would come back for visits, I noticed that the Multilin engineers and draftsmen went back to the Lenkeit habit of wearing ties at the office.

The work utterly consumed me. I would work from early mornings until late into the night over the next several years. My life became a blur of projects to do, a company structure to create, designs to refine, and design schedules to maintain (so that production schedules could be maintained) and dealing with office politics. From the very beginning of Multiline, we built a reputation for several things: creative, robust designs, high prices and always delivering later than promised. In the 1980s, the 1990s, and up to about 2005 or so, it never really mattered. The customers always kept coming back even though they had to deal with our constant problems of managing growth and production planning.

The first problems of our not being a mature equipment manufacturing business cropped up after we delivered the first machines to our customers. We didn't have an established quality control or inspection system. We didn't have the discipline of an equipment manufacturer. We were praised for our willingness to take on projects based on a good idea and a plausible chance of success, but we often sent a machine out to the customer before we had checked to see if all the screws were tightened. The very first manifestation of this was when we were contacted by customers, our distributors or even our own service technicians and told that screws loosened or even fell out during shipment with sometimes difficult to find consequences (like a lost screw blocking movement of the adjustable table on an Optiline). I recall one of our customers telling us that we were putting the industry practice of doing R & D (Research and Development) first; then developing a product; then getting to market with it on its head. He said Multiline developed and shipped. He wasn't entirely wrong, but his company was so hot to have our idea built that he ordered what we offered him based on sketches and descriptions that Mike or I had made for him! We went through a phase of training the machine assemblers and giving each of them a bottle of Loctite (a liquid that hardened in the space between screws and the threaded hole they occupied to keep the screws tightened and in place) which he should use liberally. We set up a Quality Control department and instituted inspections throughout the production process from component manufacturer to final assembly. This led to additional friction between the Lenkeit shop that was providing parts and the inspection people who worked for Multiline when parts were rejected because, the Lenkeit folks said, "The machines we make the parts on are more accurate than the machines you have to inspect with!"

The early 1980s was a very creative period in the electronics industry. The availability of integrated circuits for digital processing (Processors) and integrated circuits for digital storage of solid-state memory (ROM and RAM) led to a boom in the building of digital communications devices including digital switching computers manufactured by IBM, IT&T (Bell, Europe), AT&T, Nortel Networks, Marconi, Siemens, Fujitsu and others. Even though the communication lines of the 1970s and early 1980s were largely built to carry analogue signals, the world was discovering that local work could be done on digital devices (like word processors, telex machines and local networked computers) and subsequently be sent over communication lines via various analogue-to-digital modulation schemes. Modems, computers, telex machines, fax machines separated by walls, parking lots, blocks, miles, oceans or continents could communicate with each other. Telecommunications companies began to build out their cable networks to carry multiplexed, digitally modulated signals to carry data in a space that had earlier been exclusively the realm of voice communications. Their suppliers began to offer large refrigerator-sized boxes to take modulated or digital data in and send it out as modulated digital data into telephone cables connected to the world. Likewise, governments, companies and other large organizations started to build internal digital networks around large computers and a new classification of computers called minicomputers. Those large computers (IBM, Cray Research, Fujitsu, Hitachi, ICL, Honeywell Bull) like the CDC machine of my experience at Syracuse shrank from large room-sized machines to something that could fit in the flatbed of a pick-up truck. Minicomputers (from DEC, Wang, Prime, Data General, HP, Nixdorf, Olivetti and others) were about the size of a dormroom refrigerator (or the average refrigerator in an average German kitchen in an average German apartment). It was the demand of these companies along with additional military hardware and specialty electronics companies like Hughes, Boeing, John Fluke, Tektronix, Philips, Siemens, and AEG that fed the hunger in the world for high layer count multilayer printed circuit boards (of 12 to 40 layers or more). From the late 1970s to the early 1990s, many of these companies had their own printed circuit board factories.

It became clear that Amy and I alone could not keep up with the engineering load. There was no interest among the Lenkeit people to help us out of our stacked-up backlog of engineering and drafting work which was causing the production people (at the beginning, all Lenkeit workers) to be late on everything. With the situation as it was, all the fault could be pushed onto Amy's drawings board and my desk. We needed to hire people. In the six years I was there, we went from that group of 30 to 35 to over a 100 people. We moved the Multiline Technology Engineering

Department from the small office Amy and I had occupied into a temporary trailer in the parking lot, where we grew to a team of 11 draftsmen and engineers from the end of 1981 to 1984. We were getting so many requests for specially engineered products that we decided to split engineering responsibilities between standard machines and specially engineered products and research and development. The office load of Multiline increased to requiring a purchasing department and a department for bookkeeping which would eventually be run by a controller. Michael needed inside sales people to track all the orders and ride herd on the purchasing, engineering and production people who's ostensible task was keeping the customers' orders on track for on-time delivery. Most often, however, the job was keeping up a plausible patina of patter that might reduce embarrassment on why we were late again and just keep the customer from exploding while waiting. Mike was on the road nearly constantly. He was the father of a young daughter with a wife who wanted him to be home. In addition, he had responsibilities to be present in the office as the President of Lenkeit Industries, Royal Button and Multiline Technology. He needed help so he hired outside sales support and put together a network of manufacturer's representatives (reps) that covered the world of PCB fabrication. Inquiries and orders started coming in from Israel, the UK, China, Korea, Italy and France over the telex machine and, slowly, starting in about 1983 over the new fax machine. We hired more people to work in the front office. This led to the displacement of the Lenkeit Tool and Die Engineering group to their own trailer opposite the Multiline trailer in the parking lot. The company was obviously bursting at the seams!

Sometime during this period, Mike's younger brother Dave came on board. I think to recall that he started at Royal Button and then was brought to our factory to work in Lenkeit as an assistant to Don but eventually became responsible for inside sales at Multiline and slowly took on more and more management responsibilities as time went on. I had little interaction with Dave when I was at Farmingdale but always assumed that he would take his place next to Mike in the running of the business. It was clear that he would never be as important to the business as his brother. In part because he was the younger brother and wasn't there at the beginning of the growth of Multiline and in part because he didn't bring the same set of personal skills to the task that Mike did. There's a saying in New York about how a man can be so good a salesman, he can sell ice to Eskimos. Some people have accused me of such skills, but I don't think it's true. With Mike, it's true. Mike didn't wield this power only at customers. He wielded it at his colleagues, family, friends and anyone he encountered. He was a hard guy for anyone to follow. Dave was, and I'm sure, remains, a charming, competent guy, but he did have a problem of projecting gravitas coming into Multiline rather later than much of the long-term team did and being Mike's younger brother.

I became more interested in the fabrication of PCBs in general (beyond the problem of registering the multilayer innerlayers to one another) and I began to learn more about the photolithographic process. To me, the process of applying the image to the copper in preparation for either etching (as in single sided boards, innerlayers or panel plated outerlayers) or pattern-plating (as in conventional double-sided galvanic trace and through-hole plating) was an area of technology that I enjoyed learning more about and I tried to get myself more involved in the development of the technology. I became involved with a company called WR Grace which had developed a liquid resist for the manufacture of innerlayers (called Accutrace) and became the leading advocate at Multiline for developing a relationship with Grace. They knew that we were experts at making layers align to each other and wanted us to help them solve the problem of registering layers not only one to another but also to register one side which was imaged by itself, to the other side which was imaged separately. This liquid resist was special because it went on wet and remained wet throughout the process until it was developed after imaging. Liquid resists were used before this but the state-of-the-art had been to dry the resist after application and before imaging so that the panel could come into intimate contact with the artwork without having wet resist contaminate the artwork. The Accutrace resist required a non-contact exposure which in turn required a highly collimated light source and it required special handling of the panels which only involved touching the panels on the bottom of the layers. Our relationship with Accutrace became such that we designed and built major components of their machine over the next 10 years, became expert in the collimation system they used in their machine, built a special version of the Acculine as an automatically operated and fed machine to work in-line with the Grace Accutrace exposure machines and found ourselves invited to the table when other projects came up with other customers or suppliers of resist or automatic exposure concepts. Another bonus of the Grace/Accutrace relationship was my newfound friend Ivan Ho.

Ivan was an applications engineer at WR Grace and as such his job was to make sure that the equipment and the chemistry all worked together to deliver the results necessary to make customers happy. At the time that I met him, he was responsible for running a lab at a Grace facility in Atlanta. He was having problems with the equipment he had at his lab that we had built and wasn't sure of where his bad results were coming from. He knew that he needed help. He contacted me and asked if I could come down to help him prepare for a customer visit from Data General, who had a big PCB manufacturing facility in North Carolina in the coming days. For him, because of the importance of this customer to his management, this was a big deal. For me, it was an opportunity to travel and be helpful to Grace which would help solidify the relationship – it was in the early days of our cooperation. We worked from my arrival until about two in the morning the first day and from morning until late into the evening the second day. When he had decided that we had done as much as we could in preparation for the customer demo the next day, he took a couple of his colleagues and me out to dinner and a night on the town. I had heard of the adage, "Work hard, play hard" but had never really lived it before. That night in 1982 was the first time I'd ever come close to living the adage. As the years would pass and Ivan and I went through the phases of life that followed, we would often meet again and work hard, play hard. I didn't drink very much in those days, but I certainly enjoyed my time with Ivan.

The relationship to Accutrace would become important for my future in ways that I could not imagine at the time. Accutrace had developed a wet etching resist with some very special attributes. Liquid etching resist prior to Accutrace was like a thin paint that was applied to panels by holding the panels by the edges and dipping the panels one at a time into a tank where the resist, mixed with the likes of paint thinner or solvent would coat both sides of the panels and then the panel would be slowly withdrawn upwards out of the bath so that the excess resist could drip off back into the bath. The panel would then go through a drying process, involving heat and/or UV energy, so that it could be handled through the exposure process without leaving resist residuals on the operators hands or gloves or the artworks that were put into contact during exposure. Accutrace resist was less a liquid and more a "goop". Imagine a thick paint without any thinner, except in a nice dark blue, semitransparent hue. Accutrace resist was roller coated onto one surface of the panel. The panel was handled from under the uncoated side into the exposure machine using conveyor belts. In the exposure machine, highly collimated light (as parallel as possible with as little declination angle as possible) was projected through the artwork onto the resist surface. The artwork was held by vacuum to a piece of glass and was moved – up and down, with the glass, into close proximity to the surface of the resist but made no contact to the resist. After exposure of the first side the first side was developed and etched and the panel would either be collected and go through the same process for its other side or would go through a second machine in the line that did the opposite side. The exposure lamps, cabinets and mirrors that manipulated light into these very collimated beams of UV light that exposed the panels were the products of Optical Radiation Corporation. Multiline came to manufacture the module that handled the artworks and panels. Our job was to hold the artwork, move it up and down, move the panel in place, make sure the panels were in the proper place with respect to the image on the artwork as well as the image on the other side of the panel and the light that was being cast down upon our "tooling" module by the Optical Radiation Corporation manufactured mirrors.

Through my contacts with the people in the Accutrace organization we heard from people in a part of WR Grace that made a flexographic liquid plate making chemistry and they asked us if we would be interested in quoting a liquid plate making machine. I was interested. Mike was undecided and Don was uninterested. We didn't quote. In my research into Flexographic printing, I came across two other companies who made flexo printing plates: Hercules, who made a liquid system like WR Grace and Dupont, who made a solid, imageable plate. I contacted both Hercules and Dupont and we made the pitch that we could help solve any processing problems they might have related to processing flexo plates and making them ready for printing (a process called pre-press) and was surprised to find out that Hercules needed a registration system (Dupont already had a method). I designed a system for Hercules that involved a punch, a precision pin bar and a plate mounting system which involved two CCTV cameras and adjustment of the printing cylinder. We received an almost immediate order for 12 sets of these machines. Eventually one of the engineers was transferred over from Lenkeit's die division to take care of our print registration business. It was a spin-off of a spin-off, but that spin-off never sustained any more than that one job.

As Multiline grew and I became more certain of my place in the company, tensions grew between Don and me. I felt that his position of relative power was because of whatever he had done before I came. He occupied a position between the Angelo family and the factory. His position was secure, and he sat squarely in the seat of power and benefited greatly as Multiline grew in importance to the success of Lenkeit. Between 1981 and 1984 all the growth at Lenkeit came from the growth of Multiline. I had hoped that my power within the company would grow with Multiline's growth and, to a certain extent, it did. I would be designated the Engineering Manager of Multiline and I would oversee the growth of our product portfolio. Increasingly, customers would come to us with special wishes for equipment to solve problems of Multilayer processing or Multilayer registration. When those meetings occurred, Mike liked to have me in the room when discussions of new equipment possibilities took place. We became a good team. We had the ability to work together with our customers and anticipate their wishes. We could guide the customers to solutions that they thought only we could provide. Oftentimes when these meetings took place, Don doubted our ability to fulfill the customer's wishes and he was often the voice of caution while Mike and I wanted to charge ahead in fulfilling every wish that a customer came up with which we felt we could take on.

The very first companies in China, Taiwan and Korea purchased equipment from Multiline in 1985. If I recall correctly, they were Great Wall in China, a company called Compeq in Taiwan and Daeduck in Korea. When Daeduck bought our registration system in Korea I went back for the first time since 1959 in order to install the equipment and to train the people on the use of the equipment. The day that I flew to Korea for that trip was in late April. I remember because our house was full of guests who were there to celebrate my daughter, Laura's, first birthday. I like to travel light, so I had a carry-on bag stuffed to overfull in my one hand and my briefcase in the other as the taxi waited in front of the house to take me to the airport. Anita came to the door with me to wish me luck, and mentioned to me that I should take lots of pictures – she knowing that it was, for me, a kind of monumental trip. I told her I hadn't packed my camera but that she surely had a good idea (to take lots of pictures) – I'd buy one in Korea.

It was not only the first time back in Korea, but I hadn't been in Asia since 1959 either. I was filled with lots of impressions when the car arranged by my customer dropped me off at the hotel they had arranged for me. The customer's factory was listed as being in Seoul and was not far from the hotel, but the hotel was in the midst of an area of small squat buildings that looked like a small industrial area. The small factories looked like garages with rollup doors, many with machines seemingly spilling out of the buildings onto small paved areas in front of the rolled up doors, with some of the people working out in front of the small workshops and others working inside. Metal working, plastic cutting, painting and finishing, woodworking and fabrics all being worked on, each in their own space, along what felt to me like a country road was what I was seeing then and now remembering. I didn't have a camera yet, so I don't have any pictures. I was, for the first time in memory, only among people who looked like me and these people were all very busy and appeared to me like Asian versions of characters out of a Dickens novel. I walked a bit, and seeing a taxi leave the hotel I had checked into and about to pass me, I hailed the driver to stop and climbed in. He waited in expectation to know where he should drive me. I stammered and yammered but could not tell him. I finally blurted out that I wanted to buy a camera – in the only language I spoke competently at the time. He didn't understand and got somewhat agitated. I repeated myself. To which he reached back to open my door in hopes of getting me out of his taxi. I then pointed in a direction which took us toward downtown Seoul and he drove toward a large mountain-like hill that has Seoul's radio tower at its peak and is visible from much of the region. When we got to the roadway that wrapped itself around this hill, I signaled him to let me out and he gladly did. I held out my money and he took what his fare should have been (hopefully). Now I was walking on a sidewalk on a busy street with the radio tower to my right but I still didn't know where I should be going to find a camera to buy. I went into a building across the street that housed an office of the Goethe Institute – an NGO dedicated to the dissemination and preservation of German culture throughout the world. The young lady seated at the reception area didn't speak English but she did understand my German and knew where I should go to buy a camera. She accompanied me outside, took me back across the street, walked with me for a few strides to a bus stop, gave me some coins from her purse and told me how many stops to ride the bus to an underground shopping area in central Seoul where I bought a Samsung point and shoot 35 mm camera with a 3x optical zoom function for about $ 80 and a gold ring for Laura (because the sales lady told me, in English, that that was a traditional birthday gift for a one year girl). If this is true or not, I do not know to this day.

I did not feel any great affinity to Korea during this trip or any subsequent trip I've made there. In the intervening years, I have been back to Korea at least six or seven times on business trips or to visit our industry's annual trade fair (KPCA) there. For me, it's just another place full of people who look different to me than the people I'm used to seeing and who's language I don't speak.

What impressed me very much about the trip was my experience at the factory of Daeduck. At the time, they were the biggest producer of PCBs in Korea. They would begin the process of making multilayer PCBs immediately upon the installation of the equipment that they had purchased from us and the final installation of the multilayer press (also purchased from an American supplier) that was being commissioned in the same week I was there. A multilayer press is a big, bulky, heavy machine. It is a hydraulic press capable of applying forces of over 30 times atmospheric pressure or more than 450 pounds per square inch on surfaces of panels as big as 24 x 30 inches (and sometimes as big as 30 x 60 inches) and heat the material being pressed to normal temperatures of 350 degrees but sometimes exceed 600 degrees Fahrenheit. Because one pressing of multilayer panels can take up a cycle time of three or four hours and a large production facility might need to produce more than 1000 pressed panels per day. These presses are built with multiple openings which can each accommodate 10 to 15 panels in one pressing. (For higher technology boards only a few panels and as little as a single panel per opening might be produced). 8 openings might be able to process between 600 and 1000 panels per day depending on the complexity and material content of the multilayers being pressed. Because all the panels in one press load must be of similar materials and of the same size, to be flexible in production about what one can produce at any given time, most factories would rather buy two 4 opening presses than one 8 opening press. As I recall, Daeduck was installing two six opening presses as their starting point in the production of Multilayers. This was a major commitment and one that most western companies would have embarked on in incremental steps. The staging of material in front of a press and the removal of all the material after a press load is completed in the press requires a lot of space. Heavy duty conveyors on which the materials are brought to and from the presses require planning and, usually, a great deal of forethought. If I were to have planned the conveyor layout to this room, I would have sat at a drawing board and sketched a layout, then cut out a number of "paper-doll-type" cutouts of conveyors to test my layout within the allotted space and only when I was done ruminating about how this would all look, fit and function in the space would I have ordered the conveyor sections necessary to produce the workspace I imagined. Daeduck did it differently. They ordered a number of conveyor sections and corner units and had a number of factory workers arrange them and rearrange them until they thought they knew what they wanted. They then welded the sections together and tried the layout live with tools in and out of the press. If something intervened to show a flaw in the layout, they de-welded the assembly and started over again. They did this for two or three days until they were happy with the result. The method was strange to me but considering that it was all new to them and they didn't have any experienced people to ask, as well as having a shortage of engineers, they developed their own experience as quickly as they could. I had the feeling that such a methodology wouldn't have survived a giggle test in a western factory, but given the situation, I was impressed.

In 1985 LG was called Lucky Goldstar and was more famous in Korea as an electronics producer than Samsung. Multiline's distributor in Korea would take me on a series of visits to potential customers after the work was completed at Daeduck, so I would get a "snap-shot" of the state of the PCB industry in Korea. I went to one factory where the drilling machines were mounted on steel bearing plates, one for each of the four feet of each of the machines, on a dirt floor. I saw seas of dark-haired heads surge in and out of factory grounds at starting time and quitting times. After leaving the factory, they didn't head to cars to drive home, they walked to bus stops or waited to be picked up by vans or rode bikes away from the factory. Everyone seemed to be younger than me and they all wore overalls of the same color.

In contrast to that and at about the same period, I visited the facility that received our first post etch punches in Boise Idaho. At that time HP was in the competition for ascendancy in the minicomputer business with DEC (Digital Equipment Corporation) and Data General. Each of these companies had multiple large Multilayer PCB facilities. There was an office area full of engineers and support staff in a large open office landscape which appeared to be as big as half a football field. The cafeteria was a large airy space with glass windows opening out to scenes of natural beauty. All the people seemed to come from central casting after a call went out for tall, good-looking white people who were athletes in prep school and college. HP's facility was similar to factories all over America and Europe owned and run by large OEM (original equipment manufacturers) who operated their own PCB factories. Delco in Kokomo, DEC in Greenville SC, Boeing in Seattle, Hughes in Tucson and Fullerton, HP in Sunnyvale, Boeblingen and Loveland as well as Boise, IBM in Owego and Sindelfingen, Wang in Boston, Honeywell in Nantes, Nixdorf in Paderborn, Olivetti in Milan, Bell in Frosinone and Ghent, Philips in Evreux, Brussels, Eindhoven and Croydon, Siemens in Oostende, Karlsruhe, Erlangen and Munich – they all were well equipped, dripped excess cash and their employees reveled in well paid pride.

Two reasons exist for the very different environments I experienced at Daeduck and the HP facility in Boise (or any of the other large captive PCB shops of the time). One was definitely a difference in geography and the local cultural influences. The other was the difference in large company mentality vs. small company mentality.

We, at Multiline, generally found it easier to deal with smaller, privately owned companies. At the beginning of our experience of dealing with companies as a supplier of specialty production machinery, a smaller, privately owned company was simpler for us to deal with because their interest was to have a production problem solved with as little hassle as possible. Michael and I would sit in meetings with owners of PCB factories who had perhaps 100 employees and knew that the man (it was always a man) was successful, proud, had enough money to decide to buy a machine of ours on the spot without having to ask anyone else what they thought. A deal was often struck within a morning and we would go off to lunch along the seaside or at a nice local restaurant and then the customer was off to catch his plane home or to drive to his next visit in the area. In stark contrast to this was the experience of dealing with the decision-making apparatus of IBM, Western Electric, Delco or HP. We didn't have any personal contact with the people in the technical departments of those companies in the early 1980s. The purchasing department would send us a specification too long and detailed for anyone to want to read. It always fell to me to read these and write up a short version RFQ (request for quotation) for our engineering people to work on. The specification and the customer's version of the RFQ could be 30 to 40 pages of dense, technical jargon about what the particulars of the customer's wishes were. We knew we really were in a good position for getting the ultimate sale when the text of how they described their machine requirements were exactly taken from our own marketing materials or brochures or were simply a regurgitation of an article Michael or I had written. Nevertheless, we had to go through a long-drawn-out process to get to the order. It was as if we had to earn the respect of the customer by jumping through hoops, they held up for us to jump through, as if we were trained dogs at a local travelling circus. The larger the company, the more likely there was a set of "standard, detailed specifications" which dealt with things as inane as the color of the machine to things as important and as financially devastating as "standard terms of financial penalties for unplanned machine downtime."

Over the course of my career, I've slowly and haltingly come to the conclusion that what the big companies did to us, although it felt like they were making us do busywork (devoid of meaning or value), was actually good for us and contributed to our development as a reliable supplier of machines to the world of PCB fabricators. I suppose our reaction was that of a bunch of guys who did not come to our positions at the conference room table through "process" but rather, through reaction and "smarts." We had a good idea of what people wanted to hear and we had a good idea of what we needed to do to get to the next level of development at each stage of development. What we lacked in experience and know-how we made up for in creativity and salesmanship.

There were a small group of large companies though, where we had inroads to important technical people. These people had the power to decide on their own what they wanted the big organization to do or to have and they knew how to move the levers of their own power to cause change in their organizations and using our creativity and energy to serve their needs. Three of those companies would be critical to our development as Multiline as well as to my personal development. They were Hughes Aircraft from Tucson, Arizona and a man named Phil Hinton; Digital Equipment Corporation (DEC) from Waltham and Marlborough Massachusetts and a man named Don Newell; and Dupont, from a laboratory in Parlin, New Jersey and Bob Heiart. All three of these men came to our factory in Farmingdale during those years between 1981 and 1984 with problems that needed to be solved in their factories and they came to value and respect what they found there.

Phil needed to ease the job of laying up the multilayers' innerlayers into stacks that would be bonded together in the multilayer press and asked for our ideas on how we could help. We came up with a machine called a layup station which we sketched out for him on the blackboard. He simply asked how much money it would cost and how fast could it be made? When we answered, he said OK, he'd get us an order. When he left, we all said to each other – almost simultaneously, "We should have asked for more!"

Don Newell asked us to think about the process of handling the press plates into and out of the press and in particular the process of removing the pins that held all the panels in place. We would go through a process of "creativity" and trial-and-error testing that took us through pneumatic hammers (that could wake the dead and always attracted a kind of shocked, round-eyed surprise when we demonstrated our pneumatic depinner at trade fairs), ultrasonics and multilevel pneumatic cylinders (which scared the life out of operators as it slammed the pins out like a rifle-shot after building up pressure for a number of seconds) until we came up with our hydraulic depinner with a telescopic guide mechanism that could withstand the 5 tons of force needed to remove the approximately 5 mm diameter pin that could be as long as 3 inches. Along the way, we broke a lot of depinning pins!

The man from a big company that moved us the most was Bob Heiart. He walked and talked us through his need for a machine that became the most important creation Multiline ever made, the Post-Etch punch. He came to us in 1983 or 1984, as the developer of a new imaging system at Dupont, with a specific requirement for a punch which would punch the slots into already etched innerlayer panels by means of an optical alignment. Remember, at that time, the Acculine punched slots into unimaged panels and then those slots would be used to pin to slots punched into the imaged Artworks by the Optiline Artwork punch. In this way, the various images of the various innerlayers that made up a multilayer would be properly aligned with respect to each other. Dupont's new process could not deal with holes in the panels to be imaged. Bob wanted us to build a punch which would allow Dupont to image unpunched panels and then put the holes into the panels after the panels had been etched with the copper image in place. The idea was called a "Post Etch Punch".

Mike and I saw this as a huge step forward for registration technology and a huge opportunity for Multiline Technology. Don saw such a technology as a danger to the business of selling Acculines and Optilines and questioned our ability to successfully pull off a "Post Etch Punch". Don's resistance to the project was going to be a big problem for Mike and me. I worried that if Don could successfully kill the project at Multiline, then Dupont might go off and find someone else to build the machine. Up until Don expressed his displeasure at the project, I had convinced Bob that the project was well within our capability to achieve. It seemed to Mike and me that if the Acculine and Optiline were to be made obsolete by a Post Etch Punch, we, at Multiline should be the people to make it so. As it turned out, circumstances would intervene that would silence Don's objections. Don suffered a major heart attack which would sideline him and keep him out of the office for several months. We didn't need to deal with the objections of a man that wasn't there and this allowed us to go ahead with the project with Dupont without any further objections from Don. I only learned later how desperately Bob needed us to do what we ultimately wound up doing. Given that the Post Etch Punch was essentially created by a team, led by me (a Landscape Architect by education), which included two friends of mine (Art Brady and Lew Levy), both part-time, moonlighting electrical engineers, a team of creative draftsmen (and women) who we called "design engineers" at Multiline and the input of the tool and die business, Lenkeit Industries (which contributed the design of the Acculine laminate punch, the mechanical basis on which the Post-Etch Punch is built), I have always wondered how a company like Dupont couldn't have come up with what they needed to complete this very important project themselves. Bob Heiart was a brilliant PhD in polymer chemistry and had formulated a new kind of dry film resist that was not protected by a sheet of transparent plastic like PEN, Acrylic or PET as normal dry film resists are. This resist and the entire project at Dupont during this time was called "I-film" (probably because of the 365 nm wavelength sensitivity of the resist – this particular wavelength of the light spectrum is called the I-line).

Normal dry film resist is applied to PCB copper clad laminate at the beginning of the photolithographic process. The fact that dry film resists have this protective layer of transparent plastic means that the panels can be handled by machine operators. The plastic protection brings both advantages and disadvantages. The fact that the panels can be handled at all is an advantage over the liquid photoresists that preceded dry film resist. Although this protective aspect of the plastic layer proved to be a huge advantage to the PCB industry when dry film resist was first brought to the industry by Dupont in 1968, the protective layer can also be a problem to the fine-line imaging that some people were trying to do in the 1980s.

When I was handed my first tools for the designing of PCBs in 1974, I was given black tape of 1/16 of an inch or 0.062" which was used to represent the "normal" signal traces on a PCB artwork. Because we normally designed using a 4:1 scale, those 1/16" traces would be reduced to traces of 1/64" by the reduction camera at the PCB shop or the graphical service provider to make the actual 1:1 photo-masks (or artworks or photo-tools) which would be used in the lithographical process to form the copper tracks of a circuit. PCB people in North America speak in terms of "mils" or thousandths of inches when referring to track widths or the isolation spaces between them (gaps). A PCB person might speak of tracks and gaps of 15 mils (those tracks which were formed using black tape with a width of 1/16" or 62 mils.) Fine lines for me during the time of designing circuits for industrial and military use until the early 1980s were made using black adhesive tape of 1/32" (31 mils) which would be reduced to 7.5 mil tracks. My bosses told me to use the thin black tape only when absolutely necessary because the process of making such fine lines was more expensive than the manufacture of traces that were double so wide and the chances of creating short-circuits and breaks in such fine lines (and accompanying spaces between the lines) were greater than when the traces and gaps were bigger. I only used the thin tape when I needed to run a track between two pads of an integrated circuit (IC). In those days, most of the integrated circuits we designed for and used were called "dual-in-line" packages (DIPs). The pins, legs or leads of the DIP IC packages were separated from each other in a regular pattern of 100 mils each (about 2.5 mm). The thin tape allowed us to thread a track between two adjacent pads of an IC package. This problem of having to fit tracks between the pads of IC packages still drives the need for finer tracks today. Today's (2023) densest IC packages have pitches between IC pads of 0.4 mm (or 16 mils). The recommended pad size is 0.2 mm (or 8 mils) which means that the gap between adjacent pads is also 0.2 mm (8 mils). To fit one track between two adjacent pads means dividing the space of 0.2 mm into three equally sized widths, two of which will be isolation gaps and one of which would be a single track of 0.067 mm or (67 microns or about 2 and a half mils). To fit two tracks between the same pads one divides the available gap by five (two for tracks and three for isolation gaps) and we need to create tracks and gaps of 40 microns or 1 and a half mils). To fit three tracks between such adjacent pads, we need to create tracks and gaps of 28 microns or slightly more than 1 mil lines and spaces!

Prior to Dupont's development of dry film resist, resist was a liquid which was applied to the copper surface of the PCB. This liquid would then be dried in place on each panel using heat and/or a partial UV curing cycle. The film carrying the image of the circuit (called an "artwork" or a "photo-tool") was then placed directly on the resist surface (at the beginning of the exposure process) and UV light (I-line) would be shone through the artwork onto the resist surface. Areas of the resist surface which were not blocked from the light by the black areas of the photo-tool were radiated with the UV energy from the exposing lamp. The UV energy cross-linked the monomers of the resist turning them into polymer chains which created a strong bond between the resist and the underlying copper. The goal was to cast a perfect shadow of the image of the black areas of a photo-tool onto the surface of the resist. Perfect shadows can only be evaluated by the sharpness, amount of contrast and fineness of the border between the areas on the resist that lay under the transitions between the dark, black, opaque areas of the artwork and the clear, transparent areas of the artwork. Perfect contact of the artwork to the resist ensures that the image formed on the resist is exactly as it was on the artwork. The resist areas that fell under the black shadow were washed away during development so that the underlying copper could be etched away. Because the imaged film was in direct contact with the liquid resist, a better fidelity was achieved in imaging with liquid resists than when using dry film resist (like Riston) with its barrier layer. Better fidelity using liquid resists or a resist like the I-System resist meant closer-to-the-designed width of a track and a smaller tolerance in imaging than when a protective plastic protection sheet or barrier layer is inserted between the artwork image and the resist layer.

Dry film was applied to a panel using a lamination process. The resist was formulated to stick to the copper surface of the PCB, but because heat and pressure had to be applied from both sides of the panel and resist, it was necessary to protect the resist surface (not in contact to the panel) with a plastic film so that the resist wouldn't stick to the roller which applied the pressure and heat to the top surface of the resist. This barrier layer caused the unwanted refraction of light during exposure but also protected the tacky dry film surface from gathering dust or other contaminates which might cause defects in the imaged panel (such as unwanted short-circuits or open tracks or necked-down tracks).

At the time of I-System's introduction, Dupont had hoped to extend its domination in the photolithographic technical space throughout the world's PCB factories. During the 1960s to the 1980s Dupont shared the PCB etching and plating resist market with a very small number of competitors who also made dry film (and they all paid license fees to Dupont). Throughout the 1970s, Dupont had a commanding market share and enjoyed the highest prices for its dry film resist. Customers paid 5 to 10 times more for dry film resist in the 1970s than they do today. Dupont's market position was built on excellent support of its customers and a strategy of offering a complete technical solution to the problem of imaging of the circuit. Their knowhow extended from the pre-cleaning of the copper surface prior to applying the resist, to the application of the resist via lamination, to the proper exposure of the image, to the development of the image after exposure, the etching or plating process following exposure and the stripping of the resist. Dupont had a hand in establishing the specifications for much of the equipment that was used to apply the resist, expose the panels, develop the images or to plate or etch the panels after the structure of the circuits were created through the imaging process. Dupont's

Riston dry film resist patents helped build a dominant market share and brought high earnings to Dupont for a period spanning nearly two decades. This, even though Dupont's Riston dry film resist was imperfect in theory when compared to liquid resists. Liquid resists were not used as much as Riston. The reason was not because the liquid resist was a worse resist than Riston. It was not used because it was a better resist than Riston. If a resist's job is to reproduce exactly what is there, then evaluations of liquid resist should always rate them better than dry film resists. Every dust particle, every scratch in the artwork and every unwanted defect in the copper surface of a PCB panel to be exposed will be subject to exact reproduction. Riston succeeded; not because it was perfect, but because it was good enough. The PCB world of the 1970s and the 1980s succeeded because it had found the right balance between necessity, manufacturability, functionality and cost.

The I-System resist had no barrier sheet or protective film covering the resist surface which would contact the phototool. The advantage of this is that refraction of light was avoided at the two surfaces of the barrier cover sheet which effectively acts as a transparent spacer between the artwork image and the resist surface. No refraction of light meant less distortion of the image as the light cast from the exposure lamp of the exposure machine passed through the imaged tooling-film casting a more perfect shadow on the resist surface. To understand the full competitive issues that Dupont was facing in the early 1980s, one must understand the state of the PCB and electronics industry of the period. Personal computers were now being produced by companies in the United States, Japan and Europe and the printed circuits for them were being made in the US, Japan and Europe. Open source (RISC) software and hardware made way for revolutions in computing and communications leading to a huge burst of growth in the PCB industries of North America, Europe and Japan. While ever more multilayers were required for the large-scale communications and computing gear of those days, huge amounts of single sided boards were required for the PROM cartridges that carried the software for "applications" (todays term for software and games) that were sold to be plugged into the personal computers and game consoles of the late 1970s and early 1980s. From the late 1970s to the early 1980s, Dupont, Photocircuits, Lenkeit and Multiline Technology would benefit from both ends of this technical spectrum of PCB business growth in North America.

The I-System was targeted at large producers of print-and-etch circuits (like innerlayers). The I-System was to continue the market domination of Dupont's Riston brand of dry film resist by allowing freshly minted patents to extend their technical lead over other dry film manufacturers by addressing two problems of exposure technology with dry film resist. The first improvement was the removal of the protective film layer in I-System resist that had burdened the Riston dry film resist with refraction-created distortion of the image during exposure. Finer lines and spaces would be the result. The second major advantage of the I-System resist is that it required no vacuum to be drawn during the exposure process. To understand this advantage, one must first understand that to make as close a contact between the resist layer and the artwork or photo-tool as possible, it is necessary to create a vacuum between the resist clad panel to be exposed and the artwork or photo-tool. The creation of this vacuum ensures, in the best case, that no air exists between the artwork image and the panel which is to receive this image as a cast shadow. Air between the artwork and the resist surface creates two more refraction surfaces with accompanying diffusion or blurring of the cast shadow. Instead of a cast image with sharp edges, an image is cast on the resist which has disappointedly blurred edges. In the best of cases, the vacuum takes a good deal of time to create (often between 10 seconds and a minute-and-a-half, depending on the flatness of the surfaces involved in the exposure). In the worst of cases, one waits the time to create the vacuum, but the vacuum thereby created is imperfect and the exposure is less than acceptable. Dupont's I-System sought to solve both these problems of vacuum – the waiting time to form it and the possibility of blurry image inducing air inclusions – by doing away with vacuum. Instead, they created an ultra-thin film of water between the artwork and the resist surface which cast a near perfect shadow of the image on the photo-tool to the resist surface without any unwanted refraction. Image fidelity was improved and the 10 to 90 seconds of non-productive time to create a vacuum was reduced to the 5 seconds or so that it took to apply a mist of water between the films on both sides of the resist coated panel and the artworks for each side of the double-sided panel. The cutting of the Riston resist in conventional dry film laminators sometimes caused small slivers of resist to contaminate the panels prior to imaging. Such contaminates often converted themselves into flaws in the finished circuit via a process we have all seen live when we watch dusty old black-and-white movies. The I-Resist didn't need to be cut; it broke off in a near-perfect line when the panel pulled away from the resist roll in the automatic application section of the machine (just prior to the exposure section of the same machine). The lamps in the exposure section of the I-System machine were the kind of fluorescent lamps found in modern day tanning beds. As such they were relatively inexpensive when compared to the lamp prices for competing technologies of exposure. There are three competing schools of thought when considering what kind of light source is best for PCB exposure. If the image of the artwork is directly against the resist surface with no contamination and no refractive surfaces, then it does not matter at which angle the light comes to illuminate the image – this is the theory behind the I-System. If the distance between the image of the photo-tool surface and the resist is separated by a barrier film or air or both, and contamination from foreign particles can be eliminated, then a source of light that is always as perpendicular as possible to the imaged surface is best – this is the theory behind modern collimated light exposure technology (using expensive high pressure, short-arc lamps) and laser or LED digital direct imaging systems. The third school of thought, and that which guided and informed the Riston years, was the realization that most PCB fabricators of the time could never rid themselves completely from dust and contamination. Therefore, using a light source that was a compromise in both cost and inclination angle between fluorescents and short-arc lamps was recommended. This last school of thought worked for 90 % or more of the PCB industry into the 1980s and worked fine as long as fineline was defined as 8 mil lines and spaces (or layouts that were being taped at 4:1 with 1/32" Bishop Graphics' tapes.)

Bob Heiart arranged for Dupont to order two post-etch punches as Mike and I had described to him in our initial meetings. They were delivered to a Hewlett Packard ("HP") facility, that manufactured disc memory drives, in Boise, Idaho about nine months later. The initial testing of our machines showed that they did what we promised they would do and Dupont ordered another machine to match the needs of another "I-System" test site at an independent PCB (job shop) fabrication facility called Microfab in Massachusetts. The HP machines were manufactured to punch only six holes in a fixed pattern according to a registration concept that only HP used at factories in Fullerton and Boise. Microfab was already a customer of ours that used the Acculine/Optiline machine pair to register. Multiline Technology's Acculine/Optiline had become the state-of-the-art in multilayer registration over the course of the previous four years and would become known the world over as the Lenkeit or Multiline system. This identification was applied, not only to the specific machines, but also to the pattern of four slots that they punched and the flexibility of the system to handle and process numerous panel sizes. The slots, their size, their positions, the pins that were made to fit them and the bushings that were made to fit those pins are still known and used throughout the world today. The Engineering Manager at Microfab was a young man named David Powell. He took the opportunity to specify the Post Etch Punch to exactly match the capabilities of his existing Acculine/Optiline system. Through his (and Dupont's) demands, we were being guided through a process of forced invention which married our old flexible, four slot punching system with the newly discovered capability to capture images, computer process them, guide a mechanical system to position as desired and punch when aligned. Microfab and David Powell would receive the first standard 4-slot Multiline Technology Optiline PE.

To accomplish the engineering for the Post Etch Punch, I reached out to my friend Art Brady again. Art would design some analogue circuitry which would allow us to parse the image of two targets on the etched panels of the innerlayers to be punched. If you imagine a black round target on an otherwise white field of a camera's view, then the image of that view is represented by a long line of analogue data. The picture's long line of data starts at the upper left with a set of vertical sync pulses which denotes the beginning of the video string. At the end of each horizontal line of the video data, a horizontal sync pulse designates the right border edge of the presently completed line and the left border of the next horizontal line of video data. The key to our concept was to simplify the image to a round dot which could be described by two values per line of video. We called these two values border and chord. Border was an integer value which represented the distance from the horizontal sync pulse to the edge detection point of the round pad in the video image. Chord was an integer value which represented the length of the black portion of our horizontal line through the pad represented in the video image. Suppose the length of each horizontal line was 800 units wide and a video image had 256 horizontal lines in total. A Border which never detected an edge would be 800 and the Chord would be 0. If the pad was exactly in the middle of the horizontal screen and covered 70 horizontal lines then the first Border of interest might occur on line number 93 with a Border of 397 and a Chord of 6. The border might continue to be smaller as the lines of video represented ever fatter parts of the pad until the smallest Border is reached on line

128 with an integer value of 300 and a Chord value of 200. With each advancing horizontal line until line 163 when the Border becomes 398 and the Chord is 4. At line 164, the Border returns to the full screen width of 800 as the pad is no longer detected at all. Art's circuit delivered 256 lines of digitized data to a lookup table which was read by a small microcomputer which then calculated the positions of the two targets in the machine and compared their positions to the desired positions of the targets. After calculating each position and calculating the desired X, Y and rotational moves that the machine should make to arrive at the proper punching position, the machine directed three motors to move the panels as desired, made a new measurement of target positions and compared the result to the wished-for positions. When the actual positions matched the wished-for positions, the punch was activated to form the pattern of holes in the layer in the proper relation to the image in the layer. For the microcomputer part of the project, I involved an old colleague from Artek, Lew Levy, who used a small Motorola 6809 microprocessor board level computer to handle the calculations required of the Post Etch Punch.

The process of Post Etch Punching was well accepted by the industry and became the state-of-the-art in multilayer registration throughout the world. Every company who was serious about making high layer count multilayer PCBs wanted to have at least one and many companies bought multiple machines. With the Post Etch Punch we were building a truly advanced technology machine. People would look on in wonder as the machine positioned and punched panels automatically. It was the first optically-driven, automatic-positioning punching machine many people had ever seen. Its technology pre-dated image processing technology that would come years later which would make it easier to analyze target position data. Our simplification of using a round target in an otherwise unmarked background made our job easy and our solution was an elegant use of available technology of the time.

Although our growth had been robust before, the Post Etch Punch set us on a secure path of growth which would last over 25 years. As it was, our growth was splitting the seams of the factory we occupied with more than 20 people working in offices in trailers placed in the parking lot at the back of our building. Work began on the building of a new factory on Route 110 about a half a mile north of the where the old factory was in 1985. When we moved into the factory, what was left of the Lenkeit Tool and Die business was absorbed completely into Multiline Technology.

Dupont's I-System would not be successful for the PCB industry. There were too many problems to solve to make the system robust enough for daily production. There were possible solutions to each problem, I'm sure, but its radical designs – its very conceptual basis of doing nothing like it used to be done – were in defiance of many of PCB manufacturing's known "best practices". Therefore, there was no support in the industry for Dupont to keep trying to make the I-System work. Some of the I-resist ideas can still be found today in Dupont's deep UV resist product line for finer photolithographic processes, but the biggest success of the I-system for the PCB industry was Multiline Technology's Optiline PE. The idea of solving the resolution problem of finer lines and spaces with highly-collimated-light exposure machines using high-pressure, mercury-doped, short-arc lamps would capture the imaginations of PCB professionals of the 1980s. Dupont's attempt to fight that trend failed but we at Multiline, and in particular, Multiline in Europe, would benefit greatly from both the technical trends leading toward finer lines and spaces as well as higher layer counts.

Although Microfab wouldn't keep the I-System, they did keep the Optiline PE and David Powell would be instrumental in our early marketing efforts. He wrote an article in one of the PCB industry's technical journals in which he showed the theoretical benefits of punching already etched panels in an Optiline PE over punching the same holes in panels before exposure and pinning at exposure. His article defined the tolerance chain of our Acculine/Optiline process of:

1. Punching slots into the panels prior to imaging in an Acculine.
2. Aligning the artworks in the Optiline.
3. Punching the artworks after alignment in the Optiline.
4. Pinning the panel to the artworks during exposure using the punched holes as proxies for the image position.
5. Then exposing, developing, and etching each innerlayer.

He further showed the shortened tolerance chain of exposing panels using a simple front to back registration process for each innerlayer without the use of registration holes for the panels, but rather imaging targets on the layers which would serve as proxies for the image positions on each panel. He used the language of statistical analysis and showed by use of the "least squares method" why post etch punching had to be better than any method that preceded it. Furthermore, he theorized, looking at targets on every innerlayer and having the capability of inspection and measurement of each panel after all the processes were complete would be far better than allowing innerlayers to be bonded to each other without the benefit of being observed prior to lamination.

Multiline could build machines but we didn't have the language to describe the actual benefits of what we had built until David Powell wrote his article.

The Move to Europe

I write this from my office in the run up to Christmas in 2022. Memories of Christmas act like bookmarks on our lives – as if Christmases, by the force of remembrances, impose themselves as order-bringing-events to our stories. Each Christmas has its own set of people, gifts, background noise and its own set of responsibilities. My parents went out of their way to make Christmas a special time. My mother would turn the house into a winter wonderland full of motifs of candy canes, candles decorated with red ribbons and nestled into evergreen boughs and there was always a warm glow in the house against the backdrop of what appeared to be snow-frosted window panes on every window and door on the ground floor of the house. She'd bake Christmas cookies, the most memorable of which were "snowballs," peppermint tasting candy-cane cookies made with twisted red and white cookie dough and various shaped cookies that were pressed out of an electric cookie dough press she only used prior to Christmas. My father would build scenes in the yard of Christ at his birth, complete with farm animals, shepherds with their sheep and wise-men with their camels. One year he made life-size plywood cutouts of several reindeer (including Rudolf of the red nose), a sleigh and Santa. The most remarkable thing of all to remember about that winter is that he overcame his very real fear of heights to mount the entire scene on the roof of our house! There were several years (in the time I was 8 years old to about 11 or so and my little sister 3 to 6 years old) that my father would hide some loudspeakers outside, in our front yard, behind some bushes that were planted near our front stoop and play Christmas music into the neighborhood. If you went by our house in the evenings before Christmas and my dad was home, you'd hear Bing Crosby, Frank Sinatra, Andy Williams, Tony Bennett, Mel Tormé or Nat King Cole crooning out from behind our festively lit bushes wishing you a "Merry Little Christmas", or a "White Christmas" from our family to all those passersby who were "...kids from one to ninety-two." These Christmas traditions of my childhood have made me into a shameless, joyful crooner of Christmas songs while walking through the Christmas markets of Bad Homburg, my adopted hometown. I suppose I still feel my father's responsibility to spread our favorite crooners' Christmas Joy.

Anita's family shared the same Christmas traditions that our family practiced although I don't know if her father, Frank, was given to the over-the-top displays of workshop-display-hubris that my father practiced. It was important to her that the house was nicely decorated for Christmas and that we (generally, she) baked cookies and learned the traditions of gift-receiving (and later, as we got older, of gift-giving). We had one Christmas together in her apartment in Hicksville in 1982. I recall having a small tree on a tabletop in the apartment but as relative newlyweds, we didn't really feel the pressure of decorating like we felt in 1983 when we were in our own house. Once we were in the house in Wantagh, we started collecting the boxes and boxes of stuff labeled "Christmas Decorations" that is the fate of celebrants of Christmas the world over. Christmas 1984 was Laura's first Christmas and our first Christmas as parents. That was the Christmas that we got Laura the mechanical swing that could loll Laura to sleep, but for which no extraction method existed that didn't involve waking the peacefully sleeping child. Christmas 1985 was memorable because we had a sentient audience for our Christmas show in Laura as a child of one and a half who could appreciate receiving gifts.

Christmas 1986 was the first one with our 9-month-old twins. Memories of that Christmas that I ruined for Anita just prior to our move to Germany haunt my conscience. The move from Long Island was planned in the fall of 1986. The move to Germany began with the further deterioration of the relationship between Don, my nominal boss and me. It got to the point that I went to Michael and told him that I wanted to leave Multiline. He understood the tension between Don and me and asked me not to leave but instead to tell him what it was I'd rather do than continue doing the job that I was doing. I told him that living and working in Europe had always been a dream of mine ever since I had lived in Bremen for that semester 10 years earlier. He thought that my moving to Europe and continuing my service to Multiline from there would be a good idea. The planning began with the writing of the business plan in June or July. I took part in a trade-fair in Paris in the summer of that year and tacked on a side trip to Bulgaria where there was interest in our equipment (which took us all at Multiline completely by surprise). Based on the level of interest there seemed to be for investments in Multiline equipment in both eastern and western Europe, we concluded that having a presence in Europe would be a wise next move. At first three locations were in consideration. The UK because of language and culture, Brussels because it was central to the western European market with good driving access to most of northern western Europe and somewhere in Germany because of its role as the biggest PCB market in Europe. We settled on the Frankfurt area of Germany because I felt comfortable in a German speaking setting even though my German was not yet fluent and, in addition, Frankfurt had excellent connections to eastern Europe which was shaping up to be an interesting market.

I traveled to Frankfurt in October of 1986 and, for the first time, began serious planning for a move, along with the family, to the Frankfurt area in the first days of 1987. I stayed at a hotel in Frankfurt called the CP Plaza which later became the Marriott hotel of Frankfurt (near the trade-fair grounds). Over the period of a week, I had meetings with bankers, lawyers, real estate people, accountants, the local Chamber of Commerce, members of the American-German community and attended an English-speaking Lutheran Church full of American expatriates. The most important contact I made in the week though was with a young lady of about 20 years old, who worked at the bar at the hotel. Every evening, I would go to the bar before finding a place for a meal and speak of my day. Her name was Susi and although she worked full time in the bar, she had learned hotel administration at that hotel. The bar was the only open job they had for her when she had finished her education there, so she was working there for the time being and hoping that a better job would open there for her in the future. Her English was excellent, spoken in a British accent without a hint of a Teutonic accent, with its zis or dis for this or willage for village or burssday for birthday. In any case, we got to know each other over the course of that week and when Friday came, I told her I needed to scout out possible places to live around the Frankfurt area and I asked her where I should drive around on the weekend to look for a new hometown. She said that she had an Aunt in Koeppern and she thought that it was a nice place to live and I should look around the areas of Friedrichsdorf, Kronberg, Koenigstein, Bad Homburg, Oberursel and Bad Soden on the weekend. This turned out to be excellent advice. I had met a man visiting from Malta at the hotel bar during my time there – I think to recall that his name was Tony. He was going to be taking over the job as the German boss of Air Malta and he was interested in seeing the areas that were nice in the region and I asked him if he wanted to go exploring with me. He did. We explored those areas together and we both found Bad Homburg particularly well suited to our needs because it seemed to have plenty of homes that were suited to young family life and it was only about 10 miles from downtown Frankfurt to downtown Bad Homburg. On our way back to Frankfurt from Bad Homburg, I drove to the airport to see how long the trip was between Bad Homburg and Frankfurt airport. I found that the drive time was about 20 to 25 minutes between Bad Homburg and the airport whereas Frankfurt to the airport was about 15 to 25 minutes. On that Saturday, I contacted two real estate agents in Bad Homburg and gave them the order to find me houses and offices in Bad Homburg to look at in November so I might choose one of each and sign leases then.

I went back to Farmingdale to work in the office there and continue the planning of the European office with Michael. In essence, my head and heart were already 100 % in my new job as the managing director of the European business of Multiline. We already had a distribution and representation network in Europe with separate businesses covering the UK, France, Germany, the Benelux, Italy, Spain, Scandinavia, Israel and Eastern Europe. We were in the midst of various pieces of business that had come up during the preceding months either as a result of my trip in the summer or in the follow-up communications with the various customers or representatives (reps) since that summer trip that had included Paris and Bulgaria. I became completely immersed in European business and my original job of designing machines, building an engineering department, developing engineering processes, creating the structure of an equipment manufacturing business with a purchasing department, quality assurance and inspection departments, service capability and inhouse sales entry, order confirmation and fulfillment capabilities were all falling away from me and being given over to others. Multiline had just moved into its new building one year earlier. We had gone from being a well-respected tool and die business with about 30 people to a well-respected equipment producer with about 85 employees in a matter of six years. In 1986, there were no longer any remnants of the old Lenkeit tool and die business. Multiline Technology had all that was left of Lenkeit's legacy and it was to be found in the processes and methods of producing the mechanical core of Multiline's punching machines.

In November I returned to Germany; this time staying at the Maritim hotel in Bad Homburg. During the week that I spent there I signed a lease for an office in the old city of Bad Homburg that was normally a one bedroom apartment on the second floor of a multipurpose apartment building that contained a pub on the ground floor (who's specialty was steak grilled on a hot stone at your table – I never once set my foot in the place unless the proprietor had parked her car in the driveway blocking my way into the garage). I found a house in the village of Kirdorf, a "suburb" of Bad Homburg which was a single family residence with four bedrooms on the second floor and a first floor comprised of an entry foyer (ein Flur) with a place for coats, boots and shoes (called a "Garderobe") with an enjoining guest WC (Gästeklo), an "L" shaped living room (the small appendage thereof which became a combination music room/play room), a dining room and a small kitchen which was just barely large enough to fit our kitchen table into and, being as we were all rather small, the table could actually accommodate the five of us, but just barely! The table became the cook's (mainly Anita's) main working space because the kitchen had almost no counter space. Once we got used to the house, we normally ate in the dining room. Americans seem mostly to like to eat family meals in the kitchen if they can. Generally speaking, the house was comparable to the one we were leaving behind on Long Island. It was smaller in square meters of living space, had a smaller yard (Garten), didn't have central air conditioning and lacked our personal design touches of the Wantagh house, but it was a single-family residence and had enough bedrooms and space in general and fit into our budget. I also didn't have a lot of time to make a decision as the planned move-in date was about 7 weeks away when I signed the lease in November. The thing that I found a bit disturbing about the house and the thing that Anita immediately remarked on upon seeing the house, is that the front of the house was comprised of a wall with a door and a single row of small, prison like windows out of which we could see very little. Americans tend toward having large picture windows to look out through on the front of their houses. The picture windows looked out the back of this house onto our small backyard, our neighbor's front door and into our covered terrace.

In that same week I made arrangements for an accountant and a lawyer to do the necessary work of registering a branch office of an American company at the new company address I had (Haingasse 10) in addition to doing the necessary paperwork to register me and my family for visas to be able to stay in Germany. I had to lay the groundwork for business and private bank accounts and insurance, telephone lines, fax lines (which were different than normal telephone lines in those days in Germany!) a telex connection for communicating with some of our distributors, reps and customers (particularly in the Warsaw pact nations of eastern Europe and the Soviet Union). Mike and I had talked of me getting a company car and he thought it would be best if I got a C-class Mercedes that wasn't too ostentatious. Most of the German speaking owners of PCB companies drove Mercedes 500 S-class cars in those days whereas most of the hired factory managers or managing directors that I would be calling at in those days drove Mercedes E-class –most often the 300 E. (In France it was a comparable Citroen or Peugeot – in Italy a comparable Alfa Romeo, Audi, BMW or Mercedes – in the UK a comparable Jaguar or Mercedes and only in one case a Rolls Royce). We decided that a 240 or 280 C-class would project the right amount of success, commitment to the German market and reasonableness. I went to the Mercedes dealer to order a C-class car to lease. Inasmuch as I wasn't visiting customers and I am not used to dressing up to order a car, I went to the dealer dressed as I am always dressed – somewhat loose-fitting chino style cotton pants (with pockets big and roomy enough to carry keys, change, a wallet and a package of tissues without showing too much bulge) and either a polo shirt or a button down plaid shirt. I was at that time 32 years old and being small and Asian I probably looked to be about 10 years younger to the salesman and receptionist at the Dr. Vogler Mercedes dealer that I visited in Bad Homburg. The only explanation that I have for my treatment there is they didn't consider me a serious candidate to order a car. I stood around for about 20 minutes looking at the cars after going to the receptionist and asking her to see a salesman (in German). The salesman spent the entire time on a personal phone call that seemed to be with a wife or girlfriend looking up intermittently and looking at me as I looked back. It was almost as if he was looking at me with a certain disdain and the wish that I would just disappear. So, I did. I swore on that day that I would never, ever drive a Mercedes. I went to an Audi dealer in Frankfurt on my way to stop in at the CP Plaza bar to check in with Susi at the bar there. I hadn't changed my clothes but was greeted by a salesman in shirtsleeves who was happy to lease me an Audi 100 with a 2.3 liter engine. It was my second Audi. I had already had one in the US. That car would be the second of six Audis so far in my life. Over the years, between Multiline in the US and Multiline in Europe, we would order about 25 other Audis and about 20 additional cars manufactured by VW subsidiaries and never considered a Mercedes largely because of that haughty, lazy Mercedes salesman.

I wanted to invite Susi and her boyfriend, who also worked at the hotel, to dinner to thank her for the role she had in how my office and future life were shaping up, but her boyfriend (and future husband) couldn't make it – instead, she brought her mother. At that time it was beginning to be clear to me that Susi would be a good addition to our European project. I learned during that week that she had learned all the functions that a hotel administrator needed to do including communicating with customers, suppliers and colleagues via telephone, fax, telex and the written word in both English and German. As a bonus, she could also speak some French and Italian. After everything was planned and signed for and there was no more that I could think of that needed to be done in Germany, I went back home to wait for the beginning of January and the big move.

The move had to be planned. We were taking a two-year lease on the house and it was furnished. We told the owners of the house what furniture we wanted to keep in the house and which furniture we did not want. The twins' furniture had to be air freighted along with the kids' favorite toys and some of the household furnishings which we couldn't do without. The kitchen chairs and some of our clothes and other paraphernalia of daily life (books, records, CDs and computer for me; sewing stuff for Anita; toys and clothes for the kids) were put into a shipping container which would take three weeks to reach us in Bad Homburg along with our Chevy minivan. The rest of our house was packed up and spent the next two years in a temporary storage facility on Long Island. What made Christmas 1986 so horrible for Anita and the rest of the family was that all this needed to happen in a time period between about the 22nd of December and the 26th of December when everything would be picked up and delivered to the various destinations. We had asked the moving company if there was anything we needed to do to prepare ahead of time before they came on the 26th of December, and they said "No." We naively believed them. We wanted to celebrate Christmas in our home and we weren't willing to take down the tree or remove the decorations until the day after Christmas or "Boxing Day" as they call it in the UK or the 2nd Christmas Day (Der zweite Weihnachtsfeiertag) as they dub it in Germany. The house was fully decorated and the gifts all wrapped up and hidden away waiting to be arranged around the tree on Christmas Eve. The 26th arrived, as did the movers, and Anita started stripping the beds, washing the bedding, preparing them for packing. It was chaos. I decided that we needed to put different colored stickers on everything in the house, a different color for each of the destinations: airfreight, sea freight or storage and separated by being placed in different corners of the rooms. Laura didn't like the sound the tape dispensers made when the movers taped up a box, Frank and Julie were ....I'm not sure what they were doing ...needed tending, and Braten wandered from room to room, trying to stay out of everyone's way. What had we been thinking??? A call to Anita's mom and sister to come pick up any combination of children and dog was made and they came to the rescue. My mother-in-law thought to take in the mail for us that day and placed it on the dresser in Laura's room. The mail was packed with the sea-freight-goods and we didn't get it until about a month later! I was all juiced up about finally getting my chance to live and work in Europe, but Anita paid the price of my dream. When the movers were finished removing everything from the house she looked out our big picture window at the quaint old house across the street where friends we had made lived, and burst into tears! Although she trusted that I had everything under control and was ready to start this adventure of two years in "the Fatherland," it was upsetting to her to see our entire existence bundled up and taken away, along with the prospect of leaving much loved family and friends. We spent the last week of our life on Long Island at Anita's mother's house. I felt terrible that fulfilling my dream was taking such a toll on her. We were operating under the premise that this would be a two-year project and that after two years we would decide what was best to do then at the end of 1988. We spent until the 3rd of January at Anita's mom's (Doris's) house. At the time, Doris must have been about 64. She was probably enjoying the time she was having with her daughter and grandchildren in anticipation of a longer separation. Doris would come to visit us at least once a year in Germany for at least the next six or seven years and we would visit the US at least twice a year just about every year for the next dozen years or so, but it was difficult for us to fathom how close we would remain over the coming years despite the distance when we had been so used to seeing each other at least once a week (at church) and quite often much more frequently. It was difficult for us to foresee how cutoff from our US family we would be once we were in Germany. There were no cheap means of communication in 1987 besides the post. Telephone calls between the US and Germany cost about $ 1,00 per minute during evening hours and could be double that during the day. Personal E-mail for private, non-commercial use would take another five years for people to accept. We used the phone judicially to keep in touch regularly with calls that lasted 10 to 15 minutes each and took place on a weekly cycle with Anita's family.

What we took to Doris's for the week was what we packed up and took to the airport on the day that we flew to Frankfurt Airport from JFK in New York. Three check-in pieces of luggage; one dog (Sauerbraten) – 10 years old, in a dog carrier who would fly as live luggage in [what I suppose is a heated part of] the hold of the plane; twins – 9 months old – (Julie and Frank) with two car seats which will double as airplane seats and car seats for the end of the planned trip on the Frankfurt to Bad Homburg leg of the trip – also outfitted with a twin, side-by-side foldable baby stroller; a two year and 8 month old little girl (Laura) also outfitted with a baby car-seat and a foldable baby stroller; one 34 year old frazzled and distraught mother carrying a baby bag complete with a dozen diapers, two small tubs of Cheerios (one for Laura, who can hold them herself and one for the twins who had, by that time, learned to "grab-and-stuff"), an assortment of drinks in non-spill cups and bottles (this being the age before 9-11 related carry-on restrictions), a pile of burp cloths and several wet-nap packages; and one slightly nervous and somewhat guilty-feeling business man outfitted with a pilot bag as an attaché case and one set of fold-out/fold-up wheels piled chest high with the pilot bag and three baby-seats (with the practiced help of several bungie cords). Laura's fold-up baby buggy came in handy as Anita's wheeled contraption to carry her purse and the baby bag when Laura chose to walk.

The trip on the plane went well. The worst parts of the trip were the stress of getting to and from the plane with all that stuff in tow. The kids were fantastically well behaved though. When we arrived in Frankfurt, we had to present our passports and explain that we were entering as tourists but were planning on staying for two years to start a business and live and work in Germany. The most difficult paperwork of the trip was presenting the dog's papers that proved her vaccination and health status. We wheeled the twins, but Laura was happy to walk holding either Anita's or my hand all the way from the plane to passport control and onto the luggage carousel. I left Anita with the kids to watch out for our checked baggage and went off to get the dog. When I let Sauerbraten out of the dog carrier she had occupied for the last 10 hours she promptly shat and pissed all over the floor of the airport. A fine-looking, well-dressed example of Teutonic manhood sarcastically mentioned within my earshot how pleasant Sauerbraten's bathroom habits were to his well-dressed and sophisticated looking wife as they majestically strode by. I rushed to Anita with the dog in tow and left the dog carrier directly next to mess she'd left behind. I handed Anita the leashed Sauerbraten, collected a couple of Pampers and rushed back to Braten's impromptu toilet site to clean up after her. When I went to throw the soiled diapers away, I had to choose from four neighboring receptacles which were labelled, "Paper", "Packaging", "Bottles", "Other Garbage". I just hoped no one saw me throw the stinking but well contained waste into the "Other Garbage" bin (particularly the sophisticated couple who remarked on our lack of couth!) I wasn't doing so well with the fitting into German life part yet. I hoped to improve.

When I returned to Anita and the kids, our luggage had arrived on the carousel, but Laura had vomited down the front of her (washable, thank goodness) winter coat and on to the floor. More Pampers to the rescue! While the taxi-van (that I had ordered from America) stood in a no-parking/no-standing zone just outside the doors of the arrivals hall, a policeman came by and wrote out a ticket as we arrived. I, in my (somewhat rusty) German, tried to explain the difficulties of the last half hour and our situation. I think to remember that he threw up his hands and discarded the ticket. Had he given the ticket to the driver, I'm sure I would have felt responsible for having to pay him for the coming fine.

The driver was very helpful in getting all our stuff into the van along with Sauerbraten who was put back into the dog carrier for the 30 minute ride from Frankfurt Airport to our new home in Bad Homburg. Anita was a little worried that Laura would start to retch again. She did, depositing most of what she expelled into my hastily proffered peaked cap which just made it into position in time. I found another "Other Garbage" receptacle for my hat, discarded it and its contents, got back into the cab, slid the door closed and gave the order to drive to our taxi driver.

It was a very cold day in Bad Homburg. Later in the week I heard that it had been one of the coldest of cold snaps that Germany had had in the past 40 years. This fact became more critical to us when we had dug out the key from its pre-planned hiding place, opened the door and entered our new home. We were happy to see that our real estate agent had arranged two borrowed baby beds for us that needed assembling but gave us all something appropriate to sleep on. The house was furnished and was being sublet to us by a family that had had a son of about 10 years old, so the rest of the furnishings, although not exactly our taste, was functional. What we were not expecting though was that it was exactly as cold inside the house as it had been outside of the house. The previous tenants of the house had turned the heating system completely off. The furnace was not working. We called the real estate agent who was nice enough to come out on a Sunday to take a look, but he could do nothing but call the emergency service who could only come in several hours.

We were exhausted and cold. There were two large sized couches in the living room. Laura slept on an oversized foot stool (Hocker), her soiled, smelly coat having been removed and thrown into the washing machine in the basement; and Anita and I each took a couch and a baby to lay on top of us under blankets (we all still had our jackets/snowsuits on) and we fell asleep for a few hours. Upon awaking, I asked Anita if the stove was electric, which it was. The kitchen was small and could be closed off from the rest of the house. I turned on the oven and all the burners on the stove and opened the oven door to provide some heat. The twins remained in their snowsuits, strapped into their "umbrella stroller". I brought blankets and the mattress from one of the baby beds and put it on the floor for Laura to sleep on. Anita kept her coat on and played solitaire after feeding the twins. Braten found a free spot on the floor. Now my thoughts ran to food, drinks and provisions for the day. It was Sunday and I knew that most stores were not open on Sundays in 1987 Germany. I did recall, however seeing a grocery store at the airport, so I took a taxi back to the airport, bought groceries and enough provisions for a couple of days and came back to the cold house. The heat and coziness of our little kitchen and our proximity to each other gave us a feeling of togetherness that still warms me to this day. A repairman eventually came and got the heat turned on again and by bed time that night, we had the house up to a temperature of about 10 or 12 degrees C and warming. Our first day as immigrants to Germany ended and our German adventure had just begun.

The next day was to be my first working day. My office was on Haingasse in Bad Homburg which forms a border between the old city of Bad Homburg and the downtown shopping district of Bad Homburg. A telephone already had been installed but the apartment was completely empty. I was hoping to begin traveling immediately, I called on Susi who, luckily, had taken a week of vacation from her job at the hotel in Frankfurt and was free to come and sit in the office during that first week. She turned out to be a huge help to Anita and the children. As there was really not much for her to do in the office because there was no equipment and no communications to deal with, she went to my home to help Anita get acclimated while I struggled with the registration of the new company as a customer of the telephone company, as a new business in the town, as a customer at the bank as well as doing the necessary shopping for furniture, a phone system, a fax machine, a telex, a copier, a typewriter and all the things an office contains.

By the end of that first week, I had made an offer to Susi to come work for me as my assistant and made certain that the offer was good enough that she would gladly leave the hotel and sit in that empty office until it started to fill up with stuff and work. She became a fixture of our business for the next twenty years.

In that week Susi spent more time at our new house with Anita, the kids and Braten. Anita needed help. Laura was sick. Susi, as a local native, knew German and spoke to Anita in perfectly posh English. Susi left me alone to fight with Deutsche Telekom (the German version of AT&T) and the city of Bad Homburg. We were in contact with each other though, because the house and office were only separated by a mile. We ate lunch as a family together with Susi that week.

With the kids and Anita in Susi's good hands, I did battle with German red tape. Apparently, according to the first two people I asked, I had to get an "Aufenthaltserlaubnis" (Visa to live in Bad Homburg – like a green card in the US) and register the business (officially in the city) and sign everything at exactly the same moment in time. These two people occupied offices in the citizen's registry office and the business registry office at the Bad Homburg town hall (Rathaus). Basically, their message was that they could not offer me a document to sign until I'd signed the document offered by the other. A business could only be started by a resident of Germany. A visa (or German residency) for working at a business could only be granted to a foreign worker on behalf of an existing business. This is the classic "Catch 22". I told myself, "That's impossible!" but, nevertheless, asked myself the question, "How do you do that when the offices between these people were separated be 30 meters in three different dimensions!?" After walking up and down two flights of stairs – twice – I was furious! I reached over the visa guy's desk, picked up his telephone handset, making a gesture as if wanting to put it into his hands, looked him straight in the eyes and told him to please call his colleague upstairs and tell him that I was just now signing the necessary residency permit to be able to sign the registration of the business as the general manager of this new Bad Homburg enterprise. The knot was untied and the visa man became friendlier, prepared the document for my signature, allowed me to sign, gave me a copy and sent me upstairs to sign the paper that would register Multiline Technology's German Branch Office (Zweigniederlassung).

It was less difficult but more anger-inducing with the telephone company. I wanted to order a total of what I knew had to be five or six telephone lines. I needed one for a fax connection, maybe three or four for regular phone calls and a telex line. They told me the order for the 3 or 4 telephone lines would not be any problem at all but that I would need to rent a telephone for each of the lines. OK – that sounded like what we had to do in America. As for a fax, I'd have to order, at a higher price, and totally separately, a fax line. Furthermore, a telex line could be had with the rental of a telex terminal and a separate telex line. I never had gone through the rigmarole of arranging such basic office necessities in the US, so I really don't know if this was any worse or better than what businesses had to go through there, but I was, despite my ignorance, furious. A fax line as I understood it, was and remains to this day, an absolutely normal telephone line! The Deutsche Telekom man working at the counter is telling me, "No, the fax connections are cleaner." I wanted to grab him by the throat and throttle him because I knew that Deutsche Telekom was trying to extract more money from our enterprise through their ownership of a monopoly! I had no choice but to sign up for what was offered. I swore to myself, "Before we move back to America, vengeance will be mine!" In the meantime, they've gotten better. Deutsche Telekom has improved greatly in their product offerings, pricing policies and service attentiveness. They began to get competition from other telecom service providers in the years immediately following the opening of our office and they had to adjust to a competitive market environment. In fact, I find the present version of Deutsche Telekom much better than its oldest competitor, Vodafone. Now I'm more inclined to to seek vengeance on Vodafone!

As the winter months of 1987 passed from January to the warmer days of March, Multiline International Europa or "mie", as we began calling ourselves, began to take shape, taking on an identity all its own and becoming known throughout our representative network as their "go-to" entity. My first job was to wean the representative and distributor network away from communicating with the factory and Mike and get them to communicate with us. My first act of true genius, hiring Susi, would be a very hard act to follow. This decision, although stumbled into because

Susi worked at the hotel in Frankfurt, gave the sales reps a feeling that someone was always here for them and was looking out for their interests. Susi and I became a team that made sure that they were always getting answers to their questions, offers for their inquiries, deliveries for their orders and service for their problems. I was, from the very beginning, constantly traveling and Susi became my anchor, my mouthpiece, my scribe and the hub that connected me with the factory, our direct customers and our reps and, later, an ever-burgeoning number of suppliers. If you looked up serendipity in my personal dictionary of the time, there would be a picture of a young, attractive German lady we, who populated the European PCB community of that time, all knew as Susi.

The evaluation of my life as a husband and father during those early years in Europe drew mixed reviews from Anita. She had been convinced to try life in Germany with the idea that we would spend two years there and then see how it went and we could come back to our lives on Long Island if she didn't like it. As I've already written, I travelled constantly. Together with the travelling there was my work habit of burning my candle from both ends. I awoke early and stayed up late, entertaining as many customers or sales reps that I could talk into staying out with me during the weeks. When I came home for the weekends, I was tired and in need of sleep, even to the point of taking naps on the sofa Saturday and/or Sunday afternoons. When Monday came, I was well rested and ready to start the cycle again. We engaged "au pairs" to have another adult in the house so that Anita wasn't limited to conversations with toddlers the entire day. She became very active at Trinity Lutheran Church. Trinity was an English-speaking Lutheran Church in Frankfurt. The membership was split among expatriate businesspeople and their families, military and consulate employees and their families, and local German families that liked the idea of worshiping in English. At the beginning of our time in Germany, nearly all of our friends were from church. We also began going to events sponsored by the American Women's Club of the Taunus so that Anita would get to know some other people in the area.

The children would go to German kindergarten at three years of age and started to speak German much better than we did. They started in primary school at a public school very close to our home. Laura was in the 1st grade and the twins were four when I signed on to remain in Europe indefinitely in 1991 and Mike and I became partners in "mie". I didn't really discuss the decision with Anita. I didn't even consider that she wouldn't want for me what I wanted for me and I really don't know how I would have reacted had she said she didn't want to stay. We stayed and she made the best of it.

We learned to ski as a family through a church weekend trip in 1994. Laura was 10 and the twins, Julie and Frank, were 8 the year we learned. I was 40. Skiing became a passion for me and I started to try to find time to ski at every opportunity. After productronica in 1995, I started a tradition of skiing with business friends, customers, suppliers and salespeople directly after productronica in the odd years and electronica in the even years. These trade fairs were always scheduled in the middle of November so Stubai Glacier, about an hour and a half drive from Munich, served well as the place I would begin my ski season every year. I cannot stress how important skiing has become in my life. For me it is as much a reason to live as my work is. The feeling of speed, the crisp sharpness of the icy air streaming by, the rushing sound of speed filling my being and the rhythm of the transfer of weight from one side to the other, the view of mountains, valleys, the whiteness, greenness, blueness and shaded blackness of sunny days or the total grayness of foggy mornings all occupy a space in me dedicated to my love of skiing. My one health related wish for myself is to be able ski for the rest of my life. Beyond that there isn't much else that I wish for except to enjoy as many grandchildren and great grandchildren as I can.

My first grandchild came earlier than we were planning. Laura became an unplanned mother at 17. Her daughter, Hannah, came into the world in August of 2001. I was a 47 year old grandfather. Laura was lucky to have the support of Anita. With Anita's help, Laura was able to keep her education on track without any delays. She completed her high school (Gymnasium Abitur) education with her class and went on to study architecture at a local college in Frankfurt. Hannah lived with us until she was almost 7. Today, there are four grandchildren from my two daughters and my son hasn't settled on a woman yet, so we wait.

I left Anita in 2008 as the stresses in my life were piling up. Our relationship had gone cold. I was beginning to feel the fear of failure in business and what I was carrying around inside me, she was giving voice to. It felt like a betrayal of trust or a failure of faith in my ability to survive. I couldn't take the constant expressions of worry.

I moved into a small apartment in the old city of Bad Homburg. For the first time since my Richmond experience, I wasn't living in a single family house in the suburbs. I loved living in the city and being a stone's throw from pubs, spontaneous meetings for drinks with friends and easy access to adult conversation when I wasn't travelling. One afternoon, as I was walking from one meeting in Bad Homburg to another, walking past the outdoor tables that populate one section of our main shopping street, Louisenstrasse, I was called out to by an acquaintance. "Come," she called, "Have a coffee with us!" She was sitting at a table at a cafe with a woman I had often seen and admired but with whom I had never spoken. I'd never seen her up close but had always noticed that she was pretty, but now, as I was introduced and sat next to her, I couldn't imagine a more beautiful woman. She was introduced to me as Serpil. She was born in Istanbul and had moved to Germany with her mother in one of the early waves of Turkish "guest workers" that came for jobs in the 1960s. She had come to Germany as a five year old and had grown up in Bad

Homburg. As it turned out, she had noticed me as well, but she never admitted to being as fascinated at the sight of me as I was at the sight of her. We became two immigrants living together in Germany.

Behind the Iron Curtain

February 28, 2022 – If the news of the day keeps intervening into my consciousness and stirring up old memories, I might never get this book done.

Russia invaded Ukraine last week. I have so many memories of both Soviet and post Soviet Ukraine, Belarus and Russia that it is difficult for me to separate them all in my little ole' head. Kiev, in Ukraine as we used to write, or Kyiv as we now write, in its old town, in my memory, has at least one big hill, a big statue, several historical Orthodox churches, cold winter days with a frozen river flowing through and no open restaurants in my memories from the last time I was there in 1992. I was fed by people from the factory I visited in their homes. We always seemed to wash down dinner with home-made pepper vodka.

I have many recollections of meals in the USSR that preceded Ukrainian freedom that always featured camaraderie between me, this strange little American, and the Soviets I was visiting. Besides the obligatory "Marina" (normally attractive) who translated between English and Russian, there was good food, live music, a half- liter bottle of vodka for each man at the table, awful tasting beer and mineral water, and "champagne" from the largest bubbly wine factory in the world (I think to recall from the Crimea). The most memorable week was in Kharkiv, the second largest city of the Ukraine (as it was called then). I guess that it was 1988 or 1989. A man called Mr. Panov, (who always called me Pavel) – a Russian military officer who had attended the military academy in Kharkiv, fallen in love and stayed, had bought a whole raft of machines from me, and, as the last concession in a long whiskey fueled negotiation, extracted from me the promise that I would personally come and install the equipment and train his factory people in the use of the equipment and the manufacture of multilayer printed circuit boards. The factory was called Monolit. At the time, it was one of the biggest employers in Kharkiv. The business was a local treasure and had built subway stations, nuclear power station control systems and even TVs, radios and recording devices. Panov was responsible for the PCB factory. Panov and I had formed a friendship over the years beginning in about 1986 when I first met him at a trade fair in Moscow. Since the first meeting, he always expressed an interest in acquiring Multiline's equipment. I had arranged a visit for him to a customer of ours, Bell Alcatel in Gent, Belgium and as a result of that visit our friendship was solidified and he was able to arrange the purchase of our equipment.

My secretary, Susi, remarked to me that she had received a telex at the time to remind me that I had to go to Kharkiv in the Ukraine to install some equipment within the following four or five weeks. I asked her where Kharkiv was – her answer wasn't very enlightening. I looked it up in my atlas and realized that this was not going to be an easy trip. I flew to Sheremetyevo Airport, the international airport in Moscow and then had to take a taxi half way around Moscow to get to another airport on the other end of Moscow's ring highway that served Kharkiv and other cities to the south of the USSR from Moscow. By this time, I was a savvy enough traveler to always have about 10 US dollars in singles in my pockets and a couple of packs of Marlboro's. The taxi cost me a couple of dollars or a pack of Marlboro's – I can't remember anymore. That airport which I can't remember the name of looked like a poorly maintained train terminal. One feature of big indoor spaces like this, especially in winter, in the old Soviet Union, was the muddy floors, so that one, as a westerner, can never comfortably place one's luggage on the floor. I had my luggage for a week complete with German coffee, Marlboro cigarettes and Ballantine whisky for my friend Panov along with all my tools. At some point, I had to put stuff on the filthy floors. I checked into my flight and boarded a plane with a glass nose (like a World War II bomber) and seating for 41 people – 10 rows of two seats on each side of the aisle and one seat for a poor Schmo who sat between the two WCs at the back of the plane and had his knees banged by the doors every time somebody entered or exited one of them.

I remember a loud drunk guy – Ukrainian or Russian – with a young woman that looked like an embarrassed niece – who had a feeling of loudly expressed entitlement sitting across the aisle from me. I was happy not to have understood him. We landed and when the plane had taxied to a stop, we were picked up and taken to the terminal in this city of 1.8 million people by a wagon that resembled a school bus being pulled by a tractor. Our luggage came in a wagon that resembled a hay wagon being pulled by another tractor. The terminal was about the size of a Trailways or Greyhound Bus Terminal from my youth except that the furnishings were sparser. The guy who drove the luggage wagon just shut the motor of the tractor off and disappeared. The 41 of us just stood there looking at each other until I decided to climb up onto the wagon and hand down bags to my fellow travelers.

I took a taxi to my hotel. It was called something like the Hotel Mir or Cosmonaut or Sputnik like so many of the places that I stayed in behind the Iron Curtain of that period. I checked in, and riding the elevator up to my room, I saw a placard for a rooftop bar so I placed my luggage and tools in my hotel room and headed back to the elevator, pushed 12 for the floor where the bar was and the elevator stopped at floor 11, opened the doors and refused to go any higher. I pushed "12" several times and the doors simply closed and opened again. After awhile I stepped out on floor 11, found the stairs and ascended to what I thought would be a roof-top bar, but, it turned out only to be a roof-top.

No bar. They had advertised a bar in the elevator that was not yet built but, apparently, planned.

That was all on Sunday. From Monday through Thursday evening I installed the equipment and trained the man who was to operate the equipment, did our acceptance training and got to know the factory and its people. I was shown Kharkiv, was hosted by Panov at his house and met his wife and one of his sons. They were thankful for the gifts I had brought and gave me several bottles of home-made spicy pepper vodka to take home with me. On that Thursday evening, after all the work was done, we celebrated with the President of Monolit, the manager of the electronics department, Panov, the guy who I had spent the week training, Marina, the German-Russian translator and Tatiana, the English-Russian translator. The other four men toasted first. Each toast was punctuated with the downing of 100 milliliters of vodka (about a half of a cup or two fat fingers). Each gave wonderful words of friendship, pride, camaraderie and bonhomie and each toast was lovingly, caringly, nearly carnally whispered into my ear by the ever increasingly beautiful Tatiana. When it was my turn to give my toast, I could barely stand, no less speak. My toast: "To you, my friends; to this evening with this music, to our families and to our beautiful ladies" (I gave myself credit for remembering that Marina was sitting across the table not doing much translating!). Then, like all the other glasses of vodka that had preceded this one, down the hatch.

My head was swimming and I was kind of suspended in a thick viscous state of being that I can only accurately describe as totally, ineffably, unmitigatedly drunk. Tatiana swam out of my state of being into my consciousness and asked if I'd like to dance. I told her that you need music to dance. She pointed out that the band was playing. We danced.

Now, after 34 years or half a lifetime I wonder about the people who sat around that table and shared an evening of shared humanity not caring about where we came from. They might still be alive or not. Their hearts may pump for Ukraine or Russia, the USA, Germany or wherever they find themselves but one thing I'm certain about, none of them would want to be on opposite sides of a border and want to kill the others.

There would be another trip to the Ukraine in January 1992, in the month after the breakup of the Soviet Union. I needed to visit Kiev to conclude some negotiations that would complete a large contract that we had delivered to two Ukrainian PCB factories which were being built into barges by a large French engineering company near Marseille. Each PCB factory, once built completely into these barges in the south of France would be floated via the Mediterranean Sea, the Black Sea and rivers and canals to their final positions in the Ukraine. We had been paid 90 % of our contract through a company called Mupi in France. The contract had been negotiated in French Francs. Our suppliers of equipment wanted to be paid in dollars though. We were not very sophisticated about currency markets and really didn't have a clue what the Franc would do against the US Dollar in the six to seven months of time it would take to build the equipment. We negotiated with our suppliers that we would split the gains or losses of the currency valuation differences compared to our dollar costs. In this way we didn't need to tie up large amounts of money on any hedging strategies. We had negotiated to be paid 90 % upon completion of the equipment, 5 % upon installation of the equipment and the last 5 % after a guarantee period of one year passed without major downtime or production disruptions. Inasmuch as our prices had been calculated to pay for all the equipment (including our normal profit) 100 % upon installation, the 5 % guarantee payment was seen by us as a 5 % premium added to our profit. The contract involved equipment that we purchased from a company called TMP in Cleveland, Ohio in addition to Multiline machines and multilayer tooling. TMP made presses which laminated the multilayer PCBs together along with all the equipment to move the tooling and product in and out of the presses and the Multiline machines and Multiline tooling plates guaranteed that the process of multilayer production could be handled by our company as a single production unit. The deal was one of the biggest deals that we had ever undertaken up to that time. As I recall there were two six opening hot presses, one six opening cold press and a handling system that involved two six opening transport wagons which moved on tracks between a layup area and breakdown area for each of the two factories. The tooling plates and separator plates alone for each factory came to nearly $ 200,000. The entire package of goods came to about $ 900,000 per factory for a total of $ 1.8 million. The contract was signed for FF 11.25 million. As our deal was made in the fall of 1989, and the delivery took place in the spring of 1990, the French Franc did nothing but rise in value during the entire time it took our suppliers to build the equipment! When we delivered the equipment to the warehouse in France, we received 90 % of FF 11.25 million or FF 10.125 million. This converted to $ 1.84 million or more than 100 % of the dollar amount we originally offered the equipment for. Instead of only getting the 90 %-dollar amount of $ 1.62 million, we made a windfall currency profit of $ 220,000 which we split with our suppliers.

The reason for the meeting in Kiev was because of the collapse of the Soviet Union in December of 1991, there were no more funds for the two factory projects in the Ukraine. Ukraine was now cut off from all funding of any kind for Soviet era projects. The people at the ministry that had been responsible for the purchase of the factories wanted to cancel the last two payments for the projects. They wanted us to agree not to be paid anymore and we didn't need to do anything more. The contract was amended to make the 90 % we had already been paid, 100 % of the agreed to price and the delivery up to that point to be 100 % of our fulfilled responsibilities. We agreed. The rest of my time there on that particular trip was spent with some of the engineers from the PCB facility who I had come to know over the years from various visits to the Soviet Union. They took me to a cathedral in the center of Kiev, where we were able to witness the baptism of a grown man into the eastern Orthodox faith. For both me and the engineer that accompanied me, it was an unusual and moving sight. I had to eat at the homes of the ministry employees or at the factory canteen because, although the hotels were open to rent rooms to travelers, they had no food to cook. People still had Soviet Rubles, but while I was there, coupons were distributed which were to substitute for local currency until a new currency could be printed and distributed. Nothing really worked in the Ukraine anymore and much of everyday life was difficult. Stores which were always relatively empty during the functioning days of the Soviet Union were even emptier in this, the early post-Soviet period.

I had organized my trip to fly from Kiev to Riga after my visit. The problem popped up in the early days of the post-Soviet period that the former Soviet satellite countries like the Ukraine and Latvia that were served by Aeroflot as their "domestic" airline received no more kerosene to fuel their planes for flights from one former Soviet satellite state to another. Aeroflot aircraft were fueled in Russia and flew routes from Russian cities to non-Russian cities and back. I could not fly from Kiev to Riga no matter what my ticket said. Furthermore, it was difficult to get to Riga via a Russian hub like Moscow or Leningrad because of limited airplane capacity because so many planes were grounded in former Soviet satellite countries. My reason for traveling to Riga was to speak at a symposium on advanced electronic packaging solutions with a distributor friend of mine, Gerhard Balla. Gerhard's Russian office was based in Leningrad, and he was supposed to fly from Leningrad to Riga, but his flight was cancelled and he was working to find another way to Riga. I was supposed to speak on the Thursday of the same week where I had had my meeting with the people in Kiev on that Tuesday. The plan was for me to fly from Kiev to Riga on Tuesday night, where I would meet up with Gerhard who was scheduled to fly from Leningrad to Riga the same evening, but not getting the flight I had hoped to get on the Tuesday night meant another night in Kiev. Communicating from Kiev to Leningrad to Riga was also a difficult task even at the best of Soviet times. In these early days of the post-Soviet period, it was much more difficult than before and only worked through my office and Susi. I would have the hotel or factory in Kiev send a Telex to Susi which she would relay to Gerhard and his people in Leningrad. Leningrad would communicate with the institute in Riga and act as the relay point back to Susi who would inform me. Finally on late Wednesday afternoon, I got a flight to Leningrad where I met up with Gerhard. I spent the evening in the Hotel Astoria which is directly on the square on which St. Isaac's Cathedral stands. Gerhard and I had a nice afternoon, evening and following morning as his office people frantically sought a way to get us to Riga which did not involve walking or hitch-hiking. Finally, it was decided that we would share a first-class sleeper compartment on a train from Leningrad to Riga. We would depart sometime that evening and arrive (hopefully refreshed from a good night's sleep) around 8:00 a.m. the next morning. The symposium was pushed back one day and I was now to speak at about 10:00 a.m. Our improvised schedule had us arriving at the main train station in Riga where we would be picked up by somebody from the institute that was hosting the event. We would then shower and dress in the rooms of two of the students of the institute and then give our papers. That evening I was happily booked on a Lufthansa flight back to Frankfurt from Riga and I let the difficulties of hotels without food and airports without fuel recede into the corners of my memory.

In the years between 1986 and 1991, I had opportunities to visit major east European cities like Minsk, Moscow, Kiev, Kharkiv, Leningrad, Sofia, East Berlin, Warsaw, Ruse, Belgrade, Bucharest, Prague, and Dresden. These cities were certainly drab compared to their west European counterparts. They did, however, leave indelible memories.

During one of my earliest visits to Moscow I had some time on my hands and went to the circus. The level of entertainment at a Russian Circus has nothing to do with the sad, depressing atmosphere I have come to dread about America's travelling circuses. The entertainment is cultured and uplifting rather than evoking the sense of people and animals being exploited that permeates my thinking about the circuses of my youth. I still recall an act that filled the entire crowd at the Moscow circus with wonder. The orchestra played some dance music as a formally dressed couple entered the spotlight in the middle of the round stage area. As the couple danced, their costumes changed. As the costumes changed, so did the rhythm and style of dancing. It was an incredible sight for the eyes – absolutely and unbelievably magical – as unfathomable as it was enchanting. It was as if we were all witnesses to a dream. We watched for several minutes as the couple danced through costume change after costume change right before our eyes. Another form of entertainment that was adult entertainment in Moscow but only children's entertainment anywhere else in the world (at least according to my experience) was the puppet show at Moscow's Puppet Theatre. I think to recall that the big theatre had seating for hundreds and hundreds of people. The theatre was full, with every seat occupied; most of them by adults, and many of them using opera glasses to view a stage that, according to my recollection was only about 3 meters wide by about 1 and a half meters high. We spent an entire evening caring about the stories of these crazy fairy tale animals and people in their fantasy worlds. The access to entertainment in places like the Semper Opera in Dresden or the Bolshoi Ballet in Moscow or the Kirov Ballet in Leningrad was easy for westerners because one could always get tickets that were reserved for people who were paying in "valuta" (money exchanged at the official rates). Once while in Dresden, in 1988, having seen a poster for a performance of Coppelia, a ballet, at the Semper Opera, I asked the people at the reception desk of my hotel (the Bellevue, directly across the Elbe River from the Semper Opera) if they had any tickets to sell me. The Bellevue was a hotel for foreign visitors and sold tickets in Dmarks, instead of the local Ostmarks. The price was 20 Dmarks, which to a native New Yorker, was a bargain (at about $12,00) to see a professional ballet at one of the most famous opera houses in the world. The response from the reception lady was, unfortunately, they had not gotten their contingency of tickets that day, but if I was interested in seeing the performance, I should go to the ticket office at the theatre and take my chances at buying the tickets as a local for 20 Ostmarks. Had I exchanged all my money for 1 Dmark to 1 Ostmark as the official "valuta" rate was, the deal would have been the same. I had however (illegally) exchanged 20 Dmarks for a black-market rate of 30:1 or 600 Ostmarks (as instructed to do by my contract partners) which was a typical black-market rate in those days. With this large sum of Ostmarks, one could pay local cash for dinners out and drinks for all the locals and visiting installation crews. This helped in building the camaraderie of the future engineers and factory workers both among themselves and with the foreign "experts" who were there to set up and train people on their equipment and in their areas of expertise. This black-market money had to be spent during the visit because it was illegal to carry local currency across borders (in either direction). Black market exchanged money put pressure on us visitors to spend, not only the black-market exchanged money, but also the money we had officially exchanged. When entering East Germany from anywhere in the west, one was forced to buy 25 Ostmarks per planned day in East Germany for a "valuta" exchange rate – this means that for a five day stay, one would buy 125 Ostmarks for 125 Dmarks. To put 125 Ostmarks into perspective for the East German, this was more than two weeks salary. To put it into perspective for the West German businessman, it was the cost of three nights out at a local pub with a wife or girlfriend, or the cost of a nice dinner and a bottle of wine at a good Italian place with the wife and kids. So, the buying power of the valuta-exchanged money was, in any case, larger than the hard currency value of the money in the west. Black-market exchanges distorted this value difference even further. The translated cost of the (black-market financed) ticket was 40 cents in US money. The value of the experience was (for me, not being an expert in Ballet) every bit as valuable as the ballet tickets I would have bought for $ 60 to $ 100 in New York City to see a performance at the American Ballet Theatre.

As I became more experienced in traveling by myself to the eastern bloc nations, I would learn that the best source of exchange was the taxi driver that vied for my attention among a sea of other taxi drivers that saw me walking out of the customs control area. There was always a swarm of men waiting and as the people exited, a chorus of "Taksi, taksi...taksi?!" would go up and each potential driver's eyes scanned the eyes of those exiting with their luggage. What I wouldn't do in Spain or southern Italy or even New York, I learned to do in Sofia, Minsk, Leningrad, Kiev or Moscow. Upon climbing into the car (which was always a private car, with the smell of gasoline coming from the reserve jerry-cans these drivers always had in the trunks of their cars), I learned not to haggle the price, but just to give my wished-for destination and wait for the driver to say, "Valuta?" or something like "Exchange?" It was bound to happen and as time progressed from 1986 to 1989, it nearly always happened. The rate was most often 30:1 to the official rate. I would, most often, exchange 50 Dmarks or $ 20. For an exchange of that size, the taxi ride was included at no additional charge and the taxi driver might even give me a can of excellent canned crab or a small container of cavier. I would always give the driver an additional dollar or a pack of Marlboros as a tip when I was safely at my destination. If the driver actually wanted money for the ride, I would offer a dollar – perhaps two for a long ride or a pack of Marlboros and that usually settled the bill. I can only remember one time when I paid local currency and that was rather early in my experience. One of these men who picked me up at Sofia airport in Bulgaria spoke excellent English. It turned out that he was an engineer who worked the night shift at the local nuclear power plant. He told me he didn't need to do much except to re-act to error alarms. He gave me his telephone number and told me if I needed a driver, I should just call him. OK, I said. I called when I needed him to take me from place to place in Sofia. At the end of that trip, I called him to take me back to the airport. Before dropping me off for my flight he told me to call him before I came again and he would meet me at the airport and be my private driver. This I did. Each trip thereafter I would pay him 50 Dmarks per week to be my driver and he drove me all over Bulgaria at any time of day. We often went to Ruse (four hours away) or Pravetz (an hour or so), where I had customers. He would find things to do for the duration of my meetings and always come back a couple hours after dropping me off, often with fruit or bread or cake he found to buy while he was keeping busy exploring wherever we were. If we were in Sofia, he would drive me to dinner and come back an hour later and then he would drive me to a pub or night-club. I didn't need him after bedtime, so he could go to work and sleep. I just hoped that those alarms were not just flashing lights and were accompanied by loud noises.

On my first several visits to Moscow, I stayed at the National Hotel which is located directly across a busy thoroughfare from Red Square. It was an old grand hotel which gave the impression that it was once great and had seen better, headier days. Walking into the lobby for the first time, I was struck by how overstuffed and old the furniture was and how underlit and dingy the space felt. I had arrived later than planned and, while waiting on line to check in, witnessed several people who had had reservations, camped out on easy chairs and sofas because, apparently, having a reservation didn't guarantee that one was actually going to get a room for that night. I often think of these historical buildings possessing the well-maintained facade of an older woman that attracts a look and the fleeting thought that she was probably beautiful once. I waited quietly in my place on the line listening to furious people of various nationalities, complaining, cajoling, then fuming to no effect. Those people behind the reservations desk were made of the same stuff as the people who worked at the passport and customs control at the airport: stern, unsmiling and with a look that projected a certain sense of superiority mixed with slight constipation. (I suppose the same demeanor is reserved to the people at the Nassau County Motor Vehicle Office of my youthful memories). I was pleasantly surprised that my reservation, made by Susi with the help of the local ministry with whom I would meet during my visit, functioned to get me a room designation on the third floor which overlooked Lenin's tomb. No keys were given out by the reception lady. I was given a little slip of very thin, poorly printed, but official looking paper bearing the stamp of the reservations desk of the Grand National Hotel (picture a cross between printed and stamped thin toilet paper and wax-paper without the wax – a similar stamped document on similar paper was handed to me by the customs official at the entry border that I was to return on my exit from the USSR that showed how much money I had brought in and that I was wearing a gold ring and had a watch that had some gold plating on it when I entered). With this official guest document, I could get my key on the third floor of the hotel from the "key lady". The "key lady" always sat outside the elevator or the top of the stairs between the entrance and the exits from the hallways that led to the rooms. Sometimes if you arrived back at this control point too late or too early or at a time when the key lady just wasn't there, your key would be there; just sitting on that table that every visitor needed to pass to get to their rooms (along with any guests that they brought). In such Soviet hotels for foreigners (Intourist Hotels) of my memory, it always amazed me how a system so consciously built up upon a neurotic sense of paranoia and control could have so much personal trust of foreigners while the system tried to force us through so many hoops of official mistrust.

There was a restaurant on the second floor of the National Hotel that had the feel of the nineteenth century royal period. A pianist often accompanied dinner. The first time I sat in that restaurant, I sat at a table of people from all over the world. We had been invited by the Skibinskis, who were the owners of a company called AFIG which was one of our most important distributors in the Eastern block and with whom we must have done at least seven or eight big projects. Mr. Skibinski was born in Poland about the time of the first World War to a family that owned a large chocolate business in Poland. Being rich, well informed, and with the best advice money can buy, the family moved to Geneva, Switzerland in the 1930s. Mr. Skibinski, I think to recall, spoke Polish, French and German but no English – I recall always speaking to him in German. Mrs. (Jola) Skibinska was of Jewish and Polish heritage, but her well-to-do family fled to Brazil. She came to Europe and Geneva to study, where she passed the bar and became a lawyer in Geneva. Along the way, they married, had two children together, (both daughters who would also pass the bar in Geneva!) and build a distribution business that specialized in building turnkey factories in the former Warsaw pact nations and the Soviet Union. There were about 12 PCB people at our table for dinner that evening, and the conversation was very cosmopolitan. As guests, there were the French, who spoke French and English; the Germans who spoke German, French and English; the Swiss that spoke French, German, Italian and English; a Swede who spoke Swedish, English and German; a Brazilian who spoke Portuguese, Spanish, French and English; a couple of Russians who spoke Russian and either German or English (but not both); Mr. Skibinski's son from his first marriage who spoke French, Polish, Czech, German and English; the English who spoke English; and me, the constant immigrant, who spoke no Korean, excellent English and not-so-good German. The most remarkable part of the evening though was Mrs. Skibinska. She spoke all the languages at the table except Swedish, but did not count German among her languages although she did indeed understand and speak German, because she didn't speak it perfectly in the way she spoke all the others! Her German was, however, without a doubt, better than mine! That remarkable woman, Jola Skibinska, translated for all of us when translation was necessary, and the conversation never flagged! It was one of the most remarkable feats of a mind showing itself off I have ever witnessed, and she didn't think anything of it. She did it like treading water or swimming in place. I don't know how many of you have ever been in the position of translating for people, but I can tell you that when I need to do it, I am constantly mixing up my pathetic 1-and-three-quarter languages by speaking German to the English speaker and vice-versa! Jola was a remarkable woman!

That evening, one of my first in the former Soviet Union, felt nothing like communism. My memories of Soviet and Warsaw Pact times and places come back to me today as days of awakening. The memories are full of the mental gymnastics one was involved in in trying to fit these two divided worlds into one unified theory of humanity. On one side of the divide, in those days, I was floating along in a world of plenty and didn't often think about those who were struggling to make ends meet. On the eastern side of the divide, nobody was concerned about making ends meet because nobody felt he had the ability or possibility to pull both ends together. What I had, my Russian friend, Panov, from Kharkiv, could never dream of having. I could go where I wanted, pay for anything I wished for and help him see some of my world. In exchange, he did what he could. I met Panov through his visits to the AFIG stands at various trade fairs in the Soviet Union. He would always come to lunch on our stand and the cooks (that resembled the portly outside doll of those ubiquitous Russian stacked "matryoshka dolls" and were a fixture at every AFIG exposition stand) fed him well. We always gave him a bag full of western "treats" like a carton of Marlboro cigarettes, several ball point pens, a picture calendar of Swiss landscapes and a bottle of Ballantine's whisky. He would always have a beer or two with lunch and then I would open a bottle of whisky for the conversations after lunch. We would sit there with a Marina, or a Tatiana or some other interpreter and finish that bottle in the afternoon and talk about life, PCBs, our families and the world. Over those, my early European years, I learned to drink like a Russian through Panov's example. I experienced a little bit of his world, and I am eternally grateful to him, and the Skibinskis, that I can carry pieces of that no longer existent world around, not only in what I remember, but in the way I live and the way I view humanity.

When we were in Moscow for a trade fair, we could give Panov a taste of western life on our stand at the trade fair or invite him to dinner with us where locals normally weren't allowed. There were guards at the door of the hotel that performed a kind of face check of people going in and out of the hotel. Only people they approved of were permitted in. There were always some local women hanging out at the bar (on the second floor) who would not refuse the offer of a drink. Obviously, they were permitted in by the guards at the door – what their deal was, I never asked and I never got to know. There was also a Beriozka or hard currency store in the National Hotel where local or foreign people with US Dollars, Dmarks, Swiss Francs or other foreign currency could shop for western goods. At the National Hotel Bar there were always very interesting people to meet and chat with after a day of business. I met people who spent months at a time in places all over the Soviet Union (Siberia, Uzbekistan, Kazakhstan, Armenia or Azerbaijan, for example) doing business with furs or cashmere or oil or in cultural pursuits like music or dance. I often had one of those rooms that overlooked Lenin's tomb on Red Square. The room was always large and airy with high ceilings and interesting old furnishings. What they had in charm, these rooms missed in care and cleanliness. When I come in from outside, anywhere in the world, I am used to strip down to shorts, a t-shirt and bare feet. The thing about relatively dark colored oriental style carpets is that it isn't easy to see when they were last vacuumed clean, no less shampooed. There was a white linen towel on the floor, on top of the carpet, which was the last spot on the floor that my feet touched before picking them up and laying them down on the white sheets of my bed. A look at the bottom of my feet prevented me from putting my feet down onto the bed. Instead, I swiveled back out of the bed, took myself and the white floor mat-towel to the bathroom, cleaned my feet and the mat-towel as best I could and shuffled with my feet on the mat-towel to the bed again – launching myself into the bed without touching my bare feet onto the carpet again. The next day I found some slippers in the closet and not giving too much thought about when the last time they had been cleaned, wore them around my room until I left them next to my bed upon retiring.

I would try to return to the same room or one just above it whenever I needed to be in Moscow. I loved the view out onto Red Square and Lenin's mausoleum. When the weather wasn't bad there seemed always to be a line of people outside the tomb wanting to visit their hero Vladimir. I liked to walk out to the middle of Red Square and enjoyed the panorama view from the center of the Square. The view was particularly impressive at night with a soft snowfall. The lighting of the Kremlin, along with the numerous red stars thrust into the night sky on the end of their slender towers gave the illusion that one stood in the shadow of immense power. There was the Kremlin along one side, Lenin's tomb, St Basil's Church and this great expanse of rectangular stone paving that is the "Square". There were other hotels that I would stay at over the five years of Multiline's engagement with the Soviet Union and its satellite countries: the Mezhdunarodnyia (the "International Hotel" where there were several foreign restaurants including a Bavarian restaurant and a Sushi place); the Ukraina (A huge hotel built and financed by the German government in the muscular "victory" architectural style of post WWII Soviet domination of half of Europe (there were four such major German projects which are all identifiable today by towers of brick topped with the red star including Moscow University); and the Cosmos (a nod to Soviet's victories in the space race) where I met Jon Bon Jovi. I even stayed at a Hotel, arranged by the people of Rode, (one of the engineering companies that did turnkey projects that we were involved in), called the Budapest Hotel, near the Bolshoi Ballet Theatre, which was only meant for locals. In such a hotel, the prying eyes of the key lady were not deemed to be necessary – I got to keep my own key. There were three memorable features of this hotel: there were unrepaired (and apparently, irreparable) broken windows in the hotel room through which mosquitoes flew and feasted on me; there was a bath tub, with a drain hole of about two inches in diameter and a stopper of about 1 ½ inches in diameter; there was a restaurant, decorated in a style not very different from the restaurant in the National Hotel with the piano player, where a band played all through dinner. I don't mean quiet dinnertime, background music. This was lively dance music through the entire dinner without taking any breaks. We foreigners watched amusedly as the Russians left their food to get cold to dance their favorite pieces and returned to their food when their dance lust had run its course and left them hungry again. These people were not so jaded and cosmopolitan as we who sat through our entire dinner and ate our food hot.

I reported the broken window and the too small stopper or too big drain hole to the Reception desk at the hotel, but when it became clear that nothing was going to happen, I realized I'd have to work something out for myself. Moscow streets are cleaned with street cleaners that use what are practically fire hoses to spray the debris toward street drains. Therefore, the streets are full of puddles that double as mosquito farms. I needed to close the holes in the windows to my room, but I needed some airflow in the room that the pair of broken windows afforded. I had some ½ inch wide by about three-inch-long address labels for Multiline's office on the Haingasse 10 in Bad Homburg with me and used them as tape to cover the holes in the windows with fabric from a sacrificed tee-shirt. I used the same address labels to build up the diameter of the stopper, which together with my strategically placed foot worked to fill up the bathtub enough to get wet enough to feel clean. Traveling always makes one proud of the workarounds we need to find to be comfortable under-way – particularly behind the iron curtain. Adhesive backed address labels, paperclips, business cards, old credit-card-like plastic pieces can all be used to make life easier. Traveling, and particularly traveling in off-the-beaten-track destinations brings out the MacGyver in us all!

Not far from Red Square was the beginning of the Arbat Street. I was first introduced to this wonderful feature of Moscow on an early trip by one of my translators. I would never have had the opportunity to see normal Russians or Muscovites with-out the Angelovas, Ludmillas, Marinas, Tatianas or the Galinas who did simultaneous translating for me from Russian to English, German to Russian or Bulgarian to English, etc, etc.. The best translators are those people who, when speaking for you, give the idea that what they are saying is what you're thinking. If they are confident and translating well, and I was building my half of our dialogues well, then the communications went forward without too much delay or unnecessary misgivings. Questions came of not having a firm understanding of concepts then, not through misunderstandings or mistranslations of words. Communications in my language which were put into words and terms these women (and they were almost always women) heard and translated built ideas spoken in my language into the same exact idea in words of the language that was strange to me. One has to allow the interpreter full access into your mind and preparation was always good for this. The more they know about you as a person, the better they will translate for you as the expert when it comes to making you look smart in a meeting. On that first trip through the Arbat, I had the feeling that the people populating that street were not very different from the people shopping any Saturday on the main shopping streets of Bad Homburg, Frankfurt, New York or at a mall on Long Island or that underground shopping mall in Seoul where I bought the camera. There were a lot of sidewalk sales of artwork and handicrafts and many more disfigured or old and sorry-looking gypsy beggars than we were used to seeing in Germany or New York, but there was a sense that we were in a place that was doing well. There was a sense of people gathering in a public place to enjoy the day. A few months later I would walk to dinner from a hilltop hotel in Sofia, Bulgaria, which overlooked the downtown area. The evening was hot and staying in was uncomfortable in a place that did not boast a lot of air conditioners. The result was that everybody was outside in parks and among the trees of the city. In western cities, at that time, city planners and architects were trying to figure out how to get people to use the cities' downtown spaces because, they feared that the city centers would be hollowed out by suburban sprawl and the advent of suburban malls. Here was the answer. Right here in communist Sofia. Dense living and large generous parks with large shade trees. I began to think of Bulgarians, Russians, Belarussians, Ukraines, Poles, Czechs, Latvians and East Germans as normal people reacting to different situations in normal ways.

If you wanted to have milk for the day and there was none in your refrigerator, you needed to get to the store early to get any because the dairy store didn't store milk from one day to the next in summer and therefore never bought more than they could sell in one morning. When a truck full of socks or brown shoes were offered on the side of the road, you stood online with your plastic "everyday bag" and bought what you could or what you were allowed to buy when it was your turn. Even if you didn't need any, or the shoes or socks didn't fit. You could always trade. There were always books and records of classical music to buy. Soap was soap, not usually branded and it was sold in a bar, folded neatly in a piece of brown paper. Everyone seemed to earn 200 per month. In the Soviet Union it was 200 Rubles. In Bulgaria, 200 Leva. In the Czech Republic it was 200 Crowns. In East Germany it was 200 Ostmark. People had their pubs and restaurants where they liked to go in their neighborhoods. They had their sport clubs. Some of them secretly went to church. Life was much more than a drab brown and gray existence, although the buildings were admittedly not colorful and the whole idea of a world full of color financed by advertising was strange to them. They did, however, desire the perfumes, brand name clothes, good cigarettes, printed catalogues and calendars, shoes, jeans and cars that we had in the west – but for many, having such "stuff" was a distant wish – sort of like winning the lottery for us in the west.

Distribution in a Globalized World

At the time we opened our European business, estimates were that there were over 2000 printed circuit board companies in North America and that Europe had over 1200 companies fabricating bare printed circuits of which some 400 were in Germany. North America was estimated to be producing about 30 % of the world's PCBs. Western Europe was estimated to be producing between 20 % to 25 % and Japan was estimated to be producing somewhere between 30 % and 35 % of the world's PCBs. The rest of the world's total of about 10 % to 20 % was spread out among Hong Kong, Korea, Taiwan, China, South Africa, Australia, Brazil and Eastern Europe. By contrast, today's totals are about 60 % in China, 10 % in Korea, 10 % in Taiwan, 10 % in Japan and the remaining 10 % spread out throughout the rest of the world, with the US and Europe together producing between 6 % and 7 %. The total sales of bare (before the components are placed on them) printed circuit boards in the world (today, in 2023), in US dollars is about $ 100 billion per year. I have already stated that the PCB industry was worth about $ 5 billion in the year I entered the industry as a 20 year old. In the years it took me to finish university and start to build multilayer registration machines in 1980, the industry had grown to about $ 7 billion per year with about 15 % of that total being multilayer printed boards (largely produced in OEM or captive factories.) The next important date on my PCB timeline was the year I moved to Germany and Multiline International Europa (mie) began doing business. The world market in 1987 was about $ 17 billion and the US lead in market share had been taken over by the Japanese industry. Europe's PCB industry was in strong growth mode which would last for the next three or four years. In 1987, the big growth sector in PCBs in the world was rigid multilayers. The important products that drove growth of PCBs in the world were personal computers, mini-computers, communications infrastructure (particularly related to data connectivity and ISDN and other digital communications infrastructure.)

Through the early months and years of my time in Germany, I spent most of my time with the distributors in each country. A typical week would have me flying to two different destinations (or countries) to visit between 4 and 7 customers in each destination over the course of two or three days each. Our most important markets were the UK, where we had a company called CEMCO as our distributor; Italy with an agent organization called Plastimpianti; Scandinavia, with an organization called Wikman and Malmkjell; France with an organization called Bionic; the Benelux (or lowlands of Belgium, the Netherlands and Luxembourg) and West Germany which was handled by a company called Romex. Surprisingly, there was a great deal of interest during this time from Warsaw Pact (East European communist) countries. In these countries, including the USSR, we decided not to name a single distributor because these inquiries generally came from western companies that built entire factories to a particular specification. Over the next four years, which is more-or-less the entire period of successful East European business for Multiline, we were included in about 15 different projects in Eastern Europe with companies largely from western Europe.

1. Germany, (the company Rode) for factories in Penza, Russia and Minsk, Belarus
2. Germany, (the company Fuba) for factories in East Berlin (Marzahn) and in Dresden

3. Switzerland, (the company AFIG) for factories in Silistra, Sofia, Pravetz, and Ruse, all in Bulgaria as well as for factories in Kiev and Kharkiv in the Ukraine
4. German/Russian (a separate company Roda/Petrocommerz) Leningrad
5. France (MUPI) for two projects in the Ukraine

During the first year in Europe, I knew very few customers directly. Nearly all my contacts in the industry came through the contacts generated by our representative and distributor network. The problem of being an expert in such a narrow field like "Multilayer Registration Systems" (as I was known to be) is that it is an extremely specialized area of know-how and most people imagine that one can understand it well without the need of higher education or any special intelligence. As a New Yorker would say, "It ain't rocket science!" I am the first to admit that it is probably not a difficult intellectual feat to be an expert in multilayer registration. However, over my initial tour of the European PCB industry the managers I met were happy to meet somebody like me who had, not only an understanding of the steel plates that made up the tooling plates that were used to laminate the innerlayers to one another, but also had an understanding of what happened to the innerlayers during their production and a natural curiosity and genuine interest to know what they did to solve their problems related to multilayer production. I became an expert, not through building a good solution to the problems of punching alignment holes into innerlayer panels or putting slots into the panels instead of holes. I became an expert because: 1) I learned how everyone did what they did; 2) learned what they saw as wrong; and 3) learned to ask what made them think they were wrong. Oftentimes, I would propose a series of tests or experiments to confirm their biases about what they did wrong or, on the other hand, to show the improved efficacy of our approach to the manufacture of multilayers as compared to their own approach.

I finally was able to convince two of my customers to take part in a controlled scientific "double-blind" experiment which would prove the superiority of post etch punching with our Optiline PE when compared to registration results of innerlayers that were produced by the method of separately punching artworks (in the Optiline Artwork Punch) and innerlayers prior to exposure (in the Acculine Laminate Punch). I asked one of my customers, City Print, in Helmond, the Netherlands who had a new Optiline and Acculine to make me 50 double sided panels using a special pair of artworks in his normal way of producing in one of the two drawers of his double drawer exposure machine. These artworks contained the targets that the Optiline PE normally needed to align the panels, but in this case, the targets would only act as an indicator of the position of the image on the innerlayer with respect to the pinning locations. The other drawer contained exact copies of the artworks that were mounted in the first drawer. The only difference was, that although these artworks had been punched in the Optiline Artwork Punch, the panels would not be pinned for exposure. Rather, the panels in this second drawer were imaged by simply laying the panels between the artworks and there would be no holes in these panels as indicators of the position of the images on the innerlayers until they were punched in an Optiline PE. All the panels that were to be exposed in drawer one were punched on the Acculine Laminate Punch. The panels to be exposed in the lower or second drawer remained unpunched. So, at City Print, one panel was pinned and exposed in the first drawer, then a second panel was laid between two artworks and exposed in the second drawer. The same procedure followed for the 3rd and 4th panels and on and on until 50 sets of panels, or a total of 100 panels, had been exposed. All the panels that were printed in the first drawer were labelled CP-1 through CP-50 now contained targets and punched holes. All the panels that did not yet have holes punched into them and had been exposed in the second drawer were labelled MG-1 through MG-50. All the panels were then transported by car to Moeller-Grah, a company who had purchased our Optiline PE punch, about 1 ½ hours drive from Helmond. There, we punched the 50 panels labelled MG. After post etch punching of these 50 MG designated panels, all the panels looked exactly the same except for the designations written on the panels. We then taped over the markings that identified the panels, shuffled them well and completely randomized the position of CP and MG designated panels in the stack. We then drove the panels an additional 2 ½ hours to Wetter in Germany to a company that wished to improve their registration but wanted to have some proof of concept for the purchase of the Optiline PE. The company was Schoeller Electronic and the man with whom I was making these tests was Dr. Konrad Wundt. Dr. Wundt had access to a measuring machine that happened to be outfitted with a Multiline Technology Video Probe (a spinoff product of our development of the Optiline Artwork Punch design which was sold to manufacturers of coordinate measuring machines (CMMs)). We placed a tooling plate of the kind that is used in the pressing of the multilayer innerlayers to one another in the lamination cycle onto the surface of the CMM and placed four pins into the tooling plate to mimic the four-pin positioning of the innerlayers in the press. We placed the first panel onto the pins and moved the camera to the left target of the two targets that were etched onto all 100 panels, centered the video probe over the first target and simply called that position X=0; Y=0. We labelled that panel number 1. We removed panel number one and pinned the next panel and moved our video probe until it was centered, we noted the relative position of X and Y as it related to the first panel and recorded that relative position, labelled the panel number 2, then onto the next panel and the next until we had recorded the pinned position of every left target relative to the first left target and numbered all the panels through to 100. We repeated the process of measuring the right target positions for all 100 panels relative to the pinned position of panel number 1's right target. We then removed the tape that had hidden our CPs and MGs and collated the results accordingly. We did a statistical analysis of the 50 panels labelled CP and a separate analysis of the MG panels. The result was that the measurements of all the panels punched on the Optiline PE at Moeller-Grah had a 1 sigma standard deviation of 19.7 micron (including all uncertainty of the measurements) among all the targets on all the panels, whereas the standard deviation of the measurement of the targets on the panels processed at City Print was 52 micron (including all uncertainty of the measurements). The theoretical analysis of David Powell which he had published four years earlier was borne out and proven to be true by this test.

I turned the test into a paper that I would give as a technical presentation to both English and German speaking technical associations. It was a convincing result that caused Schoeller to place an order for the Optiline PE. Dr. Konrad Wundt would become a believer in Multiline's technology and several years later he would join our team and become the General Manager of Multiline Europe; essentially my right-hand man, until his retirement about six or seven years ago.

Most of the people that I was meeting at this time were very successful at making money fabricating PCBs. It seemed that every German owner of a small captive PCB shop, no matter how few employees he had working at his factory, had at least a normal 7-series BMW or an S class Mercedes (and most often an S-500 or bigger). A couple of my customers tooled around Europe in street versions of actual racing cars (Mr. Pagnani and Fritz Greule come to mind). My arrival in Europe coincided with the golden age of PCB manufacture in Europe (and driving fast on the autobahn). Because of the market situation throughout the world – with the healthy growth of industrial, automotive, computer and communications electronics in Europe; consumer, industrial, computer and communications electronics in Japan; and military, computer and communications electronics in North America – everyone seemed to have factories that were full and capabilities lagging behind their customers' demands.

Despite customers ordering everything independent suppliers could make, the customers were promising more orders for higher prices if the producers could fill their demands for denser circuits. There are three ways to make denser circuits. One way is density through higher resolution – make the lines and spaces of the circuits finer. The second way, density through better registration, is to increase layer counts. Of course, the third way is some combination of improving the first and second methods simultaneously. In the end, the customers of our customers, those who were designing denser circuits, were the ones who decided how they should be made.

My first trips through the PCB landscapes of Europe took me to:

- Spain: Barcelona and Madrid
- Italy: Milan and Turin
- England: Petersfield, Birmingham, Croydon, Kidsgrove
- Scotland: Ayr, Galashiels
- The Netherlands: Echt, Helmond, Eindhoven
- Belgium: Brussels, Gent
- France: Evreaux, Coutances, Nantes, Metz, Nice, Brest
- Germany: Solingen, Karlsruhe, Pforzheim, Grassau, Augsburg, Geldern, Berlin, Cologne, Erkelenz
- Sweden: Timrå, Stockholm, Kumla, Norrkoping, Oskarsham
- Denmark: Aalborg, Arhus, Billund, Copenhagen
- Yugoslavia: Belgrade
- Bulgaria: Sofia, Ruse, Pravetz
- USSR: Moscow, Leningrad, Minsk, Kiev
- Israel; Migdal HaEmek, Tel Aviv

I was usually in the company of a representative (rep) or an employee of our distributor at each meeting. As I saw it, my job at each of these visits was to put words in my representatives' (sales reps' or reps') mouths and plant ideas in their heads to make them proxy experts on our systems so they could do customer visits on their own and awaken interest in our systems. I never expected them to make our sales for us. I did expect that I would need to be there for the final sales so that each customer was buying the equipment package which was absolutely right for their needs. Although we tried to make and sell standardized equipment, we learned that the customers were hardly ever comfortable taking a standard solution devoid of personalization. They generally wanted to put things in and take things out according to their "special" cases. We grew accustomed to this but there were salesmen among our sales reps who could indeed sell customers their versions of our standard solutions without the process of adding or trimming at the end. I learned quickly that there are many kinds of sales reps and many ways to be successful as a sales rep. Every person who relies on customer contacts to make their living has their own style and survival strategy or path to success. Unfortunately, not all needed success; for some, survival was enough. Others are driven to be successful and to be seen as successful and sought recognition for their success. The Germans have a word, Ehrgeiz, that perfectly embodies this attribute – *Ehr...* means honor; *geiz* means lust or hunger. The conventional translation is ambition, but I find that ambition doesn't capture the idea as well as *Ehrgeiz*. Sometimes the sales rep wanted to show himself every bit as an expert and a great salesman as me! That was hard to accept at first, because sometimes we disagreed on the approach. If I needed my rep to communicate with the customer because I couldn't speak the customer's language, as long as he was successful in bringing about the sale, I was "all in" on him being better than I. He was not only as good as me as a salesman in my own language, he could speak the customer's language! The various markets were generally designated as national markets, largely based on language, but also because of the advantages of understanding local culture and business practices.

As an example of the effect of local culture on business practices, I'll compare pricing strategies in two different markets like Germany and Italy. We gave our reps and distributors in Italy some leeway to quote higher prices to the Italian customers. There were two reasons for this. The first is that the payment conditions could be very different for an Italian customer compared to the German customer. An Italian customer would often open negotiations with a desire to pay for the machine in one lump sum 180 days after delivery of the machine. The German customer would open up negotiations with a demand to pay for the entire machine 30 days after delivery and final acceptance. We would always open negotiations (everywhere) for a ½ payment of the total equipment amount with the order (with no work beginning until the payment was received by us) and the rest paid upon shipment from our factory. We never accepted what the customer requested first (unless they offered 100% payment with the order – which no one ever did) and the customer very seldom agreed to our wishes as first proposed. In the end, in almost 90% of the negotiations for machines over $100,000 we settled on a payment term which split our positions more-or-less halfway and shared the risks of doing business. The result was usually ⅓ down with the order; ⅓ with delivery; and ⅓ with final acceptance (often with an agreed-to delay time of 15 to 30 days). The customers who were easiest to negotiate on payment terms grounds were the eastern European customers. They were most often working with government money and payment was often tied up with documentary payments or letters of credit which were converted to cash upon fulfillment of delivery, or the signing of technical approvals which were to take place at our factory and not at the customers' factory. It appeared as if communists were used to the mistrust of their western suppliers and went out of their way to offer strong payment guarantees for equipment they deemed necessary to improve electronic production capabilities.

The second reason for a higher beginning price in Italy than in Germany, is the local demand for a "suitable" discount. In Germany a suitable discount was, in the 1980s somewhere around

3 %. I gave 1 ½ %. Such discounts did not make me a beloved figure among the purchasing managers at the captive shops in Germany (Siemens, Nixdorf, Bosch, Blaupunkt or AEG). With 20-20 hind-sight, I understand that I could've used a trimmed down version of the "Italian pricing model" to solve this problem of "managing expectations". If I ever get my life to do over again, this is something I might have to remind myself to change. I drove a hard bargain, not because I had learned to manage the customers' pricing expectations through "cost signalling" as I had learned while selling pots and pans to those unsuspecting single working girls in my youth. I drove a hard bargain because I knew I could. I was a monopolist and knew that the customer had little choice but to pay the price I demanded. At owner run PCB facilities, the owner understood this. At captive shop purchasing offices, because the companies were often big and famous, many purchasing managers expected the seller to be proud of selling to such a great company and should be willing to take $10,000 less for the honor of selling to a company the likes of Bell or IBM or Honeywell or Siemens. I didn't understand this; particularly when one could sense the amounts of money that such companies spent for their buildings and conference room furniture! The Italian customers, including the owner/managers were insulted and showed, what looked like physical pathological effects of being offered a discount less than 10 % to open a negotiation. It was a game with different rules in the two markets. Expectations drove strategy. This means that Italians expected the price to be "padded" with more ability to discount than Germans did. I tended to think that the German way was more "honest" but now in my time of age, I ask myself what "honest" in price setting even means! There was a tendency among the technical people I engaged with to believe that the price of a product should reflect the cost of making it. This means that a customer tends to think of a price being fair, when he can understand that the price reflects costs plus some amount of profit. Of course, this is not what is generally taught in business schools. From what I understand of price setting as taught in business

schools (not having attended any business schools at all in my lifetime, except for a few seminars I attended during the summers of selling Wonderware) is that the price should reflect the perceived value of the product to the customer. In all the years of selling technical products to the PCB industry, there was constant tension between the high prices manufacturers sought and the lower prices potential customers wanted to pay. The sales process for various competitive products in any negotiation hinges on value perception combined with the customer's ability to pay. A product with lower perceived value can indeed be sold if the price is right. Higher prices could be achieved if the perception of the value of the product could be convincingly shown. Some customers used return on investment (ROI) calculations to rank the various choices for investments they needed to make.

In the early stages of our time in Germany, Multiline sold two Optiline PEs (the machine developed with the help of Dupont). The largest independent (non-captive "job" shop) PCB fabricator in Europe in 1987 was a company in Ayr, Scotland (near Glasgow) called Prestwick Circuits. The machine was delivered to them at the end of November 1986 and was one of the first strategic sales of the Optiline PE. We made a "special offer" to Prestwick knowing that if they had the machine, others in Europe would follow. The second order was sold off the floor at the annual NEPCON trade fair in February of 1987 to a company called PCB Technologies from Migdal HaEmek in Israel. The owner-manager of PCB was Rafi Amit. He would go on to found the company Camtek a couple of years later. When Rafi saw the Optiline PE on our stand at the show, he knew he wanted it and just ordered it on the spot. The machine simply fascinated people who saw it for the first time. A panel placed into the machine would be clamped onto a moving table and automatically manipulated into position and punched after an optimal alignment was achieved via two targets seen through two miniature CCD closed circuit TV cameras. The progress of the target positions on the manipulated panels could be seen on two video screens containing two crosshairs with a shaded box which would perfectly frame the round targets when alignment was achieved. At the instant that the two targets were perfectly framed, the punch activated causing a whining sound of hydraulic power being applied to the punch press and the blurring of the targets in the field of view of the cameras which were now descending toward the panel until a satisfying thud was heard as the alignment holes (which would align innerlayer to innerlayer in the multilayer press cycle) were pierced into the panels. The press would then reverse itself, until the targets were again back into focus in their perfectly aligned positions, and the panel was released to be removed from the machine. The panels that went in with only an etched image and without holes, came out with holes punched in a relationship to the image to a tolerance of less than 1 mil or 25 microns of accuracy. In addition, each panel was punched with a repeatability of image-to-image (at the center of any panel) on any two compared panels of less than 12 microns. The Optiline PE was not only revolutionary, it was amazing to watch. Rafi would be the first customer to have such a reaction to our machine. Others followed. For several years, until the machine became ubiquitous, people seeing the machine for the first time would often simply fall in love with it.

Through this first go-around of all the local reps we had and the potential customers that the reps wanted me to meet, I began to get my footing as a sales manager, direct salesman, product manager and marketing manager. I began to value my time in front of customers over everything else and I began to put demands on my sales reps to put me in front of their customers. The first several months were spent by my getting to know the sales organization that had largely been built by Mike. The communications channels between the sales reps and the factory which had run through Mike and the inhouse sales organization at the front office in Farmingdale was rerouted through Susi and me. Some sales rep organizations saw this as a demotion because they didn't know me or Susi but did know that the company, Multiline, belonged to Mike. Some people in the front office didn't see me as a legitimate stand-in for Mike either and we often experienced slow responses to inquiries or requests for decisions which would somehow get lost on somebody's desk and never reach the point of being answered or responded to.

The solution to the first problem of legitimacy to the sales reps would and could only be addressed by them liking and respecting us. We needed to show them that they hadn't lost their contact to Mike and the factory but rather had gained an ally in getting from Mike and the factory whatever it was they needed to be successful in selling our products. That would take time and success with specific projects at specific customers. The second problem of us establishing legitimacy at our own factory would never really get solved. Within the middle management of Multiline Technology, I would never win the hearts of everybody to the point that they all trusted that our (or my) motives aligned with theirs. In the late 1980s, Multiline Technology in the US was a company of about 100 people. At its peak in the late 1990s and early 2000s, Multiline would grow to be a company of 180 people. All during that time the management team would be the same. There was Mike and his brother, Dave; Don, the general manager; an engineering manager (that took over my engineering duties at the factory); a sales manager for domestic sales and sales manager for Asian sales; people responsible for inside sales and people responsible for service. It was a well-organized company that built a great one-product reputation and lived well off of that for almost 30 years. What was missing was a PCB person that cared about PCB fabricators' problems. The dynamic of Mike and me sitting in the conference room with Phil Hinton, or Don Newell or Bob Heiart, or Dave Powell was gone. I was in Europe. Perhaps it was happening in Farmingdale, and I just wasn't there to see it, but it didn't seem like they were particularly happy to respond to customer requests if the requests were originating in Europe. What Don and the managers aligned with him wanted me to do was send them orders for what they liked to build. The last thing that they wanted to do was to deal with lists of what they considered special requests for all sorts of stuff that needed special attention. The problem was and continues to be that there are not enough companies in the world to continue to buy the same design of post etch punches we offered then. These punches were "tooling". They were not an "end" product. They were a "means" product. As such, they always needed to be discussed to the customers' satisfaction before any decisions were made.

We needed to institute a "work-around" to get our requests to the top of everybody's inboxes until every single one of the requests were answered or required decisions made. What we came up with was a daily fax that started with the new requests of the day entitled "new business" (each dated with its original entry on the list) and continued to a section that was entitled "old business" (each entry still dated with its original debut date). Nothing was taken off the list until a satisfactory answer was received. If something was answered but didn't satisfy the customer, the request for a change of position became a new request and the old request list was updated to delete the original request. I wish I could say that this New/Old Business list solved our problem, but the only problem it really solved was that nobody at the factory could claim that we hadn't asked before whenever we needed to call on the telephone to follow-up (usually at the behest of one of our sales reps or by the customer himself). Each day, new requests and old reminders were placed in the top of every To: and CC: person's inbox! The only thing this did was to increase the stress on those in the middle of the information chain whose job it was to nag until an answer was given. The actual managers that needed to decide on an answer felt fine with letting things slide until a telephone call could, perhaps, untie the information knot.

The first order we received as a result of having the European office came after four or five months of moving to Germany. There had been the order to PCB and Rafi Amit in Israel, but that was as a result of a visit by Rafi to California and the Nepcon fair. Somebody came to our office in the spring of 1987 and rang the doorbell. We buzzed him up to our office where Susi and I had desks facing across from each other of what would normally be the living room of a one-bedroom apartment. The bedroom held some spare parts for our already existing customers: Mommers Print Service, Prestwick, PCB, Sagem (in Lannion, France), Alcatel (in Coutance, France), CSP (in Italy), Microser (in Madrid) and Melchert (in Cologne). The sad truth is, that up to that day when that man, who's name I cannot recall – he was German – we can call him "Helmut Mueller", rang our doorbell, I could not take credit for a single order. Hr. Mueller had my latest business card that he must have collected at the NEPCON 1987 show or received from someone who had been there. He had a list of equipment that he wanted to buy that included our Acculine, Optiline film punch, Pre-Preg punch and some tooling plates. He told me that the equipment was for a factory that was being delivered to a project in Eastern Europe and that he was not at liberty to tell us where. He asked how much it would cost. I suggested $90,000. He said fine. I thought, "I should have asked for more!" He asked about when it could be delivered. I told him four to five months. He asked to which port it would be delivered. I told him we always suggested air freight because the bare metal surfaces of the tooling could rust on a three-week sea journey; therefore, JFK airport in NYC. He said fine. He asked if he could guarantee the order with a down payment of $15,000 made out to Multiline Technology. I said fine, but what about the rest? He assured me that he would open a letter of credit, payable upon presentation of the goods and an invoice at JFK airport, for the remaining $75,000 and have it confirmed on our bank over the course of the next week. My head was swimming a little bit, but I said, "Fine!" We shook hands and I invited him to lunch. He said, "No, thanks. I need to buy some drilling machines in Oberursel." (A company called Klingelnberg made PCB drilling machines in the next town over from Bad Homburg.) Just as quickly as he came, he was gone. Multiline Technology's European office had its first sale and I was elated, but to be honest, I can't remember ever having done anything to have earned it.

This would lead to the first of the many conversations that I had with the factory in Farmingdale when making a celebratory telephone call to share the good news of an order. Even at that first phone call, a pattern would emerge that would repeat itself for three and a half decades. First the joyous announcement of the sale and what the customer agreed to buy. Then:

(M)ike: How much did the customer agree to pay?
Me (P): $ 90,000.
M: Super! When do we need to deliver?
P: Five months at the longest.
M: Couldn't you get more time – we're kinda full at the moment.
P: Well, that's what I thought deliveries are running these days and you put four months delivery on the offer. Let me know how much extra time we need before I write our order confirmation.
M: No, no, that's good – so what are the payment conditions?
P: The guy wrote a check for $ 15,000 and has promised a letter of credit payable at delivery of the goods to JFK!
M: Wow! Couldn't you get $ 30,000 or $ 45,000?
P: I didn't think to ask for more because I figured it was standard equipment and we had most of the parts and assets required in stock or in the pipeline already. Should I go back and tell him the factory isn't accepting the order with such a low down-payment?
M: No, no, that's good. I think we can do it. Well that's great Paul! Thanks for the good news!

It was always joy of success seasoned with an essence of why hadn't we done better!

Now that the ice was broken with an order to my name (albeit, a bit undeserved), my confidence had a boost and I continued meeting potential customers all over Europe. Besides doing the repairs and trying to make follow-up sales on those customers we already had, I visited a long list of companies for the first time: Exacta, MEPD and Bepi in Scotland; Irlandus in Northern Ireland; Tek Sparrat in South Africa; Circa-Print, Philips, British Aerospace and ICL in England; Mannesmann, Heidenhain, Andus, Nixdorf, Ruwel, Fuba, Rode, Schoeller, Wuerth, Brockstedt and Exaprint in West Germany; Bell Alcatel and Barco in Belgium; City Print and Philips in the Netherlands; LTIS, Cimulec, Philips RTC and Nicolitch in France; Haeussermann, and Eumig in Austria, Ericsson in Sweden, Bruel & Kjaer in Denmark; PPE, Contraves and PPC in Switzerland; Olivetti, FCM, Corona, CST, CFM and Bristol in Italy. All these businesses were relatively new to the manufacture of multilayers but had enough experience to know that aligning images to drilled features and aligning images on various layers to the other images on other layers and aligning solder mask to the circuit image on the outerlayers of circuit boards were problems that needed solving.

Multiline Technology had had a representative for the Eastern bloc and for the countries of Austria and Switzerland called Fela. Fela was originally a printed circuit board fabricator that branched out into the turnkey PCB factory business to capitalize on the thirst for electronic know-how and production capability in the Eastern bloc during the 1980s. As a result of their turnkey factory business, they became acutely aware of the need for PCB registration equipment and sought Multiline out to supply the necessary machines for the turnkey factories they were building in places like the Soviet Union, Bulgaria, the Czech Republic and Hungary. It was a smart move on the part of Mike and the Uhlmann brothers, the owners of Fela, to seek each other out and do business together. At that time (1981) Mike had a couple of reps in Europe, in particular, in Italy, Israel, the UK, and one rep, Romex, that covered the lowlands or BeNeLux and West Germany but no real PCB people like Fela who saw Multiline and its equipment within the context of the void that our equipment and the accompanying know-how filled in PCB fabrication. Somewhere, over the course of the early 1980s because of the very high interest rates instituted by the Fed during the Reagan administration to dampen inflation, the US dollar became very strong in Europe. One US Dollar peaked to a value of 2.80 Swiss Francs in 1985 compared to the approximately 1.80 Swiss Francs that $ 1.00 had been worth in 1981 when the Fela/Multiline agreements had been signed. There are several things that happen when such a currency disruption occurs. Most of the time, the products manufactured in the strong currency country loses market share. Inasmuch as Multiline's market position was a monopoly, Fela would have had to absorb a 30 % increase in cost or pass the increase onto its customers. A third option presented itself to Fela because the Multiline Technology system of registration which involved the Acculine laminate punch and the Optiline film punch were not protected by any intellectual property rights or patents. All that was known to them in 1985 was that the Acculine/Optiline system of registration was the state-of-the-art in multilayer registration and their customers wanted to buy what that system could do. (The first post etch punches were still tied up in testing with the initial "I-System" test installations at Hewlett Packard and Microfab.) The Uhlmann brothers decided to copy the Acculine and Optiline and sell them as Fela machines in Europe. This was an added incentive for Mike to approve the project of our European office. We successfully defended ourselves from any real incursion of Fela competitive machines into the European market after we established our presence there.

Through that first go around to existing and potential customers in Europe, it became clear to me how important the German PCB industry was in Europe. At that time in the late 1980s, the dominance of German speaking PCB producers was not as pronounced as it is today. Then, the German speaking market probably accounted for about 30 % of the market (with much of that coming from West Germany – with very little contribution from the Swiss and Austrian markets) with the UK market coming in a close second and the French and Italian markets following. Today, the German speaking markets are over 50 % of the European PCB manufacturing market with the Swiss and Austrians contributing a significant minority portion. Our sales rep for West Germany was in the Netherlands and only through our being present in Germany did we begin to understand that we were not being represented well in the parts of Germany that were not near the Dutch border. I was receiving signs of interest from German PCB fabricators that were simply not on our "radar". Companies like Brockstedt in Kiel, Wuerth near Kuenzelsau, Schoeller near Marburg and Fuba near Hildesheim made themselves known to us or were dug up through my market research but were not suggested for visits by my designated sales rep. We decided to alter our agreement to limit the territory of Romex to a geographical territory in the lowlands of the BeNeLux plus a list of PCB fabricators in Germany known to Romex and regularly visited by them.

Orders began coming in during the summer of 1987. Orders came for either Acculine/Optiline systems or systems containing our Optiline PE post etch punch at a rate of about one order every two months and began to accelerate to an order per month in mid 1988. Notable initial European orders came from Nixdorf, a German manufacturer of minicomputers, mostly for large enterprise word processing and data processing (like Prime or Wang in New England); Mommers Print Service, an already existing Acculine/Optiline customer of ours who placed an order for an Optiline PE; City Print, a Dutch company near the German border purchased an Acculine/Optiline system, Moeller Grah, one of Romex's West German companies that purchased an Optiline PE punch; A Russian company called Technoprom purchased an Optiline PE; a Bulgarian company in Ruse purchased an Optiline PE.

We added a woman, Petra, who took over bookkeeping duties as well as helping Susi with her clerical duties. Susi became the constant in the office for all our communications to the sales reps, customers, the factory and whatever suppliers and service providers we had to deal with. As the equipment we sold began to arrive and we were getting somewhat regular visits from Farmingdale for installations, we decided to add a service engineer who would help relieve our dependence on the factory. At the time, many customers demanded service people on site within 24 hours of a production disruption caused by failure of a machine. Today, we can often troubleshoot machine problems through on-line analysis because most sophisticated machines are connected to the internet and have built-in remote diagnostic capabilities. Then, it was always necessary to troubleshoot in person. Up until we had a trained engineer we could send, I had to disrupt my schedule to be the service engineer whenever a customer had a production disruption caused by a defect in one of our machines.

It takes a deep dive into memory to remember that office life. How I communicated with the world when I traveled, was very different in the late 1980s than it is today. Today, 90 % of everything comes in on E-mail, WhatsApp, Skype or the telephone and I either deal directly or forward it on to others in the office. In those days, when I was in the office, I worked from my Inbox to my Outbox and Susi was at both ends of that process. Whatever came into the office (either by post, fax, telex or telephone messages) that needed my attention, was copied and then filed away. The copy went into my inbox. I handwrote my response or my instructions onto the copy and put the resulting marked up document in the outbox. Susi, and later whoever Susi distributed the instructions to, did the typing, faxing, sending by post or courier, telephoning, or telexing. I've already described my "old business/new business" way of communicating on faxes to and from Multiline. Eventually we did the same with all our representatives, sales reps, sales people and other suppliers. In that way, my inbox was indeed a good indicator of activity, bottlenecks and progress. When I traveled, my inbox was delivered to me in the form of my daily fax which was delivered to my hotel awaiting my arrival. On an active day the fax could be 30 or 40 pages long although not every page required a response from me. Before going to find a pub or restaurant or take a walk through the town or city I'd arrived in, I would write my instructions or responses on each page of fax and send them either to Susi or directly to the person making the inquiry if the response was being desperately sought. Once that was done, I went to enjoy my evening. Sometimes I needed to make a telephone call from underway. This was another area of communications complexity that required more thought in those days than today. Today we all have our cellular phones (or handies) with us constantly and we are totally flexible in getting to speak to people when we must. In the late 1980s it was sometimes complicated to speak to somebody when one was traveling. I had a so-called "C-Netz" (C net – analog signal) cellular telephone in my car. This is what preceded the digital or "D-Netz" cellular telephone that would be introduced to car telephones in about 1991. The service for this telephone was extremely expensive and I can recall spending thousands of Dmarks per month for the cellular phone service bills in the late 1980s. On the other hand, I drove over 60,000 kilometers per year and spent 750 hours or nearly 100 equivalent working days in my car in those years. The car phone in a moving car was OK for talking to the office or to other people that one knew well, but it was not good for having important business conversations because the phone call would invariably be disrupted in rural areas or when switching off from one cell to the next as one drove out of range of one antenna without being picked up cleanly by the next antenna. Of course there were always coin operated telephones. For those

275

important calls, I would need to stop or, mostly, keep driving until I could stop at a highway rest stop. Because so many of the calls I needed to make were expensive international calls and credit-card-accepting-pay phones were still not a thing, I often sought out telephones with call-unit-counters available at rest-stops or restaurants. There, one could ask at the cashier for a phone "cell" and the cashier would point to one of a couple or several phone booths where one could call anywhere in the world. Little audible clicks would be counted during the calls. The faster the clicks came the more expensive the call was. One would pay the cashier for the number of units or clicks. A similar system was in use at hotels throughout the world, which was a cheaper alternative than using the telephone in the room. Post offices also had such telephone cells. I often had to resort to this form of accessing telephone conversations in the Eastern Bloc. Calls made to the west could also be booked at the reception desk of a Soviet hotel, but this meant having to be physically present either in the hotel room, if the call was booked from there, or in the lobby, to wait out the up to an hour wait for the call to be made.

One day in the fall of 1987 we received a request for a visit from a small PCB fabricator in the region of Pforzheim, called Greule Gedruckte Schaltungen (the German translation of Gedruckte Schaltungen is literally Printed Circuits). The man requesting the visit was Joerg Greule, the son of the owner (Fritz). Susi said to me on the morning of the visit, "You have an appointment with a company called Greule at 11:00. You'd better leave soon!" I looked at my watch and said, "In a half an hour is good enough – it's only about a 90-minutes drive." This is what I did constantly in those days – underestimating or "optimistically" estimating the time it took to drive any place. The German Autobahn is not a single highway. It is a network of highways resembling our American interstates. One of my pleasures of moving to Germany was the possibility to drive like a crazy man, only legally. If the road was clear enough of traffic, I would drive, pedal-to-the-metal at 250 kmh or 155 mph whenever I could. But that is a big "if". Greule was 180 kilometers from our office by the shortest route. This means that, depending on traffic, the distance could be covered in less than an hour or in more than 2 ½ hours. That day was a good day. I left at about 9:15 and was back in the office at about 12:30. Susi was aghast when I returned and asked, "What happened? Didn't you find them?" My response was that there was no real problem. I had gotten there just in time.

Mr. Greule, seeing my face, introduced himself in halting English. I returned his volley in German, introducing myself and stating my pleasure to be able to visit him and telling him how lucky I had been that the Autobahn had been so empty. He beamed, obviously happy not to have had to struggle in English to tell me what he wanted to say. There are fast speakers and slow speakers (and those of us in between) in any language. Joerg Greule was (or is) a fast speaker. In the US, from the late 1970s to the early 1980s, there had been a Fed Ex ad on TV that had the tag-line, "Fed Ex – When it Absolutely, Positively has to be there overnight". The ad featured what seemed like an English-speaking version of Mr. Greule speaking from his desk, into a telephone (as I recall), at a rate impossible for the average person to duplicate. It was all, however, understandable for anyone who could understand the English language. It was just one minute of text spoken in 15 seconds in an energetic staccato. Much of what Mr. Greule said to me was, however, not understandable to me. He spoke in a local dialect. The people of Stuttgart speak Schwaebisch or Schwabian. The people of Karlsruhe speak Badisch. The people in Pforzheim are about halfway between the two and speak a dialect that, to the untrained ear, at least to my ear at that time, sounded like German heard underwater, and in Mr. Greule's case, the words came much faster than I could decipher. In Mr. Greule's defense, I think it had much more to do with me than with him. In later years, I would understand everything said by people in and around Pforzheim, even Mr. Greule. He took me for a walk around his factory and I think he told me that he was going to be expanding. He said something about exposure and Accutrace (we were making parts of that system at Multiline for WR Grace). He also mentioned something about making multilayer PCBs. So, to make a short story even shorter, I pretended to take a few notes, gave him my business card and a few pieces of technical literature, promised to get back to him with more information and left after about 10 minutes. Susi, hearing this, asked me what I was going to do. I told her I didn't know, but I would go and get some lunch and think about it.

In those days, if I was in the office, I liked to take the *International Herald Tribune* newspaper that was delivered to my house each morning under my arm and walk the 300 or 400 meters it took to go to a local café called Koflers for lunch. It was quite a change from eating a sandwich at my desk in Farmingdale while thumbing through "Machine Design" or "PC Fab". (One time, one of my friendly colleagues placed a magazine called "Abrasive Engineering" under my sandwich as suggested reading material for that day – I must have rubbed him the wrong way that day – or with the wrong stuff!). Taking an hour out of my day to enjoy a nice meal with my newspaper and a glass of wine, perhaps even having a piece of cake and a cup of coffee for dessert was a piece of heaven. I enjoyed it and tried to treat myself to that hour whenever I was in the office. After lunch on that day of Mr. Greule's visit I came back to the office and worked on a fax that Susi helped me compose with some German descriptions of our equipment for multilayer production and asked him for another meeting after he had had a chance to review the information that I had sent to him. I included our list of customers in Europe up to that point and Susi sent it off. A few days later, he would call and make another meeting date. But this time, I was prepared. First of all, I had props. The material I sent to him would serve as a basis for our further discussions. Now, with the discussion field limited to the props we were working with, it became easier to narrow down the field of possible ideas or questions being put forth. Narrowing the field of discussion has become a mantra for me ever since. The finer tuned the discussion, the more precise the understanding, is my view on difficult discussions of any kind. I am very proud of the final piece of my tactical engagement regarding the problem of understanding and communicating with Mr. Greule. Whatever he said that I didn't perfectly understand, I simply repeated in German words of my vocabulary with the preface "Sie meinen ..." (You mean ...). Now, he was getting a feed-back of how bad my German was or how well I was understanding him. Which one, depended on what I understood him to say and whether or not it had anything to do with what he had actually said. The result was a slower speaking Mr. Greule who spoke the normal "high" German he had learned to speak, (as all educated Germans do) but didn't need to speak on a daily basis in his own factory. That meeting took considerably longer than the first. Greule Gedruckte Schaltungen became a customer for our Optiline PE as well as a customer for Accutrace, the liquid resist system from WR Grace. It was also the first sale that I made without the presence or involvement of a sales representative or distributor (not counting the "Helmut Mueller" out-of-the-blue sale). Through the meetings at Greule, I met another WR Grace employee called Horst Luther. He became a bit of my "salesman Uncle". For a few years we often travelled together to customers who were contemplating purchases of the Accutrace system. Through Horst I learned to eat the local foods of each region we visited together. Until I travelled with Horst, I didn't think to eat "Maultaschen" in Pforzheim or drink "Alt" beer in Düsseldorf. We had five Accutrace customers in Europe as I recall. There were Alcatel, Coutance; Greule and Bonnert-und-Vetter, both in Pforzheim; Somacis in Ancona, Italy: and Isola in Düren. We worked together on potential orders for Accutrace Systems at the three large German independent PCB shops: Schweizer, Fuba, and Ruwel. They all came to decisions not to buy at the same productronica in 1989. Poor Horst was so looking forward to book at least two of those companies to crown the end of his career. I never felt more badly to witness anybody's disappointment and there really was nothing he could do but be totally deflated. He retired a year or two later and spent his retirement cycling as often as he could in the area near San Diego. I think to recall he had told me that he had emigrated to the US as a young man and became a citizen by enrolling into the US Army. He had, however, returned to Germany and raised his family there. At the end of his life, he chose to be in his adopted country.

The largest independent fabricator of PCBs in Germany was a company called Fuba in a place called – according to the sign upon entering the village – '"Flecken" Gittelde' near Hildesheim, which is, in turn, near Hannover. A "Flecken" is as if a place called itself a "speck" in English. Fuba had a long history of cooperation with Photocircuits and had licensed several technologies for electronic circuits and their manufacture from Photocircuits and Kollmorgen. Fuba was also in the business of technology transfer to eastern Europe (like Fela and AFIG). What they learned from the Americans, they did themselves, then sold it to the eastern Europeans. I built up a relationship among some people at Fuba and was trying to get them interested in our Multilayer registration equipment for their factory in Gittelde and thought that I was making good headway until we exhibited for the first time in the fall of 1987 with our own stand. Fuba had a stand as well because they were interested in finding people who were looking to buy PCB manufacturing capability. Normally, Fuba, as a PCB fabricator, would have been a visitor to the show for the people who had stands at productronica. The PCB fabricators, the electronic components people and the other people who were selling to the electronic OEMs (original equipment manufacturers) had their own exposition called electronica. productronica happens in odd years and electronica happens in even years in the same week in November in Munich. The first productronica was held in 1975 with 2900 square meters of exhibition space and 5000 visitors. At its peak in 1997, productronica would cover over

90,000 sq. meters of exhibition space and attract nearly 70,000 visitors. The last productronica to occur at this writing was in 2023 and attracted 42,000 visitors. The area attributed to PCB production machines and materials is about a third to a quarter what it used to be in the 1990s. In 1987, productronica was on the rise and the technology to make PCBs was expanding to meet demands of finer lines and spaces, more and smaller holes, more layers, better signal integrity (which meant more exotic materials) and the attendant better registration all of that requires. We found ourselves in a sweet spot of our potential customers' technical desire. Our initial participation at the productronica fair brought home the fact that our timing had been impeccable. What we were selling, people wanted to buy! Fuba also knew that we were in a good position. What we learned, and what totally shocked me, while at the productronica in 1987, was that Fuba had worked together with the people at a University in Berlin and an independent equipment manufacturer called Becker, to produce a copy of our Optiline artwork punch. Despite my having visited them and worked with their factory people to introduce them to our technology with the goal of gaining them as a customer (they had not asked us for a quotation to supply them a machine), but had rather, like Fela, before them, made a copy of our technology. I was livid. The people with whom I had been in discussions came by our stand and I wouldn't let them on. I wouldn't talk to them and walked away if they tried to talk further. I totally blocked them out of my life and would not have cared if I'd never have seen them again. Over the four days of the fair, they came by every day and tried at least once per day to get me to engage with them, but I was stalwartly thick-headed and wanted nothing to do with them. I was, what German kids call a "beleidigte Leberwurst" (an insulted liver sausage) and what a New Yorker would say, "totally pissed-off". Fela didn't come around at all. That bridge had been burned forever (or at least until the Uhlmann's sold their company – I sold equipment and materials to Fela in later years.)

On the last day of the fair, the particular engineer that had worked most closely with me among the Fuba engineering team, a young man called Mr. Stadelmaier, came around once more and begged me to talk to his bosses. I said through Susi (because I wouldn't talk to him) that I would only engage with Fuba if I got a letter of apology and if they eschewed any relationship with that copy-cat company Becker. A week later, I had the letter in my hand signed by the president of Fuba and an invitation to meet both the technology transfer team and the Gittelde manufacturing engineering team. What they explained to me, a couple of weeks later, at my visit, was that the manufacturing engineering team and the technology transfer team were two different groups of people who did not know everything that was happening in the other group. Mr. Stadelmaier, in particular, being a relatively young and inexperienced engineer at the time had no idea that his colleagues were seeking to get a German solution to the problem of registration because they were bidding on building two factories in East Germany. It then became evident that the technology transfer team was not aware of post etch punching or our Optiline PE. After our first meeting the technology transfer team invited me to supply all the multilayer registration equipment required for two factories that were being designed for the factories they were building in Berlin-Marzahn and Dresden in former East Germany. The highly collimated exposure machines from Optical Radiation Corporation were interesting to them as well. We became involved in the registration details of exposure and imaging for both the factories they were building as well as with their own factory in Gittelde. Once the people at Fuba understood how we had integrated the lighting units from ORC along with a concept for tooling the exposure frames in the Accutrace machines, they began to think of Multiline as a useful ally and engineering resource for integrating advanced exposure methods with advanced registration methods.

In 1988 I approached the people at Optical Radiation Corporation, where I was already known because of our work with Accutrace, to ask them if they might be interested in having Multiline Europe do for them what we were doing for Multiline Technology. They were. Here too, our timing was perfect. The electronics world, led by the communications and computer industries were seeking to manufacture finer, more densely packed circuits but were running into problems of increasing rates of defects that accompanied decreasing feature sizes. The fault for these increasing rates of defects was assigned to two specific problem areas of production: manual handling of the circuits as they were produced and unwanted contamination in the production environment. The technical response to higher defect rates thus became increasing automation to reduce handling and efforts to clean up the environment in which the circuits were produced. The OEMs led the way in building large clean-rooms for their exposure and imaging areas and at the same time sought ways to automate the exposure process to reduce human contact with the panels being produced. With this demand to automate, resist manufacturers like Dupont, WR Grace and Hercules introduced automated methods for exposure with guaranteed minimum yield rates or maximum defect rates concerning both imaging quality and registration of circuit features on one layer to holes and circuit features on other layers. Over the course of the late 1980s to the early 2000s, Multiline Europe with its Multiline Technology products and its distribution agreement with Optical Radiation Corporation was nearly always present when investments in improved technical capabilities were being considered. Initially the wave of OEM investments in Europe in automated equipment at factories like Siemens, Nixdorf, Olivetti, HP, IBM, Ericsson, Philips, AEG, Honeywell, British Aerospace, Alcatel, Marconi, Bell, Sagem and others was followed by investments in automation and/or advanced registration capabilities at job shop companies like Greule, Brockstedt, Print Service, Fuba, Ruwel, Schoeller, CSP, FCE, Bristol, Zincocelere, ISL, Exacta, Bepi, MEPD, Prestwick, PPE, Aspocomp, Printca, Graphic, Melchert, Heidenhain, Exaprint, Elco, Electotryck, Pri Dana, City Print, Italtel, Corona, Stevenage, Teltex, Eltos, Eumig, Microser, Enzmann, TW Elektrik and many more.

All of these job shop companies were not convinced to invest in automation though. There is a particular dynamic that allows OEMs an easier path to the decision to automate. An OEM factory often was able to reduce variability in their production that a job shop simply could not do. Reduced variability means an easier path to automation. Variability of productive possibilities is one way in which job shops were able to capture business from the very OEMs who had their own factories. If a new product required a new kind of surface finish that the OEM didn't already have, then they could find a job shop to make that new part. If a new product didn't fit on the panel size that the OEM factory was made to produce, then the OEM engineers could find a job shop to produce the new panel size. If the automation of the OEM made it difficult for the engineers working on a new design to break into the production schedule to get a small number of prototypes produced, they could find a job shop to make the parts in days or even hours. This idea of being ready for anything at anytime is often at odds with the conditions one would wish for when automating processes. Flexibility of capability and the demand that a factory be set up for high variability of processes became both a benefit to job shops (when they were able to use flexibility to attain customers for small production lots to begin with) and a hindrance to the same business when it became time to efficiently produce large quantities with low per unit costs associated with higher volume business.

Multiline's average customer size during this period varied from companies that had as few as 50 employees to PCB shops with up to 1000 to 1500 employees. In this latter group of larger companies or factories the best of times were the mid 1990s when there were about 10 such companies in Europe with sales in the vicinity of $150 million to $200 million dollars per year. Today, there are three PCB companies with a European production value of more than $100 million. The bulk of Multiline's sales in Europe up until 2001 were almost exclusively machines, service, spare parts and accessories for the processes involving exposure and multilayer production to these PCB companies.

Between 1987 through 1991, people running other companies supplying to the US PCB industry found out about Multiline's establishment of a successful sales and service office in Europe, those companies contacted Mike and Mike always made the introductions to me. His thinking was that the more we had to sell, the better. We were approached by a former sales representative of Lenkeit called Mel Pasternak who had the idea to market a "release film" to the multilayer industry. We took his product on even though it wasn't a machine – our product line was mostly machines and particularly, technically advanced machines. Release film is to multilayer printed circuits what baking paper is to cookies. Release film is made to contain the flow of resin that naturally seeps out of the pressed multilayers. It is placed in direct proximity to the laid up multilayers and prevents the multilayers from sticking to the separator plates. Important is that it is easily removable after the press cycle and that it doesn't leave any residue of itself on the surface of the multilayer or any impressions of itself on the copper surface of the multilayers. We started giving samples of the material to our customers. Mommers Print Service was a leading manufacturer of multilayers in Europe, as was Prestwick Circuits and PPC in Switzerland. They all tried the material, found it good and wanted to start ordering. We needed to supply the material, called "Sentrex", in packages of 100 sheets each cut to the size that each customer wanted to buy. Customers used several sizes of the material depending on the sizes of the panels they produced. We set up a supply chain that started with shipment of large master rolls of material from Mel in New Jersey to a port in Rotterdam. From there, we set up a customs warehouse at a film converting company who would cut the material to size and package them 100 per package depending on what customers ordered. If the customers needed to have the material punched (so they could be placed over our Multiline 4-slot pins) we set up a small punching operation using a small punching machine purchased from Multi-line Technology. Business boomed. We were selling about 3 to 5 master rolls every month and most of our customers who used release film purchased Sentrex from us. One day an engineer with whom we had a very good relationship in PPC, Mr. Singen-berger, called me and told me he had a problem. Sentrex had left dents in the copper of some very expensive multilayer panels. He sent me the panels and the films that had left the dents. Sure enough, there were surface defects on the films that had been transferred by the high pressures as dents into the copper foil rendering the panels useless to finish. Had my relationship with Mr. Singenberger not been as good as it was and had PPC been another kind of company, I would have been sued for damages for at least the cost of the scrapped panels. I informed Mel. Mel's material was manufactured for him by a film coating business in Chicago. Normally I would never have needed to know this but now Mel begged me to come over and visit the factory with him and discuss what happened and how we could deal with it. I was in a very tight spot now with PPC and I could wind up in the same situation with about 10 other companies that were using the material because I didn't know what was causing the defect on the film. At our visit to the film coater, we discovered that there had been some kind of clumping of the coating caused by a defective nozzle in the coating machine. They had a method to prevent it in the future but they had no idea how often the problem had happened in the past. Of all the material I had pur-chased, there was no way of sorting good rolls from bad. I liked Mel and the business we had built together had been fun and rewarding to set up but I had to give it up because I couldn't let a product like this poison the trust my customers had in me and the products we sold. I decided to give the Sentrex business up. We were able to make a deal with Romex, our Dutch and western Germany distributor to take over all the materials we had in the supply chain and take over the distribution of Sentrex in Europe from that point on. I would not sell consumable products or ma-terials until 10 years later.

A company called PAC Glass, who made glass photo-tools contacted us about selling in Europe. Mike was then relentlessly pursued by a woman called Rita Gluzman who owned a company, ECI, that made machines that analyzed plating baths. These machines were based on a principle called CVS (Cyclo-Voltometric-Stripping). We got to know TMP (the company that supplied the multilayer presses for the French projects sold to the Ukraine) and were able to at least get them some business to quote upon but it was hard going selling American presses to the Europeans with so many press manufacturers from Germany, France, Italy and other countries. These presses were modified versions of presses used to make plywood, decorative laminates, rubber or vulcanized plastics, credit cards and other flat laminated products needing heat and pressure to be properly formed.

In 1991, Mike and I came to an agreement to start the company Multiline International Europa L.P. which would make us partners and make me a permanent resident of Europe although I've remained a US citizen all these years.

Most of the products that we sold fit well together. That is to say that interest in one product often overlapped into interest in the others and those discussions dealing with one product often led to discussions about the others because of the way that the technology of each influenced the results achieved by the rest of the products in our portfolio. It all seemed somehow complementary. The exception was the CVS machines from ECI. ECI was a small company with one very narrow idea and one product based on that narrow idea. A CVS machine measured the efficacy of the organic additives in plating baths. Organic additives such as brighteners or levelers were sold by specialty chemical companies such as Schering (Atotech), Lea Ronal, Dow, Uyemura, Shipley, MacDermid, OMR, Blasberg, Schloetter, etc., etc., etc. Nobody at Multiline (including me) had any idea about plating at that time. All our knowledge was in things that could be seen, lined up and counted, cut, bent and weighed, controlled through sets of easily understood instructions or explained in mechanical terms. Electro-plating, until that phase of my life, went under the heading "magic" in my mind. I recall going to a company, called Circuit Foils, that manufactured copper foil in an electroplating process in Luxembourg around this time. (Copper foil is laminated to the outsides of multilayer printed circuit boards during the multilayer press cycle. The copper foil must be flawless and to see its perfection when it is laid upon a multilayer being prepared for the press is truly remarkable – this reddish copper-colored shimmering, glistening but slightly matte appearing perfection of surface embodying a thinness and fragileness always in danger of being torn to uselessness never ceases to amaze me.) Electro-deposited copper foil starts life as used copper wires, old foils or discarded copper bought and sold by copper recovery businesses which is then transformed into an acid copper electrolyte. Indeed, the factory I visited had mounds of scrap copper in various forms in untidy piles at the back of their factory. A large, perfectly polished drum of polished metal acts as a slowly rotating cathode within an electrolyte bath. An anode and a DC current drives copper ions from the electrolyte onto the cathode drum. As the cathode completes a rotation in the electrolyte bath, the film of copper which has formed on the drum is simply pulled from the drum and rolled onto a collection spool that winds up the copper foil into a roll. The process really does appear to be magic as copper foil is pulled off the drum in a continuous process which continues as the "harvested" drum continues its stationary journey into the electrolyte to begin the process of slow deposition again. This particular Copper Foils factory that I visited had at least 30 such drums creating copper foil rolls of nearly two meters width in a large room with strangely little activity. Large, submerged cathodes rotated out of the bath bearing copper. A take up roll peeled the copper off of the cathode and wound it up continuously onto an ever-growing spool of shiny copper foil as the now naked part of the cathode rotated itself into the electrolyte bath once again. In a printed circuit board factory this magic is harder to appreciate because the panels that are being plated-upon already have copper visibly present. The process of electroplating in the PCB shop involves clamping the panels which are to be electroplated to a metal frame. The metal frame containing the panels and the panels themselves thus become the cathode. Anodes in the electrolyte and a DC current applied to the electrolyte drive copper ions from the anodes to the cathodes causing the deposition of copper on the metallic, electrically conductive parts of the panels. In this way, copper is applied wherever resist is not blocking its deposition on the surface and in the holes of the panel. Without the use of organic additives like brighteners and levelers, copper would form in an uncontrolled way, too quickly, with too many defects, with the wrong crystalline structure and the wrong surface characteristics. I was absolutely convinced that the use of CVS is a good idea for companies to maintain good plating baths and insure good plating results. I, however, did not feel that we could sell the technology because we didn't know the right people to talk to about the technology at our customers and we didn't understand the product in the first place. The President of the company, Rita Gluzman, was insistent though. She was sure that we were the right partner to help her company expand into the European market. Rita was not only an attractive lady, but remarkable in many ways. She was relentless about getting her own way. Whatever got into her mind was going to happen some way, somehow, someday.

Her story is easily found today on the internet, one only needs to google her name. She told me of being left alone by her parents in the Ukraine for a couple of years (in the former Soviet Union) and how she had cared for her sister and herself during those years. Sometime later, after having married and having a son, her father finally received permission to emigrate to Israel with his family. In Israel, she made herself heard and became known as an activist as she cajoled, harangued, and begged the government of Israel to get her husband out of the USSR. When she came up with no success in Israel, she received a temporary visa to the US where she petitioned everybody she could, including congress people, ambassadors, UN officials, prominent politicians, and the Jewish community in America to intervene with the government of the Soviet Union to let her husband emigrate to Israel. Eventually, the Soviet Union let her husband go. He emigrated to Israel where he received his PhD in biology. He eventually would be invited to the United States and become a staff member at the Cold Spring Harbor Laboratory (run by James D Watson, of double-helix-DNA fame) as an expert in the newly burgeoning area of pharmaceutical biotechnology. In that way, Rita came to Long Island. She made the Soviet Union bend to her will and used everyone she could find to help her. If the USSR bent to her will, what chance did I have? We took ECI on and tried to learn how to sell plating analysis equipment. My initial thoughts of caution in the face of ignorance proved prescient. I truly didn't know how to sell CVS equipment and Rita convinced me to hire someone who might be able to help us sell her equipment. I found the ad of a man who had placed a "man seeking job" ad in the technical journal called "Galvotechnik". I invited him to come to an interview and upon meeting him, I knew that I had been struck by serendipity again. The man's name was Dr. Karsten Andrae and he had done his PhD. dissertation on the applications of CVS in analyzing organic additives of plating baths at the Ilmenau University in East Germany. I had, through dumb luck, found one of the best qualified people in Europe, at least from a technical stand-point, for the job that I needed to fill to make Rita happy. I also must admit, I had to free myself of Rita's constant attention. From the time we took her product on until I had made my decision to hire Karsten Andrae, a year or more had passed. In that time, she had come to visit and spent time with me travelling to potential customers and people with whom she was already acquainted. I would often take a week's time to travel with her. But the week was not the only time I was taking away from other business and my family to make sure she was happy. She orchestrated the planning for the weeks of visits in advance of her trip. To do so she would call on the tie-line I had had installed in my home so that I could easily communicate with the factory in Farmingdale during their days, so that we wouldn't lose the afternoon hours to the six-hour time difference. Once she was on the phone, it was hard to politely get off. During the trip, it was 100% time devoted to Rita and her potential customers. It would have been easier for me to take if I didn't have to hold doors and play the constant gentleman and if we weren't always late. Rita spent an inordinate amount of time during mornings before breakfast, mornings after breakfast, afternoons before meetings, before dinner or evenings just prior to dinner in her hotel room either on her phone or not (one never knew and I never asked). She always arrived at a preplanned event like breakfast, checking out of the hotel, drinks before dinner, dinner itself, or anything else, late. I was constantly calling and begging forgiveness for our tardiness and pushing back meetings or dinner reservations or drinking coffee after extra coffee at the breakfast table. These are things we travelling-business people do all the time when travelling together but it was never so stressful as with Rita. There was a certain amount of relief that I felt when she was on her flight back to the US at the end of these trips. When she had gone from Europe though, I had the follow-up phone calls at least once or twice per week to navigate, until she thought it would be a good idea to come again. Then, the whole cycle began again. By hiring Karsten Andrae to be our ECI product manager, I was freeing myself from being Rita's contact person at Multiline and making him the contact person. He didn't have a tie-line phone at his home, and he could set limits that I found difficult to set. I never asked him about his experiences of travelling with her. I just figured it was his job.

Rita became famous in the New York area in the spring of 1996, because she murdered her husband with the help of a cousin. She was convicted of the murder and spent her life in a Texas federal prison until 2020 when she was released for reasons of poor health and humanitarian considerations. The news of the murder centered on the divorce-filing her husband had made and Rita's knowledge of his affair with another woman, but I do believe that much of the animus toward her husband was also because of PCB related problems she was going through at the same time. ECI had sold a plating line to Boeing, she had told me during her last visit to Europe. The plating line was manufactured by a company in Switzerland and was sold for something close to $2 million, according to what she told me. Boeing had paid ECI a ⅓ down payment and ECI had paid what they owed to the Swiss supplier their portion of the ⅓ down payment. The Swiss company subsequently declared bankruptcy and Rita was at a loss as to what to do. Besides his other misdeeds concerning Rita, her husband refused to help her bail out ECI. After the murder, she hid herself in an unoccupied dwelling on the grounds of the Cold Spring Harbor Laboratory where she had learned to love Long Island along with the husband for whom she had moved heaven and earth to have with her. She was captured there.

We were relatively successful with ECI throughout the 1990s, but it is doubtful if we ever earned enough profit to pay for the full-time salary of a PhD. employee, his car and his travelling expenses. We wound up giving Karsten other tasks in the sale of other products and as a regional salesperson responsible for northern Germany. At some point in the early years of the 2000s, he took a job directly with ECI and moved to New Jersey. Rita's sister hired him. A few years later ECI cancelled our distribution contract and signed with another company that, hopefully, knew what they were doing.

My "Captain-of-Industry" days of turbocharged equipment sales, hyper-energetic travel, constant business action and total market engagement began in 1981 and continued its assent until the year 1999. In November of that year, at the biennial productronica trade fair, I had my first indication that the party wasn't going to last forever. The VP for sales and marketing (a guy called Mike, with a second name that sounded to us like "Fiasco") of Optical Radiation Corporation cancelled our European distribution contract. They were still present on our stand for the trade fair, but they had informed us prior to the fair that they thought that they could do better by themselves, than they could do with us. From their perspective we were too expensive.

This is a similar dynamic that I had gone through with Multiline machines in the early days of Multiline sales in Europe. I also had cancelled contracts or reduced territories when I thought that the policies of our sales reps or distributors worked against our interests in particular markets. As examples, I can cite two instances where I cancelled distribution agreements. One of these, I regret. The other, I don't. In France we had a distributor which had grown out of a customer of ours called Bionic. Bionic had grown out of the fusion of two existing distribution companies in France that had both equipment and materials to sell. The two businesses decided to fuse their equipment businesses into one business and the materials businesses would go into another business. When I came to Europe, Bionic had decided to hire a sales engineer that would be responsible for dealing with us. We had a good deal of activity on the French market concerning inquiries and customer interest, but I had the feeling that we should have been selling more. After an analysis of our lost opportunities, I concluded that the pricing policies of Bionic were too aggressively seeking high margins at the cost of more sales at lower margins. I felt if we could manage the negotiations completely, we would be able to find the right prices and do better at making sales. I got along well with the man that Bionic had hired and he seemed to agree with my assessment of the French market, so I hired him away from Bionic and established my own office in France. It was a bonehead move on my part and I regret it to this day. Knowing now what I didn't know then, I should have sat down with the people at Bionic and communicated more about margins and should have told them that

I wanted to be involved directly in negotiations. They had been long year PCB people and understood their market. Had I sat in the same room with them during negotiations we would have all gotten what we wanted, more sales. We had a similar problem in Scandinavia, but hiring a salesman for the territory was out of the question because we couldn't picture ourselves being able to sustain a full-time salesman on sales to PCB fabricators in Denmark and Sweden, which made up 90% of the Nordic market at that time in the late 1980s and early 1990s. The only avenue open to us there, was to sign on a new distributor with whom we could set up pricing, commission, margin and discount policies clearly from the very beginning. We did well with our new distributor, a company called PC Trading with whom we had an extremely open communication. I remain friends with Mogens Medegaard, who ran the Danish PC Trading for a good 25 years and who told me once directly before going into the customer for a negotiation, "When it comes time to speak about payment terms, don't say the word risk!" Of course, I said it and of course Mogens had been right and we didn't get the order that day. But, we did eventually get the order. That is the difference between the power of a monopolist and a good salesman who doesn't have a monopoly.

The difference though, among these three cases of France and Sweden for 1989's Multiline and 1999's Optical Radiation Corporation, was that we had been successful with the Optical Radiation product line. For us, the imaging products of Optical Radiation had become an integral part of our identity. Our customers identified Multiline Europe with imaging and registration and it was unclear to Optical Radiation Corp where their success was coming from. Their technology was good but our sales and marketing to the industry had introduced them to all the customers they had in Europe over the course of more than 10 years. We had a salesman in the UK who had been with us since the mid 1990s called Ged Laing. At one point in the late 1990s our UK office in Ayr, Scotland had four or five people who took care mostly of the service requirements of the UK and Scandinavian customers. Ged had an excellent relationship with the people at Aspocomp, Finland. He told me when he arrived at the stand at that 1999 productronica that he felt good about getting the order he had been working on at Aspocomp. He thought they were going to go for three fully automated exposure machines. The order was estimated for between $1.8 million and $2.1 million. "Wow!" I remarked. "That's great! We'll have to celebrate!" As the week progressed, the news of our pending order mixed with the news of ORC's seeming betrayal of us made for a bittersweet combination of pride, hurt feelings, and a kind of defiance because we were certain that ORC could not have done what we had done. (In fact, they never sold a machine in Europe again after they cancelled our contract). The people who were now responsible for sales at ORC didn't have the people skills we did. They didn't have the ability to react to communications from potential customers the way we did. What we did well in the best of times was to know how to combine what the customer wanted with what we knew we could do or what we knew our suppliers could do. We felt badly because we knew in our heart of hearts, how bad this ORC decision was.

These productronicas always ran to a certain rhythm and with our normal traditions. We always started building up the stand with our technical service crew travelling to Munich on the previous Wednesday or Thursday before the week of the expo. They would start by setting up the equipment and building the walls and displays of the stand. I would usually arrive on Saturday or Sunday. The salespeople and sales reps would arrive on Monday. We would normally have dinner at Trader Vics, in the basement of the Bayerischer Hof Hotel with the service crew on Monday evening because it didn't seem fair to me that the sales people always got to have the great celebratory meals and the service guys never did. The fair began on Tuesday and among the first visitors to the stand were always Mogens and his sidekick, Christian and our first official action was to each drink a shot of the Gamal

Dansk that Mogens brought. Tuesday and Wednesday evenings were often spent eating out with customers or suppliers, but productronica Thursday evenings were always reserved for our celebration of the Multiline team. The team usually included all our salespeople, the sales people of our suppliers, our stand staff (including Susi and who ever else was there to help out on the stand), our representatives and their sales people (or customers if they wanted to bring them along). In the 1999 version, we invited the Aspocomp team who had given us a $ 1.9 million order for three automatic exposure machines as Ged had expected on that very day. As I recall, three of Aspocomp's people wanted to join us for dinner. Susi had found a large Thai restaurant to fit about 40 people who were to join us for our "Multiline Team" celebration. It was a typical Multiline celebration. Great company, good and plentiful food, beer, wine, schnapps, vodka, good and open conversations, jokes and bonhomie like it is supposed to be among people enjoying their particular place in the world in that particular moment in time. The party began to breakup around midnight. As we walked out of our space at the restaurant, Ged and at least one of the Aspocomp guys discovered a guitar playing musician at the bar accompanying our exit. About half of us decided to stay and listen and drink and laugh and talk and sing! It all was getting to become a blur to me when Ged told me that the Aspocomp guy wanted to go dancing with the girls in our group. Aiy, aiy, aiy, I thought – we could try the nightclub at the Bayerischer Hof. So the twenty of us made our way to the Bayerischer Hof. When we got there we were told by the bouncer who was standing at the door of the night club, that there was a private party in the club and only invited guests with their printed invitations and hotel guests and their guests could enter. "Huh?" I asked, "I can bring my friends in if I have a room here?" "Do you have a room key?" he asked. "I gotta pee, I'll be right back," I responded. I went upstairs, booked myself a room and went back downstairs with my key and we were all allowed to continue our celebration. The celebration went on until about 7:00 on Friday morning. We all headed back to the hotel rooms we had spread out across Munich, showered, dressed and made our way to the fair for the last day of the expo. At about 16:00 it was our tradition to leave the stand to the service team to break the exhibit down, pack the machines and send them on to our customers or back to the factories they had come from or to our warehouse to await onward sales there. The Multiline sales people, some of our suppliers and some of our customers would then travel on to another traditional stop associated with Multiline's participation at productronica and electronica since 1995; the beginning of our ski season at Stubai Glacier in Austria.

I can draw a straight line from that celebration of Multiline's team (complete with the presence of that particular customer, Aspocomp) to my situation of today. At the same fair, we would get an order for another automatic ORC exposure machine from our old customer Melchert. After the fair was over and our hangovers had been traded over to a good night's sleep, we carried on descending from what we were to what we are today. I just couldn't see it until about eight or nine years later. Had I been a more astute businessman, I might have seen it. Had I not been so optimistic, I might have seen it. Had I not been so damned wrapped up in my same old, same old, I might have seen it. But I didn't. On New Year's Eve's day in 1999, just before the night we thought we were celebrating the coming of a new millenium, about seven weeks after our Thursday celebration, I went into the office and found a fax on the fax machine from the purchasing manager of Melchert cancelling the order they had placed at productronica. That was, I even knew then, a bad omen. Our halcyon days were over but I still thought that I and we (as Multiline) would continue to be what I and we had always been since that day in 1980 when I saw that CCTV camera on a test bench in Mike Angelo's Lenkeit office.

I spent the next couple of years trying to develop a better exposure machine than ORC offered. For that, I needed a company who had experience in collimated light exposure machines.

Through friends in Japan, I came upon a company called Dai Nippon Kaken (Great Japan Scientific – I think). In Japan there are the old traditional Zaibatsu (vertically integrated, family owned businesses like Mitsui, Mitsubishi, Sumitomo, and Yasuda and their modern version Keiretsu (closely related companies what have cross ownership relationships and largely compete with other Keiretsu). Large companies often fit themselves into allegiance with one of these or other, smaller modern Keiretsu like Toyota, Hitachi, Fujifilm, National (Panasonic), Sony, Kawasaki and others. Supporting each of these major companies are excellent companies who supply engineering and products on a more-or-less exclusive basis to these Keiretsu. Dai Nippon Kaken (DNK) was a Kyoto company of about 200 employees that manufactured exposure components and machines for the larger company Dai Nippon Screen (DNS), in a Keiretsu like relationship. Practically all that DNK produced was either sold in Japan through DNS' distribution system or integrated into a DNS product which was then sold by DNS sales channels either in Japan or through trading companies for export. DNK saw the possibility to add to their growth and end-market knowledge through a cooperation with Multiline. They trusted that I knew what PCB customers wanted in our markets because I could show them the success we had had with ORC and their machines. ORC never sold machines in Japan successfully because Dai Nippon Screen's exposure machines dominated the high end of exposure technology in Japan, and those machine exposure components were manufactured by DNK. When it came to more advanced features like automated optical alignment, DNS added those components themselves denying DNK the opportunity to make their own. They couldn't sell me or my customers the machines that DNS sold in Japan because they didn't own the complete rights to those machines or they didn't have the technology to build it by themselves.

At my first meetings with them, it became clear that they had an eager young engineering group who wanted to build a first-rate

PCB exposure machine of their own. I worked together with a Japanese woman in my office who was specifically hired to communicate with our Japanese suppliers of wet process equipment (Ishii Hyoki, with whom we had worked since 1995) and a local woman in Kyoto who became my translator whenever I was in Kyoto and that young engineering team to develop a state-of-the-art exposure machine. Over a period of two years, we designed and built a proto-type. Unfortunately, this timing coincided exactly with the transfer of PCB production from Europe and North America to China. Our market for state-of-the-art exposure machines had shrunk to two or three customers. Those people who wanted to buy a machine that worked automatically and used collimated light bought a machine that cost 40% less than the machine prices we used to get for ORC machines and half the price of DNK's machine from a French competitor. The only markets left for DNK's machines were in Asia where DNS had exclusive distribution rights. I had wasted two to three years of my own time and money and DNK's time and money to develop a machine that we sold one of, ironically, to a French customer.

The only costlier product development story was my work on laser drilling between 1994 and 1997. Working in registration of multilayer PCBs automatically brought me face-to-face with something called "blind-hole" drilling. A blind hole in the parlance of machinists is a hole that is drilled into one side of a workpiece and doesn't exit the other side. A hole that starts on one side and exits the other side is a through-hole or thru-hole. Before blind holes were used in PCBs, they went all the way through and were plated all the way through to connect to the other side whether they needed to connect to the other side or not. If one were designing an 8 layer multilayer and one only needed to connect layer one to layer two, it would be easier for the designer to use the space saved by not having to deal with an unnecessary hole extension on layers three to layers eight. So, for a designer being able to use blind holes in a PCB design is a definite benefit. It could be so much of a benefit that the 8 layer multilayer might be reduced to a 6 layer multilayer, or, perhaps, even a four layer multilayer. Now, two problems emerge and one further technical possibility. The problems are: how do I drill the blind holes and how do I plate them? In the early 1990s, the idea of blind holes was being converted into the reality of blind holes by Japanese fabricators of PCBs and most of the technology was coming from Mitsubishi for the Japanese, one of the largest manufacturer of CO_2 lasers in the world. In the western world, during the early 1990s fast flow CO_2 lasers, smaller sealed beam CO_2, TEA CO_2 and solid state YAG/UV lasers began to enter the market for drilling small, blind holes (or vias) in PCBs. There was one man from Switzerland, from a company called Dyconex (a spinoff of the Swiss defense contractor, Contraves), Dr. Schmidt, who advocated for a method of plasma drilling (or dry etching) of organic substrates to form what became widely known as microvias. Of course, one could also simply do controlled depth drilling with mechanical drilling processes as well to form blind holes. With all these methods of forming blind vias or microvias, the solution to the second problem of "how to plate" such holes became the more important question to answer. All the methods could make holes but they all had different effects on the plating problem depending on the sizes of the holes, the depths of the holes and number of holes one needed in a second, minute, panel or day and the composition of the materials being drilled and plated. (The spectrum in Europe of companies that produce blind vias or microvias in only one of these variables, number of holes required, varies from tens of thousands per day to several hundred thousand holes per panel)! In the early 1990s, my goal was to be there where my most advanced customers wanted to be with the products they needed to have. I felt that everybody who was anybody in the field of PCB fabrication would need to have at least one laser drilling machine and I worked diligently to educate myself about the technology required and to position Multiline Europe to profit. I aligned Multiline with a company called Convergent

Energy in Sturbridge Massachusetts and we set about working with them to design and build a machine to drill microvias using their patented "Diamond" 200W sealed beam CO_2 laser. Convergent Energy was a spinoff company of Coherent, one of the great laser companies in the world. This laser, although quite small (about the size of portable keyboard carried in its case) when we first saw it work, could create holes at a rate of 1000 per second. The holes looked spectacular in certain homogeneous materials on a good day. On a bad day or in the wrong materials the holes could look charred or spattered with rehardened droplets of liquefied solids. And so it went from day to day, week to week, month to month. We added a scanner (called a galvanometer in those days) to free the rate of drilling from the layout of the holes – the 1000 holes per second could only be achieved when the holes were perfectly aligned and spaced in the pre-galvo machine. We wanted to add a collimating lens, then an f-theta lens when we learned how much a collimating lens cost. We added pulse shaping optics and pulse selection software to give users flexibility to control the beam. We had to design a user interface that the customer could use to select the path of a beam within one galvo field and to move the table from one galvo field to the next. We had to adapt the machines which Convergent would normally build as stand-alone machines made to be loaded and unloaded from the front to be automatically fed from one side and unloaded to the other side. We did this all over the course of three years and finally sold our first machine to Aspocomp at the 1997 productronica, only to have Convergent Energy declare bankruptcy in the weeks after the fair. After three years of work and investment, we had no product to sell. What made the pill even more bitter to swallow was that a Japanese manufacturer of drilling machines made over 1000 machines using the laser we had selected. I would have been happy to have sold 50 in Europe. After the bankruptcy, Coherent took back the IP for the "Diamond" sealed beam product line and worked together with Hitachi to make it one of the most successful laser drilling machines of its time. I am not saying we could have done anything like Hitachi did. Hitachi had a lot of resources we didn't have including being the most successful PCB drilling machine manufacturer of the 1990s. I suppose it's one way for me to take some consolation in the failure of Convergent Energy and to take some pride that we had made a lot of good and correct decisions in the design of the machine for which we did indeed get an order. After that we worked with various laser machine manufacturers trying to get to a machine that fit the technology, price points, and flexibility that the European and North American PCB fabricators were seeking and that these relatively small markets required. In the end, our influence in the area of laser drilling would never generate success in our market. The large manufacturers of Asia have not entered the western markets because they see the markets as too expensive to enter and the sales potential of up to 20 machines per year as too small. These companies have single customers in Asia that will take as many machines (or more) in a year.

I travelled constantly between 1986 and 2010. At the beginning, it was mostly between Europe and North America or within Europe. Beginning in about the year 1994, the travel began to regularly include Asia and particularly, at first, Japan. I found that my initial travels to Japan were much different than my initial travels to Europe. Up until then, I was not only inexperienced regarding Asia, but I had also had very little experience of being among Asians. I think of myself as a Eurocentric American. I am used to thinking of myself as culturally German-American. I consider my philosophical roots as shaped most of all by the teachings of Martin Luther. I consider a good evening meal a piece of meat, some vegetables, and a mound of potatoes. When I go to a pub, I drink a beer and feel comfortable in my German or American skin. What others see in me; I don't see in myself. This is most true when I am travelling in Asia. I look like a local Asian to most people in most of Asia. Americans might call me an Asian "Everyman". In Germany you could call me the "Max Mustermann" of Asians. I have been taken for Filipino, Vietnamese, Chinese, Mongolian, American Indian, Thai, Japanese, and strangely enough, Korean. I had my gene test done by Ancestry.com and the result was 99 % to 100 % Korean, but put me in the middle of Asia and chances are someone will talk to me in the local language thinking I'm one of them. The funniest anecdote in this direction is that I met a Korean woman recently at the birthday party of a German friend of mine and she remarked, "I couldn't figure out Korean or Japanese? Japanese or Korean? Then I decided you must be Japanese." "Why?" I asked. "Because you have gray hair! All the Korean men your age I know color their hair!" she replied. The Japanese take me for Japanese and many strangers, particularly men, I run up against in pubs or clubs seem to have a problem with me not being Japanese when they find out, as if I was trying to be an imposter. My experience of Japan is filled with cognitive dissonance because things are so different from what I am used to. I am used to and prefer social flexibility and Japan is a place of social rigidity. I have been travelling to cities all over the world and I have the same daily habits no matter where I am. I work my days and when my work is done, I walk the town or city I'm in and I try to find a pub, café, wine shop or restaurant where I can engage locals and have a nice conversation and learn about the place I'm in. Obviously, it's easier for me to do this in Europe or North America. Partly because most of us understand that pubs, cafes and clubs are there partly to serve this very function. Finding a place in Europe or North America is so much easier because they are normally easy to find and are made to be welcoming. In Japan, access is usually achieved by making your way through a barrier. The barrier is often cloth curtains that hang in the way of you seeing past them causing one to have to force them open to peek inside. Whereas most pubs and restaurants in Europe and North America are ground floor or second floor establishments and finding one involves walking along and looking right and left, in Japan finding a pub or restaurant involves walking along and looking right, left, and up. Most of the entertainment districts of cities are a collection of six to 12 story buildings with their signs sticking out from the sides of buildings from the floors they occupy. Hierarchy means more in Japan than in any other culture I have ever experienced. I enjoy the kind of establishment in Germany (and particularly my hometown) where the local baker and the investment banker can sit together and enjoy each other's company or play cards as they please. I doubt that there are many of those kinds of places in Japan. I have been at countless dinners with management groups in simple restaurants where the working staff were present, and everyone enjoyed some time together as a team. Usually when dinner was done, the top manager, if he wanted to continue the evening with me or with other higher managers present, he would dismiss the lower echelons and we would repair to an exclusive space where he had his own bottle of whiskey and his favorite serving woman. I am sure that there have been people who took me for a fake Asian, but there is little I can do about what they thought and there is little I can do to change myself at this late date.

I remember Japanese people telling me that they really miss their soya sauce when they are in Korea. I suppose that sometimes I missed my salt and pepper, but most often, I found something to like wherever I was. There were times that I was in China that I recall looking forward to a cheeseburger but in China that was really the exception because for so much of the time I was in China, I was with my friend Ivan,

In 2000, Japan was still the leading country in the world in Printed Circuit production and, in my view, in the technology of fabricating bare boards. The shake-up of electronics production in the world which had started with personal computers (where Japan was able to hold its own until about 2010) and cellular phones (where Japan decidedly could not hold its own beyond about 2005). I was mostly travelling to Japan for two reasons: to try to open the market up to post etch punching (which I totally failed at) and to maintain good relations with the PCB supplier base. Over the years we have had supply agreements with

Somar (manufacturers of dry-film laminating machines), Ishii Hyoki (horizontal wet process machines and planarizing brushing machines), Dai Nippon Kaken (exposure machines) and Fujifilm (PCB silver halide films for artwork production). I found that engaging the world of technology was fun and spoke to my natural curiosity of how people in different countries faced with different problems reacted in different ways. A look at the Japanese approach to multilayer production and registration is a good case in point.

Multiline has tried to convince the Japanese producers of telecommunications multilayers, network multilayers and high layer count computer multilayers that post etch punching is a superior way of registration. The Japanese way relied on superior base materials, smaller panel sizes and a process that used holes drilled in the base materials as the first process of fabricating innerlayers as reference points for everything that happened to an innerlayer or production panel. This methodology of always applying a new process to an already existent set of references will always give a best fit between the old reference and the new process. Now, if the universe of registration problems can be reduced to this relationship between existent reference and new process, then there will never be a registration problem. This is the way of semiconductors and this is the way of Japanese-style sequential process registration. The Multiline method of fabricating a six layer multilayer is to produce two double sided innerlayers, punch them to be in registration with respect to each other, combine them in a press with two pieces of copper foil to form a six layer structure, structure the outerlayers to be in registration with the innerlayers and then plate up and plate-thru the entire six layer structure. Compare that with the sequential build-up method in which each layer is built up on the basis of the last layer and each layer is plated individually. Layer 2 is aligned and produced on top of and in registration with layer 1. Layer 3 is aligned and produced on top of and in registration with layer 2. Layer 4 is aligned and produced on top of and in registration with layer 3. Layer 5 is aligned and produced on top of and in registration with layer 4. Finally, Layer 6 is aligned and produced on top of and in registration with layer 5. As long as layer 1 doesn't need to align with layers 3, 4, 5 or 6, the part is perfect. Both methods work. The Japanese way is closer in concept to semiconductor manufacturing and so is seen as "higher tech" and used in the costliest, most advanced PCB products on the planet. The Multiline method is still used on most of the multilayers produced in the world, including by advanced shops in Taiwan and Korea. Why? Cost, productivity and lower scrap costs. Should the Japanese have looked closer to our technology? Probably, but they most likely had other incremental problems to solve at the moment I visited at each factory or they never understood with any clarity what I was proposing.

One of the best ways to keep up on technology trends that I learned to do when I started at Multiline was to visit trade fairs and walk around (as if one were window shopping). If there was something interesting, just ask questions. I was flying to the NEP-CON show in Anaheim, California from Frankfurt in February of 1990. I was looking out the window of the plane and enjoying the view of our westward approach to the shoreline, before the plane banked rightward for the final approach. The man sitting behind me was looking out his window and, seeing me doing the same through the gap between my seatback and my window, he remarked how nice the view was. Noticing his German accent, I answered in German how I never could get enough of the view of a shoreline no matter where it was. He was astounded that I spoke German. As one does when one has just started a conversation before deplaning, we continued our conversation as we exited the plane. His name was Heinz Rembold and he introduced himself to me as the boss of Ciba Geigy's Electronics Products business and the Chairman of the EIPC. We shared a taxi to our hotel because we were both staying at the Marriot Hotel in Anaheim and we became industry friends. He told me before we parted from that trip that I should join the EIPC to get plugged into the European PCB industry. That I did. In 1991, I began my engagement in the industry association world. I began attending EIPC, VdL (Verein der Deutschen Leiterplatten, or the German Printed Circuit Association) and PCIF (the English Printed Circuits Industry Federation) meetings and events. I found the EIPC the best organization to spend my time on because it was pan-European, basically a combination of social, business and technical club and in English. The VdL was a bigger organization in the first years of my involvement but as companies such as Mommers Print Service, Ericsson, Zincocelere, Prestwick, ISL, Exacta and Microser grew in size and influence, the other associations and particularly PCIF and the EIPC became more active and more influential. I joined the board of directors of the EIPC in 1995 and remained on the board until 2022. I served as chairman for the years between 2000 and 2006. The rest of the world tended to see Europe as one entity and I liked that the EIPC truly represented Europe during my time there. An umbrella world organization had been founded to host a World Printed Circuits Conference with the name ECWC which stood for the "Electronics Council World Conference" in 1978. The member organizations that brought this world conference into being were the ICT (of the UK), the EIPC, the IPC (of North America) and the JPCA (of Japan). The initial world conference was held in London. Today, the ECWC has been renamed to the WECC or the World Electronics Council Conference and includes as its host organizations: the EIPC, IPC, CPCA (China), JPCA, HKPCA (Hong Kong), KPCA (Kirea), TPCA (Taiwan), THPCA (Thailand), and ELCINA (India). For your interest, the next world conference takes place in Anaheim in April of 2024 and will be hosted by the IPC, the Institute of Printed Circuits of the USA.

I became very active in 1997 together with another member of the EIPC board, Umberto Aiassa, the president of a company called IS at that time. IS was a manufacturer of wet process equipment from Parma, Italy which made him a competitor of mine because of Multiline's relationship to Ishii Hyoki, the Japanese producer of horizontal wet process equipment. Umberto and I became partners in the planning of the trade fair called EPC. Our idea was to have a trade fair combined with a technical conference in the even, non-productronica years. Umberto and I created a group within the EIPC called the supplier's council which would collectively guide the planning of each EPC event. EPC exhibitions would be held in 1998 in Wiesbaden, 2000 in Maastricht, 2002 in conjunction with the WECC World Meeting in Cologne. productronica offered to turn over one of their halls to the EIPC so that we could run the EPC within the productronica Expo in 2003. In an agreement with the productronica management within the Messe Muenchen Gesellschaft (MMG), EPC could be held within the productronica Fair, the EIPC would organize, plan, and administer a Conference for the attendees of productronica. The concession by MMG which showed us just how much they wanted to engage the EIPC in the planning of the Conference was their willingness to fund the gala evening of the Conference and EPC. They gave us a very nice party which was catered by the famous catering company "Kaefer". The last EPC was held in 2004, again in Cologne. The EPC was imagined and brought into life in a time that we could all be optimistic about our futures in the European PCB industry in 1997 but seven years later, when we pulled the plug on the event after the 2004 event, it was clear that the European PCB industry was in decline.

There had been a time between 2004 and 2009 when I spent a week every month at Multiline trying to help them in product development and strategic planning. Those weeks were spent with the engineering, sales or management teams trying to find ways back to the success we had had in the time before the turn of the millennium. I also took over day-to-day sales responsibilities for all export sales, including Asia. I found myself travelling to Asia once a month as well. Mike and I were trying to extend life for a business that we both knew was in critical condition but we both believed was possible to save. In retrospect, nothing I was going to say or do was going to move anyone in the organization to do anything except what they were already doing. I wasn't coming in with any real power to change anything. I couldn't spend money (we didn't have any). I was nobody's boss in the Multiline Technology organization. I could cajole, complain, admonish, or praise, but that was about it. There was a product idea which could have brought us some level of success had we performed better in both design and workmanship. That product was a new version of our existing X-Ray drilling machine. In my view, we brought that product to about 80 % completion to what it had to be to be successful and then we dropped the ball just before crossing the goal line. The design suffered from being seen by our customers as too lightly built and not robust enough. The machines we built and delivered were plagued by reliability problems and our competitors were able to capture this market segment with a design based on conventional PCB drilling machines.

The time that I was travelling each month to North America coincided roughly with my most active time in the EIPC and my efforts to bind the EIPC to the Asian and North American PCB industries in the loose confederation of PCB organizations which was the WECC. If you recall, I had a friendship with a guy named Ivan Ho who had worked for Accutrace during the early 1980s. In the intervening years, he would move from Accutrace to Ciba Geigy then Shipley. He would also move from his home in Massachusetts, separating himself from his wife and family and moving back to Hong Kong when he took over the job of Cimnet Systems Asian manager at about the turn of the millenium. When I started to travel to China regularly in about 2002, I picked up my friendship with Ivan again. We wound up seeing each other for one week at a time perhaps 6 to 8 times per year between the years 2004 and 2009. I would take an around the world trip in one direction – eastward, for example – from Frankfurt to Hong Kong, Hong Kong to New York, then returning home via Frankfurt. The following month, I would do the same trip in reverse flying westward from Frankfurt to New York, then to Hong Kong. To save money I would buy these tickets as round trip tickets between Frankfurt & Hong Kong, between Hong Kong & New York and New York & Frankfurt. Sometimes I would substitute Shanghai for Hong Kong or LA or San Francisco for New York, but the trips were always planned well ahead of time, and I always had industry association people to meet, customers to see, suppliers to visit and Ivan to spend time with during my visits to Hong Kong, Shenzhen, Shanghai, Kunshan or Suzhou. He had offices in Hong Kong, Shenzhen and Suzhou, so we were always able to coordinate our schedules to be with each other. An evening with Ivan always started with cocktails, often for happy hour at one of our regular bars in Suzhou or Lan Kwai Fong in Hong Kong, then on to dinner and karaoke or a bar somewhere and, at the end of the evening, sitting at a table across from each other, with the final bottle of the red wine he loved so much between us, doing the e-mails that had come in from Europe or the United States on each of our notebooks. Ivan and I together was like a travelling party in a bottle (or several bottles).

Ivan and I started a regular feature of PCB trips sponsored and planned by the EIPC (which meant organized by Ivan and his Cimnet colleagues and made available to our EIPC membership to take part in). For several years during the weeks that the HK-PCA (Hong Kong Printed Circuit Association) trade fairs in Hong Kong, Shenzhen or Dongguan or the CPCA (Chinese Printed Circuit Association) trade fair in Shanghai took place, this Chinese PCB technology tour was offered to western PCB professionals. It became a vehicle through which European and Chinese PCB people met each other and the Europeans got a sense of what the Chinese PCB industry was all about. Through this trip I made many new PCB industry friends from both Europe and China and I solidified or expanded and extended friendships of Europeans that were already acquaintances. We arranged for people to see factories of both very sophisticated well financed fabricators as well as simple factories where investment took a back seat to cheap labor and 'cut corners.' During those years I could imagine Ivan and I growing old together. If I was anywhere in China and I needed to get in a cab and needed to tell the cab-driver about where I needed to go, or arrange a pickup later in the day, I'd call Ivan and he would be my Chinese translator. If he needed to know anything from me, he knew I was always on the other end of the line from his phone and was always happy to hear his voice. Getting old together was not to be though with Ivan and I. He died in the summer of 2012 of a massive heart attack that struck him down on a late-night sidewalk in Hong Kong. He was walking home from another one of those wonder-ful nights that he did so much to light up for the people he was with. Just like that, he was gone. It's been 12 years now. He was 58 years old and the best friend that I have ever had. I miss him greatly.

While doing this work to try to revive equipment sales for Multi-line in Asia, the sales of registration equipment in North Amer-ica and Europe were collapsing as the method of registration we preached was becoming less and less necessary in the west. Whereas the most difficult multilayer PCBs were being made in North America and Europe through the years up to about 1997, the technical level of multilayers and layer counts in North Amer-ica and Europe were declining as the late 1990s progressed. The product mix of the OEMs purchasing their boards in these west-ern markets were the industrial, medical, prototype automotive, military and instruments manufacturers who were using lower layer counts and semiconductors with fewer interconnects and less densely packed interconnects that simply didn't require the layer counts and the tight lines and spacings of the telecommu-nications, computer and network industries. The most difficult multilayer PCBs were being made by only a few companies in the west as much of the expertise had moved to Asia, and in particular, Taiwan, Korea, Japan and China. The most difficult of these circuits, the chip packages, were being made by increas-ingly chip-like, sequential methods mostly by Japanese, Korean and Taiwanese companies. China became the home of high layer count multilayer production through Anglo-American style libertarian capitalism. It is interesting to note that the USA created the technical competition with China which seems, today, to be such a threat to western style liberal social democracy and five centuries of western economic hegemony. I had a front row seat throughout my career of the long migration of the PCB world from west to east. My life's migration story was east to west but my PCB life began in North America and followed its progress to east Asia. The western world gave the eastern world the tools to beat us in the production of electronics. How and why are the important questions to ask in this our questioning of globalization in the shadow of trench warfare in Europe (Russia's invasion of Ukraine) for the first time in a hundred years. How and why are the important questions to ask as the world seems to shatter into regional economic and political fragments and the idea of peaceful globalization seems to be receding.

Where from here?

Consolidation in the Printed Circuit Board industry began in the mid 1990s as large competitors in Canada, the USA and the UK began to combine to form larger entities in reaction to the ever-growing demands of the telecommunications and networking industries. For the first time, big money looked at the PCB industry as a subset of the electronics manufacturing business. A company called Hicks, Muse, Tate and Furst (HMTF), fresh from the successful financial restructuring of a significant portion of the US electrical connector industry, set its eyes upon the PCB industry. They had used leveraged buyouts of several connector companies (including Berg Electronics from Dupont) and consolidated them into Berg Electronics Corp. which they had then taken public. The Berg experience had made the partners at HMTF a lot of money and made them believe that they could do the same for the western PCB industry. The PCB industry was to them simply another branch of the electronics industry that was experiencing massive growth and seemed to them fragmented and undervalued. In order to unlock the full value of their target acquisitions, they believed they only needed to acquire a significant market share of PCB producers to the communications and networking OEMs (the customers of the PCB fabricators that were fueling much of the growth of the electronics industry at the time), consolidate them into one large entity, cut out redundancies in the various organizations that they purchased thereby unlocking value which could be harvested in a future sale of the company just as they had done successfully with Berg. HMTF was the biggest of these consolidating companies in the PCB industry of this time, but they were not the only ones. There was also Tyco, Sanmina, Multek, Merix, TTM and others.

HMTF began with the acquisitions of the former Western Electric (AT&T or Lucent) PCB factory in Richmond (a big Accutrace customer) and the Canadian PCB manufacturer, Circo Craft. In doing so, they had a number of factories which were able to produce about $ 600 million of sales volume per year which would have made it one of the largest producers of PCBs in North America along with Hadco, Zycon, IBM and Sanmina (The estimated size of the North American PCB market in 1995 was approximately $ 7.5 billion, the European market about $ 5 to $ 6 billion, with the world market at between $ 25 and $ 30 billion). They renamed their company Viasystems and then went on a buying rampage in Europe. They began their European acquisitions spree with the purchases of Forward Circuits and ISL in the UK in 1997. Sales Revenue for 1997 was nearly $ 800 million (with a net loss of nearly $ 330 million). They then added Ericsson Telecom AB's PCB factory in Norrkoping, Mommers Print Service B.V., in Echt, the Netherlands and Zincocelere S.p.A., from Milan, with a number of facilities in Italy and the UK all in 1998. To understand the magnitude of these acquisitions on the European PCB marketplace, one must understand that Viasystems owned

⅓ of the production capacity of PCBs of Europe in 1998. To understand the magnitude of these acquisitions to Multiline Europe, one must understand that these companies were our biggest and truest customers. ISL, Zincocelere and Mommers Print Service were companies that each purchased machines worth at least $ 500,000 from us each year and sometimes as much as three times that much. To have them consolidated and then see how the people I was used to seeing in one place turn up in total different places because of management changes that were made willy-nilly gave me the business version of vertigo. It was interesting to note but difficult to understand.

The year 2000 brought good news to Viasystems as the public sale of the company raised $ 900 million which was more than expected. Revenues were over $ 1.6 billion and they earned $ 136 million. After that, it was all bad news for both Viasystems, the various factories they had purchased in Europe, Multiline and me. Sales dropped to $ 1.2 billion and they reported losses totaling $ 500 million in 2001. They entered a pre-packaged bankruptcy agreement that eliminated $ 720 million of debt and they began closing factories and shipping production assets from Europe to China (where they had bought a PCB business and were building a large new factory). By 2005, the closing of Mommers Print Service factory was the final act of Viasystems in Europe. An American company had bought many of the best high layer count multilayer PCB facilities in Europe and, during one disruptive decade, not only closed it all down, but transferred the know-how to China. Multiline's customer base for high layer count multilayer PCB registration equipment and fine line production equipment was reduced to a fraction of what it had been.

The German PCB industry escaped Viasystem's influence and money machinations and the larger producers there now became the largest producers in Europe. Germany's experience was that their major OEM customers from the automobile industry wanted to pay the lowest possible prices for their large volume purchases of PCBs but, at the same time, they wanted to have the support of local experts to help in the development of the next generations of PCBs for their future products. German companies like Continental, Bosch and Hella that supply electrical and electronic subassemblies to the Automobile manufacturers like VW, Mercedes and BMW are constantly under pressure to keep the prices down and their technology, reliability and quality up. Four major German PCB companies (Schweizer, Ruwel, KSG and Wuerth) and one Austrian company (AT&S) would emerge from the Viasystems era as the largest PCB fabricators of Europe. Fuba, who had traditionally held a position as one of the most important PCB companies in Germany would close their doors in Germany in 2005. Fuba still operates in Tunisia as a PCB manufacturing unit of the company OneTech. The PCB manufacturing base of Germany today and most of the rest of Europe is centered on supplying the industrial, automotive, medical and, instruments businesses. There is a small base of PCB companies in the UK and France who are capable to supply the military and aerospace businesses. Multiline's strength was always as a supplier to the high layer count multilayer PCB sector. That sector's end customers are the computer, telecommunications, and networking industries. That supply of PCBs to those industry sectors is largely from China, Taiwan, Korea and to a lesser extent from North America today.

In the last several years several events and new ways of thinking about them have caused the world's business and political leaders to rethink the rightness of globalization as the goal of economic development in the world. Previous to 2020 and the Covid pandemic, the world simply took it on faith that world supply chains would become stronger and more immune to disruption as time went on. The conventional wisdom said that lower delivery costs combined with our ability to exploit low wage regions to reduce the costs of our manufactured goods was both inevitable and good and desirable for all people everywhere.

Prior to the invasion of the Ukraine by Russia in February of 2022, we overlooked "shared values" as an important factor in how we do business and with whom we do business. Before we were confronted with the very real impact of CO_2 on our climate and the catastrophic effects of continuing to burn fossil fuels, sustainability wasn't something that most of us thought about. The people who have advanced the technology of Printed Circuits throughout the world in my generation and the generation that preceded mine have much to be proud of. On the other hand, we are also partially responsible for the advent of easily accessible social media and the democratization of the means of information dissemination. The world we helped create makes it possible to manipulate what people think by exploiting each person's biases. The world of social media platforms that profits from engagement and can custom tailor what a person sees based on his own biases has uncovered a new way of keeping people "tuned in." Social media, search, and news media monetizes our interests and biases. This has given tools to opportunists, despots and populists that bend people's attention toward disruptive, often false or misleading, unhealthy, dangerous and ultimately self-serving ideas, propaganda or conspiracy theories. It seems to me that our creation of an interconnected world has brought into sharp focus the dangers of nationalism and the identification of religion within national identity among many of us while at the same time reinforcing nationalism, religious and cultural identity in others.

The automobile industry in Europe suffered from disruptions of production and delivery of semiconductors during the pandemic. This has led to some discussion among the producers of automotive electronics whether it may make sense to make Europe more proficient in the production of semiconductors. The real question comes down to the answer to the following question, "How much is supply-chain security worth?" The German automobile industry has proven itself to be a less than model citizen in the last several years as it showed in the diesel scandals.

The industry still supports no speed limits on our German Autobahns as it hangs onto old ideas of how an automobile industry makes money. The industry itself must be dragged back into thinking in the interests of society as a whole and be prevented from reacting to future trends only informed by self-interest. Because of our natural emotional attachment to automobiles and particularly our beloved, powerful German Audis, BMWs, Porsches and Mercedes, we are easily manipulated by the reactionary view of what it means to own a "real" car and what it means to be "free." In my opinion, nothing better could happen to the PCB industry in Europe in the coming years than if the industry would jump completely and whole-heartedly into the manufacture of Electric Vehicles (EVs) beginning as soon as possible.

Mike and Dave Angelo and Multiline Technology gave up trying to survive in 2015 and simply closed up business. We had become estranged over the previous several years as they increasingly looked to Asia in general and China in particular for their survival. Our Chinese distributor, WKK, had purchased a license to produce the simpler post etch punching machines in 2009 and become proficient in producing ever more sophisticated machines over the intervening years. The original license involved Multiline Technology building some of the critical components of the more advanced machines for WKK. They were to slowly and incrementally take over the manufacture of ever more advanced machines as time passed and their competence grew. WKK and one of our customers, TTM, had unfinished machines at Multiline Technology when the factory closed. These unfinished products, the drawings and technical data and the manufacturing methods for producing our precision components and how we combined those components into machines that could punch materials as big as telecommunication back-panel boards with accuracies of plus or minus 10 microns (0.0004") and repeatability of position of 8 micron at production rates of 6 to 8 panels per minute were what was left of Multiline Technology's assets. Today, WKK, TTM and a Korean company, one of our customers called ISU Petasys, share the legacy of producing Multiline's Post Etch Punch. Each of those companies took from Multiline Technology the methods and practices used to make our machines and now make our machines in their own factories. In addition there are copies of our machines made in China and Taiwan as well as competitors from Germany and the United States who have designed their own versions of post etch punching machines. I am proud of my part in creating the technological landscape of the PCB world as it is. I have often described my role as a front row observer of our industry's development and its comings and goings, but I'd like to be remembered as a contributor to the PCB landscape everywhere as one of the industry's constant immigrants.

Multiline Europe's focus on being an equipment supplier blurred at the turn of the millennium. We began to sell dry film resist for Dupont as well as taking over the spare parts and service businesses of Dupont's "Riston" brand of equipment that included laminators and exposure machines. Along with the resist, we took on Agfa silver film for artwork or photo-tool production. We added a plotter and film processing machines to our product base and we came to be experts in the manufacture of Artworks. After 10 years with Dupont, Dupont decided to consolidate all their sales in Europe with an exclusive contract to a competitive distributor. Agfa followed suit. We started a cooperation with Fujifilm in 2011 and built up their market share of film to the PCB industry from nearly non-existent to about 40 %. Price pressures and the additional costs of delivery during the Covid pandemic led to Fujifilm's decision to abandon the European market after 2022 which in turn left us with no more major products to sell.

Today we still have a relationship with the Spanish company, Chemplate, which manufactures a series of machines called Indubond. Among those machines, of particular interest to me is a lamination press which uses inductive energy generated in each separator plate to heat each multilayer by direct conduction instead of the old method (devised to manufacture plywood) which heats a stack of panels by indirect conduction via oil, steam, or electrically heated press platens. We sell tooling and accessories for Multilayer production as well as products used in the exposure process. I continue to work with WKK to try to keep the Multiline Technology machine brand viable and successful throughout the world.

I have a view of the coming world of PCB manufacture that I hope to see come to reality. The view is based on a lifetime of experience of the PCB world through personal experience and how I understand the events of the world during the time it has taken me to write this book and what their lessons for us should be.

In my view, the printed circuit industry of the world developed simultaneously in North America and Europe and was picked up by Japan as an important element of the engine of export development for their economy that electronics manufacturing became. To have a local electronics industry must be in the interest to all regions and countries when they evaluate their own strategic goals concerning self-sufficiency in defense, protecting important local industries and maintaining manufacturing jobs. We have not heeded our own sensible thoughts about what would be in our own strategic best interests because of big business, governments, and libertarian economics. The underlying principle of capitalism as it is practiced today by big business and government is to minimize costs to increase profits. Big business has convinced governments that increased profits are in the interest of all. However, there is an ever-growing body of research with a preponderance of data showing that the world is becoming less fair in the distribution of accumulated wealth. If one believes that the profits of growth as it is achieved today do not accrue to the creators of the growth equally or fairly, wouldn't that be a reason to think of how we could make it fairer? The PCB industry's move to China was the result of Big Business defined as the computer, networking and telecommunications manufacturers of North

America and Europe and the automobile industry of Europe exercising their will. We, in the PCB industry in North America and Europe, never really had a chance to grow and prosper in Europe after 1995. We were part of the imbalance of the unfairly distributed profits of libertarian capitalism. Once "big money" looked our way, we were toast. We, in the western PCB world, were always going to be too expensive, too small, and too regulated from that point on. The mantra that growth in a global economy raises all boats turned out to be a fantasy. We have learned through the Covid pandemic that a globalized economy where end customers are spread around the world and production is controlled in one region of the world causes ridiculous imbalances of costs and logistics. Examples of imbalances that came to our attention during the pandemic for which we have no elegant solutions are:

1. Ships awaiting unloading at ports for weeks on end.
2. Countless containers clogging up ports to the point that there was literally no place to put more of them.
3. The shipping cost of shipment from east to west far exceeding the cost of shipment from west to east.
4. Getting shipping containers back to Asia to circumvent the need to build new containers in the East became increasingly difficult. Empty containers languished, uselessly stacked like children's blocks in expensively acquired paved fields covering hectares of expensive land near ports throughout the world.

Beyond these logistical conundrums with no easy logical solutions, there is the very real fact that the entire industry of sending stuff from one continent to another is built on a need to burn fossil fuels that are contributing to global warming and not properly priced to account for the damage that the additional CO_2 in the environment costs the inhabitants of our planet.

Once the Covid pandemic abated, we were confronted with a war in Europe. A thought that had been unthinkable at the turn of the millennium became reality. For the first time since the cold war, we were confronted with the presence of evil, embodied in Putin's government, let loose on the world. Those people, companies and governments who didn't immediately condemn the actions of the Russian government became, for me, incomprehensible. They represented a way of thinking that could not align with the way I think about good and evil. I saw the world bifurcated along a line between those that shared our modern social democratic values and those that didn't. When China's government didn't condemn Putin's war, I asked myself, "how is it that we can do business with them?" The answer to my question is of course, because it's cheaper to buy from there than from many other places and because they do a good job of making what they make. "Is it worth it?" is the question that follows. Then, obviously, "Does it make sense in the overall scheme of things?"

For a local electronics industry one needs engineers, access to components and integrated circuits, designers, and printed circuit boards. The best of all worlds or in any region is to have the PCBs available the day after they were designed so that the design process can be accelerated when necessary. The USSR had the right idea to try to invest to catch up to the western world during the end of the cold war. It was, however, too little too late and they learned ultimately that they couldn't buy an electronics industry. A country needs to grow an electronics industry or, it can do what the Chinese did. The Chinese got western companies to transplant the PCB industry to China as one element of many transplanted manufacturing technologies required to have an electronics industry from the western world. The electronics industry centers in Guangzhou province and the area west of Shanghai were developed through transplanted technology from Hong Kong, Taiwan and the US and to a lesser degree from Europe. The Chinese understood how to use western greed and its economic system to accelerate the development of the PCB industry in their country. PCB production became an important component of their hegemony in computer production, cellular telephone production and now, through their increasing dominance in battery production and the manufacture of photovoltaic cells, the renewable energy and EV production. The Japanese, Koreans, Taiwanese, and Thais are the last frontier of competition to China's manufacturing might in PCBs and there is still a chance that India will enter the world competition of PCB manufacturing nations. But to only see these possibilities for braking China's power over the world in general and the electronics and PCB industries in particular is to continue to think of upholding the libertarian global economic policies of the past and ignore the lessons we have learned over the last several years.

My hope is for a de-globalized electronics industry and with that, a world of PCB production which is distributed along geographically, and values defined regions. The US and Europe have passed legislation which would give incentives to companies to build semi-conductors in the US and Europe. The US version of the "CHIPS and Science Act" foresees some support of PCB manufacturers, but I don't see it as a very effective way to support those businesses in the US who have seen their businesses hollowed out by Chinese competition. I fear that much of the incentive money will disappear into the coffers of large companies and not be converted into additional investment in new technology improvements or capacity improvements for the US based PCB businesses most hurt by globalization. One way to look at what the PCB means to the costs of a product is to see how PCBs have developed as the total cost of manufacture of an electronic product. When I started in PCBs in the 1970s, the rule of thumb was that PCBs comprised about 3% of the value of a product. Estimates of the size of the electronics products manufacturing industry today run about $3.7 trillion. (There are estimates that vary from $800 billion to $5 trillion. The lowest number only counts the production of Electronic Manufacturing Services (EMS) businesses which doesn't capture OEM direct manufacturing and the highest includes all IT spending including software – I chose the $ 3.7 trillion because it makes the most sense given the 3 % PCB rule of thumb, along with the logic of combining consumer electronics market size of $ 1.1 trillion, an automobile electronics market size of $ 1 trillion, a non-consumer telecommunications business of about $ 1 trillion, and a global computer industry of about $ 450 million. Another indicator that this estimate is closest to being the most accurate is that it fits well with a known semiconductor industry size of about $ 700 billion). Comparing the size of the global PCB market ($ 100 billion) to this number gives us a sense that this 3 % rule of thumb still seems to hold today. If anything, the value ratio of PCBs compared to the value of the products they enable has gone down in the intervening 50 years. I would like to point out that although the value ratio shows the PCB industry is of minor value compared to the value of the complete electronic product, the PCB is, nevertheless, irreplaceable, and necessary to every electronics product. The US and Europe's CHIPS initiatives were informed by two different lessons learned from recent events. The US position is much more a protective impulse to react to Chinese competition in the geopolitical and economic arenas. The Russian invasion of Ukraine and Chinese saber-rattling concerning Taiwan added to the fact that the US has much to protect in its home-grown semiconductor industry led US policy makers to the political will to pass their legislation. Europe's impulse for action, although also a reaction to Russia's invasion of Ukraine and Chinese aggressive posture in Asia seems to have more to do with the lessons of the difficulties of maintaining global supply chains in a world far from guaranteed to be free of future disruptions. My view is that Europe's position of seeking regional sustainability is a reaction to understanding national vulnerabilities whereas America's position is in wanting to maintain national self-reliance. Each of the regions have concluded that protecting local electronic industries is important for slightly different reasons. Each gives their local producers slightly different motivations for actions in the future.

For all the reasons given above, we are moving to an electronics industry that will have regional support to grow locally in the future. We, who should have a value of 3% of the electronics industry of North America and Europe – the industry that manufactures a little over 5% of the world's PCBs although the electronics industries we serve in America and Europe add up to 39% of the world's electronics production according to a 2020 report by the European Commission (20% in the EU and 19% in North America). Starting from our $3.7 trillion global market for electronics products, this translates to markets for electronics production of $740 billion in Europe and $700 billion for North America. Chinese electronics production comprises 24% of world electronics production which would translate to a size of $900 billion. Applying our 3% rule-of-thumb, Europe needs about $22.2 billion of PCBs for the electronics that are built into European products and North America would need about $21 billion for their products manufactured in North America. Today, about half of the PCBs used in the EU are imported as bare boards from China, Hong Kong and Thailand whereas about 10% are produced here in Europe, the rest are imported into the EU as already assembled or populated PCBs. Wouldn't it be great if these PCBs could be manufactured in Europe and North America?

What the PCB industries in North America and Europe need is not protection from the Chinese but the friendship and support of our government supported big businesses. If we can't get big business's friendship and support, then we should seek protection from their worst profit-seeking and cost-cutting impulses. We should take a page from the instruction book of much smaller European businesses who seek support through cultural support and an appeal to pride-in-local-production from local customers. The food and wine industry in Europe and the UK has passed legislation to protect the interests of farmers, grape growers and food processors in Parma, Bologna, Bordeaux, Champagne, or Dijon under the "Protected Designation of Origin" or PDO to protect local growers and producers from the largest players in the $2 trillion European food and grocery market. It seems to me that applying an idea like the PDO to PCBs would not be impossible to implement but it would need to get the attention of policy makers who might be able to convert the idea into a set of tariff agreements or industry support programs. I could imagine a system in which products with a "PCBs fabricated in the EU" designation could be subject to a tariff between 1% and 3% lower than products without that designation. The tariff savings should compensate the importing OEM an amount to reimburse him for the 20% to 40% difference in the price of Chinese fabricated PCBs as compared to the costs of fabrication in the EU or North America. Imposing direct tariffs on PCBs would be another way to address the problem, but the tariff would have to be in the region of 40% to have the same effect as a 1.2% tariff on the finished subassembly or product.

If big business will continue to be allowed to roam the world and transplant local technologies to exploit differences in regional costs to extract additional profits with impunity, then they should be forced to pay the future costs of global warming by paying a suitable CO_2 tax which would bring logistical costs more into the realm of fair and equitable when comparing the costs of a long supply chain to the benefits of a short one.

Throughout the writing of my story, I've been worried about my future as if the past wasn't good enough. Relaying the story has brought home the fact that I have always been and continue to be, in the immortal words of Lou Gehrig, "...the luckiest man on the face of the earth." He stood and stated this simple thought facing his friends, family, colleagues and fans at Yankee Stadium. He was looking back at his story-book life, with the knowledge that his chapter as the "Iron-man of baseball" was at an end and he had been diagnosed with Amyotrophic Lateral Sclerosis (ALS – which would come to be called Lou Gehrig's disease by all

Yankee's fans and most Americans). No, I don't have ALS, but I might have the business version of it. I am hoping that I will be able to carry on with my life in PCBs and continue solving problems of technology, capability, capacity, quality improvement and cost containment with creativity and energy for as long as I can ski no matter what happens to Multiline Europe in the coming months or years. I have exited planes and trains and climbed out of automobiles in so many interesting situations and in so many new places, I suppose I can continue exiting and entering. I've had the pleasure to observe the world in all its variability and still always appreciated whatever came next. I wish myself more of the same and hope that this constant immigrant's tale has entertained and informed you. I also hope that the next time you hold or operate, watch or listen to a device or product that contains a PCB, that you'll smile and have an appreciation for all of us that have done our parts to make them cheap, plentiful, reliable, functional and beautiful.

Hopefully, to be continued...

Paul Waldner short biography

On the fifth of May 1959, a good citizen of Seoul, South Korea, came across a small child who had a bleeding injury to his right leg which stretched from his buttock to his heel. The "good Samaritan" took the little boy to a hospital and left him there. I was that child. I was sewn up, given medical attention for whooping cough, ring worm and chicken pox; given a name (Choi Bi Bum), given a birth certificate (May 5th, 1954 – because they thought I must have been about five years old) and sent to the Holt Children's Service in Seoul where I would await adoption. I was adopted several months later and sent to the US on August 11, 1959.

I grew up on Long Island in my parents' home in East Meadow, staying there until April of 1971 when I abruptly ran away to Richmond, Virginia. I returned to Long Island where I stayed with my older sister until I graduated from high school. I attended the State University of New York College of Environmental Science and Forestry at Syracuse University between 1972 and 1977.

I married the mother of my children, Anita, in 1982, had three children: Laura, Julie and Frank in the years 1984 and 1986 (Julie and Frank are twins). The family moved to Bad Homburg, Germany in 1987 where I started Multiline International Europa (mie). I have been running mie ever since.

Today, I still live in Bad Homburg, but now with my girlfriend/partner, Serpil. I am happy and proud of every expansion of my family with the additions of two sons-in-law (Eric and Joe) and four grandchildren: Hannah, Timothy, Amy and Lily. I am also happy and proud to have Serpil's daughter, Senem, son-in-law, Marcus and grandson Ferdinand as extended family members.